Drieu La Rochelle and the Picture Gallery Novel

Drieu La Rochelle and the Picture Gallery Novel

FRENCH MODERNISM IN THE INTERWAR YEARS

Rima Drell Reck

LOUISIANA STATE UNIVERSITY PRESS
Baton Rouge and London

First printing
99 98 97 96 95 94 93 92 91 90   5 4 3 2 1

Designer: Laura Roubique Gleason
Typeface: Janson Text
Typesetter: G & S Typesetters, Inc.
Printer and binder: Thomson-Shore, Inc.

Library of Congress Cataloging-in-Publication Data
Reck, Rima Drell.
    Drieu La Rochelle and the picture gallery novel: French modernism
in the interwar years / Rima Drell Reck.
        p.   cm.
    Includes bibliographical references (p.   ).
    ISBN 0-8071-1584-3
    1. Drieu La Rochelle, Pierre, 1893–1945—Criticism and
interpretation.   2. Drieu La Rochelle, Pierre, 1893–1945—Knowledge—
Art.   3. Art and literature—France—History—20th century.
4. Modernism (Literature)—France.   5. Painting in literature.
I. Title.
PQ2607.R5Z864   1990
843'.912—dc20   89-48255
                                                                        CIP

Chapter 2 first appeared as "Drieu's Theater Criticism of the Twenties: Rituals, Spectators, and Subtext," in the *French Review*, LXI (October, 1987), 50–59. The author is
grateful to the editors of that journal for permission to reprint that essay in somewhat
different form.

For Richard Collin
and
In memory of Jacob Drell

Contents

Figures

Preface

This book has evolved gradually, from the discovery years ago in the pages of the *Nouvelle Revue Française* of an extraordinary article on Malraux's earliest novels by an unfamiliar writer with a very long name, Pierre Drieu La Rochelle; through an intellectual odyssey into World War II and its literary aftermath, chronicled in *Literature and Responsibility: The French Novelist in the Twentieth Century;* then backward in time to the artistic contexts of World War I and the question of literary modernism. No scholar-critic deliberately sets out, I suspect, to write extensively on "marginal" writers. I, at least, did not. But the act of exploring and trying to understand what still remains clouded by neglect or misperception can lead in such directions. And so, I have confronted Céline, Aragon, and, now, Drieu, original and difficult novelists who were slow to find their audience.

A child of "museum culture"; a writer nourished on texts; a Parisian to the tips of his fashionable shoes; a journalist extraordinaire; a critic of prescient insight and luminous style; a writer who cared most about art, literature, Paris, and politics, in that order; in his last years a "traitor," a fascist, a pariah; and after his death a writer stripped of his context and read into another era—this was the figure of Drieu I began to track many years ago. The results of that journey are recorded in the pages of this book.

Along the way, I was aided by many organizations and people. A John Simon Guggenheim Memorial Foundation Fellowship in 1972 provided me with my first period of concentrated study of the literature of the collaboration and its most distinguished writer, Drieu. Research grants from the American Council of Learned Societies and the American Philosophical Society supported research and travel to France at several points. In the final stages the University of New Orleans Research Council awarded me grants in 1985 and 1987 that supported the writing of specific chapters and travel related to the selection of illustrations. To all of these institutions I am deeply grateful.

To the museum curators and *documentalistes* who shared their knowledge, textual resources, and photographic services and who offered valuable advice and encouragement, I owe an immense debt. I wish to thank the staff at the National Gallery of Art Library, Washington, D.C., in particular, Ted Dalziel and Carolyn Backlund; at the Courtauld Institute of Art, William Bradford and John House; at the Man Ray Trust, Jerome Gold; the staff at the Musée d'Orsay, in particular Anne Roquebert, Marie-Madeleine Massé, Isabelle Cahn, and Monique Nonne. The debt of a literary scholar to research librarians is beyond measure. I wish here to express my gratitude to Evelyn Timberlake at the Library of Congress; Marie-France Bougie at the Musée d'Orsay; Barbara Everly at the Howard Tilton Memorial Library, Tulane University; and the staff of the Earl K. Long Library, University of New Orleans, with special thanks to Evelyn Chandler and Anthony Tassin and to Robert Heriard, for his deep knowledge of books and art and for his friendship.

Themes developed in this book were presented in earlier versions before responsive critical audiences: Drieu's mythologies of national temperaments, at the South Atlantic Modern Language Association in Atlanta, Georgia, in 1969; his poetic-iconic myth of Germany, at the International Comparative Literature Association in Bordeaux in 1970; his place in World War I literature, at a special session on "La Littérature et la guerre" at the American Association of Teachers of French in Chicago in 1985; rituals, spectators, and Paris spectacles of the twenties, at the Third Colloquium on Twentieth Century Literature in French in Baton Rouge, Louisiana, in 1986; modernism, realist collage, and *Gilles*, at the South Central Modern Language Association in New Orleans in 1986; Drieu, Barthes, and the music hall, at the South Atlantic Modern Language Association in Atlanta in 1986; fiction in the Paris wasteland and postwar art quarrels, at the South Atlantic Modern Language Association in Atlanta in 1989. Other themes were shared and developed in contact with my students at the University of New Orleans in seminars on modernist fiction, Henry James, James Joyce, and Marcel Proust.

Throughout this book, all translations from the French are mine. Chapter 2 first appeared in the pages of the *French Review*. I wish to thank the editors of that journal for permission to reprint that essay here in slightly expanded form.

To Margaret Dalrymple and John Easterly of Louisiana State University Press, for their commitment to reliable and handsome books and their *gentillesse* with authors, and to my copy editor, Trudie Calvert, for a sharp eye for detail, my sincere gratitude.

Personal debts incurred in the gestation of a wide-ranging, long-ripening project are many. For dialogue, debate, encouragement, and counsel, I take this opportunity to thank, publicly and warmly, Roy Jay Nelson, Catharine Savage Brosman, Ronald Tobin, David O'Connell, William Savage, Jerah Johnson, Jack O'Connor, Elizabeth Penfield, John Williams, and the late Henri Peyre.

And to my husband, Richard Collin, who listened, shared, encouraged, and took joy in my joy, all the warmth a wife and scholar can put into words.

Chronology

1893   Born Pierre-Eugène Drieu La Rochelle in Paris, tenth arrondissement, on January 3, to Emmanuel Drieu La Rochelle, a lawyer, and Eugénie-Marie Lefèvre, daughter of an architect. Both parents of Norman origin; childhood visits to the northern coasts.

1902   Enrolled in Sainte-Marie-de-Monceau, a Marist private school.

1903   Birth of brother Jean, whom Drieu later introduced to painting and encouraged to become an architect.

1907   First enthusiasm for Nietzsche, aroused by copy of *Thus Spake Zarathustra.*

1908   Spends holidays in Shrewsbury, England, with family of pastor of St. Giles vicarage. First signs of lifelong attachment to the English language, English literature, English men's clothes.

1909   Second visit to England. Dazzled by collection of Turner at Tate Gallery in London.

1910   Enters Ecole Libre des Sciences Politiques in Paris, for career as diplomat or bureaucrat; concurrently prepares *licence* in English at the Sorbonne. Reads traditional French literary criticism and history. Introduced to avant-garde *Nouvelle Revue Française* by schoolmate Raymond Lefebvre; counseled on writing Parnassian sonnets by Raoul Dumas. Visits wealthy Jewish family of schoolmate André Jeramec; meets André's sister Colette.

1913   Fails final examination at Sciences Politiques. Becomes secretly engaged to Colette. Enters the army to serve three years of compulsory military service; persuades André Jeramec to join him. Stationed in Paris for nine months, promoted to corporal.

1914 April, on convalescent leave to recover from jaundice, visits Pinakothek in Munich, thinks museum ideal setting for a novel. June 28, Àrchduke Ferdinand assassinated. August 1, general mobilization announced. Drieu's company sent onto Paris boulevards to control crowds pillaging shops with German names. August 6, regiment leaves Paris, takes train to Amagne. August 15–18, completes forced march over Belgian border. In battle of Charleroi, receives shrapnel wound in head; André Jeramec is killed. Hospitalized at Deauville, then Falaise, begins to compose first war poems. October, rejoins regiment in Champagne. Promoted to sergeant. October, sustains deep wound in left arm; three-month hospital stay in Toulouse.

1915 Convalescent leave in Paris. Second operation on arm. Official engagement to Colette announced. Becomes depressed, volunteers to fight in the Dardenelles. Spends months in trench, seriously ill with dysentery. Removed to hospital in Toulon, then Paris; reads Claudel, begins to write new, freer poems.

1916 Attached to shock regiment, sent to Verdun. February, fights in battle of Verdun. February 25, wounded by exploding shell; soldiers walk over his prone body. Removed to hospital in Montbrison. March–December, convalescent leave in Paris. August, publishes poem in dadaist periodical *SIC*. Introduced by Colette to her fellow medical student Louis Aragon. Reads poems aloud at avant-garde salons; is encouraged to publish a volume by Léon-Paul Fargue.

1917 Classified auxiliary service. August, *Interrogation*, collection of war poems, published by Editions de la Nouvelle Revue Française in edition of 150 copies. Drieu hailed critically as voice of the "sacrificed generation," a French Whitman. October, marries Colette Jeramec; she settles half of her fortune on him.

1918 Bored with civilian life, resumes active duty. June, becomes interpreter for American division stationed near Swiss frontier. September, promoted to adjutant. October, American division recalled.

1919 March, demobilized. Contributes to *Littérature*, founded by Aragon, Breton, and Soupault. Meets Aldous Huxley in Brussels. Awarded Croix de Guerre.

1920   Publishes *Fond de cantine*, second collection of poetry. Frequents Paris theater, music halls, circus, and brothels with Aragon. Separates from Colette, acquires expensive English clothes, participates in dadaist activities. Begins publishing in *Nouvelle Revue Française* (*NRF*); work admired by Gide.

1921   Publishes *Etat civil*, a portrait of the artist as a young Frenchman, praised in *NRF*. Publishes review of Aragon's first novel, *Anicet ou le panorama*. Participates in mock trial of Barrès organized by André Breton, literary parades and demonstrations. Attends Jacques Rigaut's reading of dramatic apology for suicide. Is officially divorced from Colette; they remain friends. Argues with Aragon about surrealist painting on occasion of first Max Ernst exhibition at Galerie Sans Pareil, avenue Kléber.

1922   Publishes *Mesure de la France*, an analysis of the declining moral and physical strength of France. Literary reputation continues to grow.

1923   November, initiates in *NRF* "Chronique des spectacles," monthly reviews of theater, music hall, circus performances.

1924   March, publishes fifth and last "Chronique des spectacles." Publishes *Plainte contre inconnu*, first collection of short stories, influenced by Hemingway. Rents villa in south of France, houses Aragon and other friends. Buys yellow roadster. Has stormy love affair with American Constance Walsh; she fails to divorce husband, returns home. Finances surrealist pamphlet attacking Anatole France, who had been recently honored by national funeral.

1925   Publishes first novel, *L'Homme couvert de femmes*, dedicated to Aragon; critical reception poor. August, publishes open letter to surrealists in *NRF*, attacking their political sympathy with the communists and their betrayal of the surrealist ideal of artistic freedom.

1926   Publicly deplores poor critical reception of Aragon's surrealist novel *Le Paysan de Paris*.

1927   Publishes *Le Jeune Européen, La Suite dans les idées*. Critics attack "unacceptable mixture of self-analysis and political analysis," decline of Drieu's creative talent. With Emmanuel Berl, founds and writes *Les Derniers Jours*, political magazine that runs seven issues; publishes there second and third letters to surrealists. Marries Alexandra Sienkiewicz, daughter of Parisian banker; after barely six months, resumes solitary travels. Meets André Malraux, who shares his passion for art and for historical and cultural generalization.

1928   Publishes *Genève ou Moscou*, political essay on behalf of European unity. Travels to Greece; impressed by Parthenon, "American" Athenian suburbs; finds lobby of hotel ideal setting for movie, novel. Publishes second novel, *Blèche*; grudgingly praised for author's new-found order and clarity.

1929   Publishes *Une Femme à sa fenêtre*, novel set in Greece in 1924; lukewarm reception. Meets Victoria Ocampo, Argentinian woman of letters, in Paris; begins affair; they travel to England. November 5, surrealist Jacques Rigaut commits suicide.

1930   Continues to explore Europe, visits Germany. Publishes major critical articles on Malraux and Huxley in *NRF*. March, Aragon publishes *La Peinture au défi*, preface to catalogue of exhibition of collage at Galerie Goemans, 49, rue de Seine.

1931   Writes preface to French translation of Hemingway's *Farewell to Arms*. New political essay, *L'Europe contre les patries*, admired by Mann, Bertrand Russell, and Croce. Play *L'Eau fraîche* produced by Louis Jouvet, runs fifty-two performances. Book sales poor, sporadically worries about money. Separates officially from Alexandra. Lives off advances against future books from Gaston Gallimard and cash gifts from friends. Rents Ile-Saint-Louis apartment with extraordinary view at 45, quai Bourbon, described in Aragon's *Aurélien*. Publishes *Le Feu follet*, novel inspired by suicide of Rigaut; subject of drug addiction shocks critics. Ocampo founds literary magazine *Sur* in Buenos Aires, Drieu on editorial board. Refuses Légion d'Honneur. Writes unpublished play *Gille*.

1932   June to October, trip to South America. In Argentina gives series of public lectures on current state of Europe. Introduced by Ocampo to Jorge Luis Borges, shares with him long nocturnal walks through Buenos Aires, hears tale of Bolivian dictator that will reappear in 1943 novel *L'Homme à cheval*. Makes lecture tour to Germany.

1933   Publishes *Drôle de voyage*, novel-comedy-ballet influenced by Gide and Joyce; critical reception most favorable to date. Divorced from Alexandra. Watches rise of Hitler. Begins work on stories of *La Comédie de Charleroi*. Writes play *Le Chef.*

1934   February, Stavisky riots in Paris. Travels to Berlin, meets Otto Abetz. Cotranslates, writes preface to French translation of D. H. Lawrence's *The Man Who Died*. Play *Le Chef* produced by Georges Pitoëff, runs for five performances. Begins series of newspaper articles on nationalism in troubled European capitals, visits Italy, Czechoslovakia, and Hungary. Publishes *Socialisme fasciste*. Publishes *La Comédie de Charleroi*, orchestrated collection of stories, which is awarded Prix de la Renaissance, biggest literary success to date. Publishes new collection of short stories, *Journal d'un homme trompé.*

1935   Travels to Germany and Russia. At Nazi congress in Nuremberg meets American journalist Janet Flanner, enjoys staging of parades, speeches, Wagnerian music. Finds Moscow disappointing, with bad movies, *pompier* art. Meets Christiane Renault, wife of French industrialist, and begins ten-year liaison.

1936   Publishes exotic novel *Beloukia;* ignored critically. Joins former communist Jacques Doriot's new fascist group, delivers several ineffective speeches before political gatherings. Makes journalistic expeditions to North Africa and to Spain, where civil war is stirring. Aragon's second socialist realist novel *Les Beaux Quartiers* widely acclaimed.

1937   Publishes long family novel *Rêveuse bourgeoisie;* ignored by critics. Begins work on *Gilles*. Watches with distaste as Paris Exposition Universelle is erected along banks of Seine; sees again Watteau's *L'Enseigne de Gersaint* on loan from Berlin, visits exhibition of modern French painting since Cézanne at Petit Palais; is unsettled by Picasso's *Guernica* at Spanish pavilion, greatly moved by major Van Gogh exhibition at Palais de Tokio.

1938   January, first International Surrealist Exhibition held in Paris opens at Galerie des Beaux Arts. August, completes first draft of *Gilles*. Resigns from Doriot's party. Begins extensive rewriting of *Gilles.*

1939   July, first part of *Gilles* published in *Revue de Paris*. August, corrects proofs. Writes play about Charlotte Corday. September, World War II begins. December, *Gilles* published in censored edition.

1940   *Gilles* reviewed unfavorably in *NRF*, admired by Mauriac in personal letter to Drieu, generally ignored. June, *NRF* shuts down, Drieu leaves Paris for the Dordogne. June 17, French surrender to Germans; June 19, Himmler arrives in Paris; June 25, Pétain announces armistice. July, Drieu returns to Paris, visits Abetz, now German ambassador to France. December, *NRF* revived with Drieu as editor, helped quietly by previous editor Jean Paulhan.

1941   Aragon, Gide, and Eluard disappear from *NRF* contributors' list. Drieu begins private journal. Publishes *Notes pour comprendre le siècle*, analysis of French temperament, literature, and art from the Middle Ages. May, Drieu secures Paulhan's release from prison for resistance activities. Has Gerhard Heller, German literary censor in Paris, agree to watch over personal safety of Aragon, Malraux, Paulhan, Sartre, and Gallimard.

1942   *Gilles* republished in complete text, with new author's preface. Works on novel set in Bolivia. Has play *Charlotte Corday* performed in provincial tour; hostile reviews. November, depressed, rejoins Doriot's party briefly. Dreams of dying on battlefield.

1943   March, publishes *L'Homme à cheval*; reception cool. Publishes *Chronique politique 1934–1942*. Works on play *Judas*, never completed. Colette and her two children imprisoned; secures their release. Malraux visits Drieu in Paris, urges him to drop *NRF*, get out of politics. Considers leaving France, travels to Switzerland, dislikes it, returns to Paris. Arranges papers, begins memoirs. Begins *Les Chiens de paille*, novel set in occupied France. Begins series of articles in *Révolution Nationale* that become increasingly critical of Germans. June, resigns from *NRF*; review shuts down.

1944   Journal plots Allied advance, notes pitiful reality of fascism, disappointment at Sartre's new play *Huis clos*. Completes short story collection *Histoires déplaisantes* (published posthumously). Composes *Récit secret*. May, *Les Chiens de paille*, *Le Français d'Europe*, collection of articles, published. August 11, first suicide attempt; found still alive by housekeeper next morning, taken to hospital. Slashes wrists in hospital, again saved. Colette finds him shelter in Paris. August 25–27, Paris liberated. *Les Chiens de paille*, *Le Français d'Europe* seized and destroyed. Hides out in friends' country homes near Paris. October, begins new novel based on life of Van Gogh.

1945   Mid-January, completes four of seven planned parts of *Mémoires de Dirk Raspe*. January 19, Robert Brasillach convicted of collaboration in Paris; executed February 6. Drieu returns to Paris, lodges in apartment near the Etoile belonging to Colette. March, reads in newspaper of warrant issued for his arrest. Leaves instructions for preservation, publication of manuscripts with Malraux as literary executor. March 15, commits suicide.

1951   *Récit secret* published.

1963   *Histoires déplaisantes*, short story collection, published.

1964   *Les Chiens de paille* reissued. *Sur les écrivains*, anthology of scattered excerpts, published.

1966   *Mémoires de Dirk Raspe* published.

Drieu La Rochelle and the Picture Gallery Novel

1

The Other Drieu

"J'aurais voulu être peintre," 'I would have wanted to be a painter,' declares Gille, the hero of *L'Homme couvert de femmes* (The man covered with women, 1925), Pierre Drieu La Rochelle's first novel. Gille, named after the enigmatic clown of Antoine Watteau's late masterpiece, reappears in *Drôle de voyage* (Strange journey, 1933) and—with an "s" on his name—in *Gilles* (1939). The hero of Drieu's unfinished last novel, *Mémoires de Dirk Raspe* (Memoirs of Dirk Raspe, 1966), is a painter. The narrator of "Journal d'un délicat" (Diary of a sensitive man, *ca.* 1936) works in an art gallery and writes for the illustrated magazine *L'Art au XXe Siècle* (Twentieth-century art). Characters throughout Drieu's fiction debate the significance of contemporary painting. Thousands of references to painters, important and lesser known, French and foreign, appear in his novels, letters, notebooks, essays, and newspaper articles. He repeatedly compares other art forms to painting and judges them in its light. Illustrations from childhood books appear superimposed over scenes in *La Comédie de Charleroi* (The comedy of Charleroi, 1934) as iconographic or emblematic devices. Drieu's critical reviews of music halls, circuses, and plays in the early twenties build on aesthetic comparisons with contemporary painting and on visual intertexts drawn from nineteenth-century caricature. Drieu attempts to have "Le Music-Hall," the last part of *Le Jeune Européen* (The young European, 1927), an intergenre work, reissued in 1931 with illustrations by George Grosz. Major painters—Picasso, Turner, Giotto, Piero, Poussin, Rubens, Goya, Delacroix, Manet, Daumier, Matisse—appear as the key figures in an evolving semiotics of French and European cultural history. From his youthful amazement in 1909 before the Turner canvases at the Tate Gallery, Drieu's private writings evoke the mu-

1

seums of London, Munich, and Paris as enveloping, intoxicating worlds of forms and colors. With expert visual detail he describes a riveting painting by an unfamiliar artist, Chaïm Soutine, glimpsed in 1930 in a Paris gallery window.

Drieu's novels and stories are saturated with painting, with tableaux and scenes pictorially conceived, with actions described as painted gestures animated. His most memorable fiction combines complementary and contrasting modulations of tone and form—the concise, intensely modern sound of an ironic central viewpoint (at times first person, more often third) and the expansive, spatial rhythms of a strongly visual imagination experiencing the world—in narratives that are densely self-reflexive, full of mirror effects and shaded reflections, disturbed by shifting planes of focus. The French term *mise en abyme*, sometimes translated as specularity, comes close to suggesting the art of composition-as-vision that characterizes Drieu's best work, a fruitful confusion of light, form, color, framing elements, transforming mirror devices, and pictorial fragments.

Drieu was born in 1893 and died in 1945. The historical contours of his life—as veteran of World War I, as self-declared fascist in the thirties, as collaborationist under the occupation, as a suicide at the age of fifty-two—have tended to attract political, ideological, and psychological critics, while his aesthetic vision has remained largely unexamined, although its signs are clearly visible, readily displayed like the paintings in a gallery or museum. It would be possible, as Adeline R. Tintner has done for Henry James, to catalog the museum of Drieu's images.[1] The visual contrasts between the stately collection of America's great aesthetic novelist and the acidic-comic gallery of one of France's most interesting modernist writers would provide some striking insights into the cultural and historical differences between the two nations. My purpose here, however, is different from Tintner's. James's interest in the visual arts was encyclopedic and to a large degree acquisitive, that is, a way of consciously appropriating to his expanding practice of the American novel, whose first professional man of letters he rightly conceived himself to be, the accumulated art of the Western world.

Drieu, on the other hand, was following and expanding the grand

1. Adeline R. Tintner, *The Museum World of Henry James* (Ann Arbor, 1986), 235.

tradition of the French nineteenth-century novelists, absorbing and fusing intimately into his work a direct and continuous visual experience of the art housed in Paris and other European cities. Ultimately, Drieu's intense sensitivity to the physical aesthetics of the French capital, to its map and its seasons, to its complex physical layers of historical *signs*, would lead to his exploration of a new fictional form. The seeds were there early on. As the hero of *Gilles* puts it, even before he became wealthy through marriage, as a child growing up in Paris he had inestimable treasures at his disposal in the books, parks, museums, and streets. What was unique to Drieu was the intensity of his plastic experience, the degree to which he interpreted the visible world through his perception of art and the extent to which he fundamentally conceived his life and his fiction as largely visual experiences. This study is directed toward reading Drieu's most striking novels as they demand to be read, seeing rather than shutting our eyes to what they so clearly put before us.

Jean Hagstrum in his classic study of the relationship between literature and painting noted that in eighteenth-century England pictorialist writers tended to breed pictorialist readers.[2] In the forty-odd years since his death, Pierre Drieu La Rochelle has not found his pictorialist readers, although the prose works of Louis Aragon and André Malraux, his contemporaries and friends, have at last begun to receive some of the close aesthetic attention they invite. Critical studies of modernist writing and its interartistic dimensions have tended to focus on the work of poets such as Ezra Pound, T. S. Eliot, William Carlos Williams, E. E. Cummings, Wallace Stevens, René Char, Yves Bonnefoy, and Max Jacob. Studies of prose writers have developed more slowly with discussions of literary cubism in James Joyce, Virginia Woolf, Gertrude Stein,

---

2. Jean H. Hagstrum, *The Sister Arts: The Tradition of Literary Pictorialism and English Poetry from Dryden to Gray* (Chicago, 1958). Other useful works on the relationship between literature and painting include Mary Ann Caws, *The Eye in the Text: Essays on Perception, Mannerist to Modern* (Princeton, 1981); Bram Dijkstra, *Cubism, Stieglitz, and the Early Poetry of William Carlos Williams* (Princeton, 1969); Roger Fry, *Vision and Design* (London, 1923); William Heckscher, *Art and Literature: Studies in Relationship* (Durham, 1985); Archie K. Loss, *Joyce's Visible Art: The Work of Joyce and the Visual Arts* (Ann Arbor, 1984); Jeffrey Meyers, *Painting and the Novel* (Manchester, 1975); Mario Praz, *Mnemosyne* (Princeton, 1970); and Wylie Sypher, *Rococo to Cubism in Art and Literature* (New York, 1960).

William Faulkner, Wyndham Lewis, and Alain Robbe-Grillet in the lead. Reexaminations of nineteenth-century art in works such as *Romanticism and Realism* by Charles Rosen and Henri Zerner encourage new readings of the history of artistic movements and the interrelationships between cultural history and painting. Wendy Steiner's *The Colors of Rhetoric* suggests an exciting painterly analogy for reconceiving the periodization of twentieth-century art. In *The Painting of Modern Life* T. J. Clark proposes a striking rereading of early modernist painting, connecting his interpretation directly to the literary and critical texts of the time.[3]

Unfortunately, the current creative ferment in art history and in literary studies has left the major French novelists of the post–World War I period largely untouched by the light of aesthetic vision. Much of this narrowness of approach stems from the influence of Jean-Paul Sartre, the defining genius of the decades that include World War II, the literature of engagement, and the opening years of the new watershed of the sixties. Sartre's ideas, novels, plays, and sheer intellectual presence defined the literary tastes and ideological concerns that dominated criticism of French literature for over thirty years. When Roland Barthes took over the mantle of intellectual pope of France, which he wore in a far milder and more playful style, he defined himself at once in opposition to and as a heritor of Sartre. But everything Sartre touched with his pen and massive moral vision remains heavily under his shadow. And Sartre was clearly not a descendant of the French aesthetic tradition, whatever attention he may have devoted to a few Italian and French painters and to the psycho-historical portraiture of Jean Genet and Gustave Flaubert. Sartre was a moralist, and on the winning side in World War II. He could not, understandably, condone what Pierre Drieu La Rochelle had done under the occupation, and he could not, understandably, acknowledge openly the massive influence of Drieu's writings on his own work. Drieu was Sartre's great moral exemplum of the writer gone wrong, and that he has largely remained even for his most sympathetic critics during the sporadic revival of his works during

3. Charles Rosen and Henri Zerner, *Romanticism and Realism: The Mythology of Nineteenth-Century Art* (New York, 1984); Wendy Steiner, *The Colors of Rhetoric* (Chicago, 1982); T. J. Clark, *The Painting of Modern Life: Paris in the Art of Manet and His Followers* (New York, 1985).

the sixties, seventies, and eighties.[4] As the most significant precursor of the literature of engagement, Drieu served admirably to highlight the anxieties of choice and the dangers of bad political allegiances. Luminously aware of the possible consequences, Drieu analyzed them in a few late autobiographical texts whose discovery, republication, and analysis have almost totally obscured his literary work and perpetuated the repetition of a few narrow critical lines of approach: literature as testimony, fiction as confession, unity of the self as the single theme of all Drieu's writings. The resulting books and articles have perpetuated Sartre's Drieu minus the demonic glow.

Which brings me to the focus of this study, the pictorial dimension of Drieu's fiction. Although *Gilles* is recorded in most French literary histories as an important novel of this century,[5] and scattered studies of individual novels suggest that somewhere behind a maze of highly per-

4. Sartre's initial attack on Drieu appeared anonymously as "Drieu La Rochelle ou la haine de soi," in *Les Lettres Françaises*, No. 6 (April, 1943), 3–4. The key works of the Drieu revival are Pierre Andreu, *Drieu, témoin et visionnaire* (Paris, 1952); *La Parisienne*, special issue on Drieu La Rochelle, October, 1955; Frédéric Grover, *Drieu La Rochelle and the Fiction of Testimony* (Berkeley, 1958); *Défense de l'Occident*, special issue on Drieu La Rochelle, L (February, 1958); Paul Sérant, *Le Romantisme fasciste* (Paris, 1959); Grover, *Drieu La Rochelle* (Paris, 1962); Marc Hanrez, "Le Dernier Drieu," *French Review*, XLIII, special number (Winter, 1970), 144–57; Allen Thiher, "*Le Feu follet:* The Drug Addict as Tragic Hero," *PMLA*, LXXXVIII (January, 1973), 34–40; M. D. Gallagher, "Drieu et Constant: Une parenté," *Revue d'Histoire Littéraire de la France*, LXXIII (July–August, 1973), 666–75; Frank Field, *Three French Writers and the Great War: Studies in the Rise of Communism and Fascism* (Cambridge, Eng., 1975); Jonathan Dale, "Drieu La Rochelle: The War as 'Comedy'," in *The First World War in Fiction*, ed. Holger Klein (London, 1976), 63–72; *Magazine Littéraire*, special issue on Drieu La Rochelle, CXLIII (December, 1978); Julien Hervier, *Deux individus contre l'histoire: Drieu La Rochelle, Ernst Jünger* (Paris, 1978); Dominique Desanti, *Drieu La Rochelle ou le séducteur mystifié* (Paris, 1978); Pierre Andreu and Frédéric Grover, *Drieu La Rochelle* (Paris, 1979); *Drieu La Rochelle, Cahiers de l'Herne*, ed. Marc Hanrez (Paris, 1982); Robert Barry Leal, *Drieu La Rochelle* (Boston, 1982); Jean Lansard, *Drieu La Rochelle ou la passion tragique de l'unité: Essai sur son théâtre joué et inédit* (2 vols.; Paris, 1985–87); Rima Drell Reck, "Drieu La Rochelle's *Etat civil* and the French Lost Generation," *French Review*, LVIII (February, 1985), 368–76; Reck, "Drieu La Rochelle's *La Comédie de Charleroi:* A Long View on the Great War," *Romance Quarterly*, XXXIV (August, 1987), 285–96; Reck, "Drieu's Theater Criticism of the Twenties: Rituals, Spectators, and Subtext," *French Review*, LXI (October, 1987), 50–59; Reck, "Pierre Drieu La Rochelle," *Dictionary of Literary Biography*, LXXII (1988), 148–69.

5. R.-M. Albérès, *Histoire du roman moderne* (Paris, 1962); Gaëtan Picon, *Panorama de la nouvelle littérature française* (Paris, 1949); Henri Peyre, *French Novelists of Today* (New York, 1967).

sonal writing can be found an occasional glint of good French prose and a few memorable fictional moments, without a perception of their visual dimension the task of reading Drieu's novels remains largely impossible. Once that dimension—characteristic of the entire artistic milieu of Drieu's formative years—is restored, light comes in through all the windows at once. The specularity of Drieu's fiction—its fundamental pictorial conception—is so obvious as to be largely inescapable. When one sees Drieu in his own context and not in Sartre's, things become infinitely clearer.

Drieu was a post–World War I romantic, a participant in the French *années folles* and contemporary of the American lost generation, a modernist whose apocalyptic view of Europe in the twenties resembled the world of Eliot's *Waste Land*, of Joyce's *Ulysses*, of Picasso's *Demoiselles d'Avignon*. Like Aragon's and Malraux's, Drieu's work bridged several genres and art forms. His characteristic artistic vision was plastic, relational, and theatrical, an irregular and unstable structure of interrelationships he called "la comédie des formes," 'the comedy of forms.' The phrase itself is typically "Drieutique," an artfully distanced description with a slightly acidic note of intense emotion. Drieu's fiction has a strong afterimage, one projected by a constant theatrical interplay of human desires, actions, and social structures with the visible world of nature and art. Painting and spectacles are intertwined for Drieu, as they were for his artistic and spiritual patron saints: in literature Stendhal, Baudelaire, and Flaubert; in painting Watteau, Daumier, Manet, and the cubist, futurist, and expressionist artists of his own time. The best of Drieu's novels are complex pictural fictions that successfully fuse the French romantic and realist traditions with a strikingly fractionalized and spare modernist vision.

The selection of texts in this study reflects a personal perception of the total shape of Drieu's oeuvre based on reading all the novels, stories, journalism, essay-meditations, criticism, and most of the letters and journals. I have put my emphasis where Drieu appears to have put his—on a select gallery of works that might comfortably be viewed in the company of the novels and paintings he most admired. After a chapter devoted to Drieu's first significant literary venture, the five "Chroniques des spectacles" he published in the *Nouvelle Revue Fran-çaise* in 1923–1924, the analysis moves chronologically through the five novels that trace his evolving practice of that peculiar and endlessly fascinating structure I call the picture gallery novel—*L'Homme couvert de femmes* (1925), *Blèche* (1928), *Le Feu follet* (*The fire within*, 1931), *Gilles* (1939), *Mémoires de Dirk Raspe*—with reference where relevant to some of the short stories, nonfictional works, critical pieces, and newspaper articles. The other essential texts of these chapters are some of the paintings—many of them illustrated by the figures included here—and some of the art exhibits and art quarrels that directly influenced Drieu's conceptions of his novels or that paralleled their iconology.

There is no pretense at exhaustive coverage of all of Drieu's writings, which were massive in quantity like Aragon's and Sartre's. Aragon lived to eighty-five, Sartre to seventy-five. Drieu, who died at fifty-two, published some forty books and almost six hundred articles. Several plays, a voluminous correspondence, and thousands of pages of journals presently remain unpublished. This profusion of writing suggests that the persistent image of Drieu as an accidental author is false. He did do some other things besides write—fight in three major battles and suffer three wounds in World War I (Charleroi, Champagne, and Verdun), marry and divorce twice, have numerous love affairs, spend time with friends, travel widely, involve himself in politics, edit a literary magazine, walk millions of miles through the streets of Paris, visit museums and art galleries constantly, and meditate on the fate of France and on world affairs. But most of the time Drieu wrote, rewrote, planned what he would write next, and worried about the immediate and long-range fate of his work. To ignore the fact that Drieu was a professional writer is to misunderstand both the nature and depth of his commitment to art. If the description of Drieu—who in 1934 declared his choice of a utopian "fascist socialism," in late 1940 became editor of the *Nouvelle Revue Française* for two and a half years under the German occupation, and in August, 1945, committed suicide—as a dedicated artist seems incongruous with the facts of his life and his era, the imbalance was characteristic of his time. It was almost impossible to be French in the first four decades of this century without living many of the incongruities that characterize the life of a Drieu, a Malraux, or an Aragon.[6]

One of the thorniest and most intriguing aspects of Drieu's fiction is his studied incorporation of debate, polemics, and political commentary into the text. The literary methodologies of these artistic responses

---

6. For a detailed account of Drieu's life, see Reck, "Pierre Drieu La Rochelle."

to external events became increasingly complex as Drieu the novelist began to absorb and accommodate Drieu the political essayist, critic, and journalist within the very substance of the novels. By the time he published *Gilles* in December, 1939, Drieu had discovered—by means of deepening insight into the plastic arts of the nineteenth and twentieth centuries—ways of combining cubism with the satirical tradition of Daumier. Significantly, the incursion of journalism and polemics into Drieu's fiction was paralleled by developments in the plastic arts. The composition of the first three parts of *Gilles* and the painting of *Guernica* were contemporaneous—the year 1937.

Drieu began early on to write in several genres at once, as did Aragon and Malraux. This proliferation of forms affected his novels in a decisive way. Contrary to the contentions of many of his critics, the nonfictional texts—political essays, newspaper articles, journal entries, letters, critical pieces—did not bury the novels; instead, they often freed them of much of the extraneous detail that Drieu felt compelled to put on paper. Another skewed critical perspective assumes that because Drieu frequently invoked something he called history, because he claimed to be a philosopher, he was in fact a historian-philosopher and, as a result, less of a novelist. Quite the contrary. Drieu tended to confuse the artist and the intellectual, and to want to be both. He never functioned—as did Sartre—as a critical intellectual, and he systematically revolted against being formally trained as a critic, political thinker, philosopher, or historian. Drieu's dramatic failure on the examination that would have earned him a degree from the Ecole des Sciences Politiques in 1913 was clearly an unconscious declaration of vocation much like Balzac's illness when working in the law offices and Flaubert's flareup of epilepsy that ended a possible legal career.

Drieu's early novels provide a visual inventory of the iconology of early modernist art—the brothel, newspapers, music halls and circuses, cafés, country chateaux in the south of France, art dealers, Paris streets and apartments, windows and mirrors, monuments and nudes. His early contacts with dada and surrealism and his ten-year friendship with Aragon (they met in the winter of 1916–1917) are inseparable from the fabric of his novels, where the approach to visual imagery, the underlying spirit of revolt, and an amused but deep-seated respect for the avant-garde mirror a fund of commonly held assumptions. Indeed, it might be suggested that Drieu's taste for debate, polemics, and dialogic rating schemes reflects the grand tradition of the surrealist *enquête* (investigation) that gave birth to numerous published surveys on literary, sexual, and cultural-political subjects in dadaist and surrealist periodicals. Drieu broke with the surrealists between 1925 and 1927 ostensibly because he disapproved of their meddling in political matters and of their drift toward communism. However, his most serious objections were to what he perceived as their betrayal of literary values.[7] While he continued to travel a highly personal road to fictional form, his friends played with some collectively oriented enterprises such as automatic writing that he found particularly offensive. The surrealist spirit of combat that often disintegrated into low farce left in its wake Drieu's heightened perception of the literary life as an odd form of theater.

While still defining his own fictional voice, Drieu also began to write criticism. His early analyses of form, language, and the conception of fictional character in new works by Aragon, Malraux, and Louis-Ferdinand Céline are among the most perceptive assessments of these gifted and flawed novelists ever published. Intensely open to the inter-artistic visions of the early twenties, Drieu followed closely the colorful drama that culminated in the Paris publication of Joyce's *Ulysses* in 1922, wrote regularly for the *Nouvelle Revue Française*, and expanded his contacts well beyond the surrealist group. He came to know Ernest Hemingway, Aldous Huxley, Malraux, Jorge Luis Borges, Picasso, Henri Matisse, Georges Braque, Jean Cocteau, and other major artists of his time. The French reading public was introduced to Hemingway, Huxley, and D. H. Lawrence through Drieu's critical essays and prefaces. Drieu was one of the first writers to notice the radical differences between the American and the French Paris of the twenties and to incorporate a vision of the artistic, moral, and economic contrasts between these coexisting cities into his work.

As an avant-garde novelist, as a shockingly frank chronicler of the twenties' games of sex, money, liquor, and drugs, as a *moderniste malgré lui*, Drieu grappled with the painterly vision of disintegration that he called *la décadence*. This perception of the death of grand composition is best illustrated in the third part of *Gilles* with the visual revelation that

7. For the three public disagreements with the surrealists, see Pierre Drieu La Rochelle, "La Véritable erreur des surréalistes," *Nouvelle Revue Française*, XXV (August, 1925), 166–71; "Deuxième lettre aux surréalistes," *Les Derniers Jours*, February 15, 1927, pp. 3–5; "Troisième lettre aux surréalistes," *Les Derniers Jours*, July 8, 1927, pp. 1–17.

Delacroix's manner is no longer possible in the France of 1934. An interesting recent critical study of modernism has focused on the "ruin of representation" in a group of literary and critical texts conceived during Drieu's coming of age as an artist.[8] Placed within the context of the writers he considered his contemporaries—Joyce, Eliot, Woolf, Hemingway, F. Scott Fitzgerald, and the Aragon of the twenties— Drieu appears as the paradigmatic figure of the French lost generation. He was, as Borges noted, "the Frenchman of Paris," an early twentieth-century dandy in the best Baudelairean tradition who had managed to survive the Great War and begin a literary career in that strange corridor of time between the first world war and the next.

In these pages I examine and attempt to make visible the look, sound, and feel of a "Drieu novel," a unique entity that has had a more striking fortune than has yet been perceived, within the blood and bones of other more famous works such as *L'Age de raison*, *L'Etranger* and *La Chute*, *Le Voyeur* and *Les Gommes*. Ideally, we should learn to identify a work of fiction as we do a painting, by its creator's name. We say "a Picasso," "a Matisse." Why not "an Aragon," "a Sartre," "a Malraux," "a Drieu"? The internal signatures of original novelists are as clearly visible as those of painters. The signatures of paintings are in the forms, colors, textures, the ensemble of elements. In the same way the words, pages, chapters, images and arrangements, sounds and voices and silences of a novel come together into a recognizable form that is in fact a creature that stands for and stands in place of its creator. To identify "a Drieu" one must also see in relief some of its basic intertexts— novels of the French nineteenth century; an incomplete but persistent vision of Dostoyevsky; the evolving art of film; the popularized theories of Freud and Einstein; the rhetorical voices of a long line of French moralists, nationalists, and philosophes; an interest in ethnology and the philosophy of art; the rhetorical modes of journalism and the new *musée imaginaire* of the popular arts; the tenacious, brilliant, often wrongheaded voices of Aragon and Malraux. And last but far from least, the painterly intertexts—general or specific, historically or practically perceived—that made Gilles and his creator want to be painters.

8. Jo Anna Isaak, *The Ruin of Representation in Modernist Art and Texts* (Ann Arbor, 1986).

2

"Chronique des Spectacles": Rituals, Spectators, and Subtexts

History as theater, event as spectacle, the writer as actor-author in a comedy of culture—these characteristic metaphors of modernist literature became the formative structures of Drieu's writing during the initial years of his career. His immersion in the experimental art forms of the twenties would continue to shape all he viewed, from art and literature to the history of his time. In 1944 Drieu would describe in his journal the disintegration of Hitler from the perspective of a disillusioned surrealist: "Ainsi va l'Histoire, qui construit de vastes perspectives avec de sales petits bouts de décor."[1] 'So goes history, building vast perspectives with dirty little scraps of scenery.' This view of a cataclysmic historical moment as a piece of inferior theatrical staging had its roots in Drieu's brief but intense adventure as a critic of Paris spectacles in the early nineteen twenties.

In that luminous moment when literary surrealism still remained—for a brief time—unpoliticized, Drieu, a decorated veteran of the war and already a noted young poet, memorialist, and essayist, participated in the mock trial of Maurice Barrès, published poems and fragments in *SIC*, *Littérature*, and *L'Oeuf dur*, and with his friends Louis Aragon and André Breton argued about the nature and direction of contemporary art forms.[2] Stage productions were a favorite topic of conversation. The brilliant innovations of cubist painting and the liberating accents of the new dada-surrealist poetry had made existing theatrical forms—from

1. Pierre Drieu La Rochelle, unpublished journal, quoted in Andreu and Grover, *Drieu La Rochelle*, 539.
2. Drieu's earliest works include two volumes of poetry, *Interrogation* (Paris, 1917), published while he was still in the army, and *Fond de cantine* (Paris, 1920); and a fictionalized memoir, *Etat civil* (Paris, 1921).

11

the set pieces of the Comédie Française to experimental prewar theater—appear dull or irrelevant. After fighting in the war, Drieu explained in a 1922 interview with the *Revue Hebdomadaire*, "Voulant avant
tout m'accorder avec mon temps . . . je me suis jeté avec ardeur vers
ceux qui exaltaient le moderne, vers ceux qui acceptaient toute notre
époque, vers ceux même qui s'hallucinaient uniquement sur ce qui est
propre à cette époque." [3] 'Wanting above all to come to terms with my
time . . . I rushed ardently to join those who exalted the modern, those
who accepted our epoch in its entirety, to join those who even went so
far as to hallucinate solely about all that is truly contemporary.' Drieu
intensely admired the surrealists for their individual poetic talents and
for their conception of literature as independent from external forces.
When Aragon returned from a summer visit to Berlin in 1922 convinced by the frenetic vitality of German music halls that real stage art
was to be found where the "public" went, the ongoing discussion about
contemporary art forms expanded in a new direction.[4]

Systematic criticism was an uncharacteristic venture for a surrealist.
Breton's manifestos and Aragon's pastiches on literary works were both
essentially modes of avoiding or subverting direct analysis. Drieu, by
temperament and talent more a critic and satirist than an enthusiast,
had already brought off some startling performances, including a 1921
review of Aragon's *Anicet ou le panorama* identifying the radical thrust of
that first novel and predicting its author's literary future in two dazzling
pages.[5] A practical and theoretical text on the still uncanonized art
forms of music halls and circuses, applauded by the public and lionized
by his fellow writers, seemed a worthy enterprise in the modernist
spirit.

In November, 1923, Drieu initiated in the *Nouvelle Revue Française* a
series of articles entitled "Chronique des spectacles" dealing with a wide

3. Pierre Drieu La Rochelle, "Réponse à Pierre Varillon," in "Enquête sur les maîtres de la jeune littérature," *Revue Hebdomadaire*, IV (November 4, 1922), 93–94.
4. Aragon's description of "expressionism and cubism applied to bars and music halls
. . . [compared] with the contempt expressed by the pretty little chatter-chatter-chatter of
our *artistes*" made the music hall seem an authentic repository of the modernist vision.
See Louis Aragon, "Le dernier été," *Littérature*, November, 1, 1922, p. 22; and also the
analysis of Aragon's Berlin trip in Pierre Daix, *Aragon, une vie à changer* (Paris, 1975),
134–35.
5. Pierre Drieu La Rochelle, "*Anicet ou le panorama*, par Louis Aragon," *Nouvelle Revue Française*, XVII (July, 1921), 97–99.

range of stage entertainments. Unlike the traditional dramatic chronicle that treated formal plays as spoken literary exercises, Drieu's moody, impressionistic reviews of Paris music halls, circuses, and theaters analyzed popular rituals and their audiences using aesthetic theory, literary history, and an early form of semiological analysis. His open museum of arts included the plays of Racine, the medieval churches, the noblemen-actors of the Sun King's court, the surrealist poets, British chorus girls, American jazz singers, and the totems of primitive art. The chronicles, which ran from November, 1923, through March, 1924, viewed the stage performances of Paris and their audiences as an experimental laboratory of cultural forms. Drieu's text provided a reading of French society through its entertainments, while his subtext dealt with the surrealist debate over popular art. Drieu's series of articles evoked the performances by juxtaposing diverse elements—stage props and poems, dance movements and typewriters, paintings and autos—against traditional French arts. Writers and painters appeared in the text as characters on a limitless stage standing just behind the main one. The performances appeared doubled, tripled; they became mirrors of the essential forms of rituals and their participants. At moments the stage reflections disappeared, and the critic-observing-and-writing took center stage, his words the transposition of a secret verbal ritual accidentally overheard.

With their immense variations of tone, theme, and synesthetic devices and their dazzling range of historical and literary references, Drieu's chronicles typify that extraordinary form, the *Nouvelle Revue Française* essay of the early interwar years, that protean, Gidian, intellectual-cultural sonata that became the basic model for Roland Barthes' later virtuoso performances.[6] Indeed, Drieu's spectacle reviews are arguably his first real novel, a sequential, unified text, a concealed fiction with strong roots in surrealism and new historical-aesthetic accents that foreshadow André Malraux's *La Tentation de l'Occident* and suggest the critical directions Malraux would later follow in his writings

6. Drieu's and Barthes' similar use of the discursive-analytical form, their common choice of the music hall as subject, and their semiological readings of spectacles strongly suggest that Barthes knew Drieu's "Chronique des spectacles." Susan Sontag's characterization of Barthes' form as the "complex, comma-ridden and colon-prone . . . style of exposition . . . whose parent tradition is to be found in the tense, idiosyncratic essays published between the two world wars in the *Nouvelle Revue Française*," supports this view. See Sontag, "Writing Itself: On Roland Barthes," in *A Roland Barthes Reader*, ed. Susan Sontag (New York, 1980), ix.

on art and his *Antimémoires*.[7] While Malraux a few years later would set out to find keys to the eternal image of man in the faces of Cambodian stone figures, Drieu—the quintessential rooted Parisian writer—looked to the more immediate, to the strangely blank faces in the stalls at the Comédie Française and to the popular rituals of Paris. In the course of his critical inquiry into the psychology and sociology of spectatorship and its rituals and into the relation between popular and elite culture Drieu began to develop his own characteristic nonfiction form, a special strain of the French essay-meditation fusing literary and historical commentary with cultural-political journalism.[8]

Monthly reviews offered a challenging exercise in practical criticism and in literary infighting. Using the very substance of the productions, Drieu could confront the enthusiasms of his friends with the visible reality. He dissected the routines, assessed the dancing and sets, and compared the techniques of popular spectacles with the evolving theatrical enterprise of Jean Cocteau, whom Drieu greatly admired for his fusion of painting, poetry, spectacle, and theater. When the evening's show lacked substance or form, Drieu tried to imagine ways of transforming it into a durable, authentically modern art. His speculations on directions for improvement broadly pointed in two directions: toward more intense physical and emotional involvement on both sides of the footlights and toward greater mythic and verbal conceptualization. Interestingly, Drieu's suggestions for exploiting the more violent dramatic potentials of ritual and his calls for objectified mythical speech and action on the stage suggested two major innovative directions theater would follow in the years to come, the nonverbal theater of cruelty of Antonin Artaud and the epic theater of Bertold Brecht.[9] Applying his formidable intelligence to the criticism of popular art forms, Drieu also

7. Drieu's *Mesure de la France* (1922) is the earliest work in the Drieu-Malraux vein of historical-aesthetic meditation, continued by Malraux's *La Tentation de l'Occident* (1926) and his "D'une jeunesse européenne" (1927), both of which bear strong similarities to Drieu's *Le Jeune Européen* (1927). In this connection, see Rima Drell Reck, "Malraux and the Duality of Western Man," *Personalist*, XLVIII (Summer, 1967), 345–60; and Reck, "The *Antimémoires*: Malraux's Ultimate Form," *Kentucky Romance Quarterly*, XVI (Winter, 1969), 155–62.

8. Drieu described his political-historical writings as essays or meditations written in the margins of newspapers and journals. See Pierre Drieu La Rochelle, "En marge II," *Révolution Nationale*, July 15, 1944, p. 1.

9. See Neil Kenny, "Changing the Language of the Theater: A Comparison of Brecht and Artaud," *Journal of European Studies*, XIII, Pt. 3, No. 52 (1983), 169–86.

anticipated significant later trends in the study of mass culture and entertainment.[10]

The initial and longest critique, a detailed analysis of a music hall revue at the Casino de Paris, establishes the form and methodology of the text. As Drieu creates in the act of writing an idiom for an unfamiliar subject, the text takes on the shape of a *roman d'aventures* of the voyage of criticism with all its inflections—setting out, discovery, stops, retreats, new beginnings. As he meticulously enumerates and describes the "numbers" of this Paris ritual—the chanteuse singing in English, the comic sketches, the rows of naked women, the ordered waves of dancers, the full troupe "freeze"—the prose list and its annotated commentary stretch the sense of time elapsed and minutes literally grow longer in the dark room. Watching this relentless array of horrors at first in amazement and then with a rising sense of dismay, Drieu wonders about the origins of such a bastardized show. Is it English, French, American?[11] He remembers attributing the impression of cultural fractionalization to his own disorientation when he first visited the Casino de Paris right after the war in 1918. All this dreadful stuff is obviously enormously popular. The dark room is filled. Now the subtext rises to the surface: why did his fellow writers urge Drieu to observe and write about the Paris music hall? The question is too unsettling to contemplate at this moment: the subtext disappears again. Drieu will face the evening alone, a critic armed only with his perceptions and his words.

Drieu concentrates on the visible subject as he carefully sets down the aggregates of signs: the physical accessories of expensive pomp, the grotesque gestures of poorly trained dancers, the deformed conceptualization of the tableaux, the connotative scams of predictable comic sketches and vaguely familiar musical forms, the dismal "modern" sets ineffectively influenced by the revolution in painting. How does all this appear to another spectator? The textual focus suddenly veers away

10. Two illuminating studies following out these lines of investigation are Richard Altick, *The Shows of London* (Cambridge, Mass., 1978); and Maurice Descotes, *Le Public du théâtre et son histoire* (Paris, 1964).

11. Recent interest in the scholarly and historical study of popular spectacles is reflected in Guy Dumur (ed.), *Histoire des spectacles*, Encyclopédie de la Pléiade (Paris, 1965). See in particular Jacques Damase, "Le Music-Hall," 1543–75; and Michèle Richet, "Le Cirque," 1520–42. In his preface Dumur notes that the circus and music hall have only recently achieved an autonomy that justifies their being studied as independent forms of spectacle (vii).

from the stage as Drieu turns to look at the audience. The wildly staring eyes of the man seated next to him, trying to make out individual faces onstage, reflect a futile struggle. The critic defends himself by *naming* the groups on both sides of the footlights crowds, like a malediction: "Deux *foules* s'opposent aveuglement, c'est la démocratie qui se fend par le milieu et qui expulse un plaisir bruyant, clinquant, et vague" (italics added). 'Two *crowds* stand against one another. It's democracy cracking open at the center and discharging a noisy, garish, vague pleasure.' He calls the whole house, on both sides of the footlights, nothing more than "un étalage de corps tués . . . de viande morte anonyme," 'a display of lifeless bodies . . . of anonymous dead meat.' The music hall performance itself suddenly takes on a clear shape; it is in fact a complicated machine of destruction, "un des laminoirs qui écrasent le mieux les âmes," 'one of the rolling machines . . . most efficient at crushing souls,' a ritual of the "other Paris," the one threatened by urban demolition, by invading barbarians, by the pursuit of novelty and money.[12]

The spectacle, with its offending emptiness, anonymity, and vulgarity, seems gradually to disintegrate as Drieu watches it. There is a pause, almost a respite; then the components of the evening suddenly reappear translated: the ultimate carnage left uncleared from the war, the two crowds of dead meat lost, blank-eyed, unable to find themselves or one another. As Drieu rereads the signs of the music hall revue, he recognizes it as an *obverse ritual*, one degraded from its original regenerative function, by communion and participation, to the level of a poorly staged ritual of death, a weak parody of mass murder that serves no one but the cash counters. Novelty and modernism have reached their apogee in a bloodless death pageant with bad music, few meaningful gestures, and a crushing quotient of boredom.

Drieu's analysis of the music hall revue illustrates vividly some of the central issues raised by contemporary theorists of theater. His reading of the signs recognizes the fact that rituals function as a fundamental form of social encounter and as a reflection of the inherent structure of a society.[13] His detailed analysis of sets, audience reaction, patterns of presentation, connotative devices, and historical connections also an-

12. Pierre Drieu La Rochelle, "Chronique des spectacles," *Nouvelle Revue Française,* XXI (November, 1923), 590.
13. See Richard Schechner, *Between Theater and Anthropology* (Philadelphia, 1985); and Victor Turner, *From Ritual to Theater* (New York, 1982).

ticipates major areas of inquiry in contemporary audience and performance theory, areas such as the psychology of stagecraft, the interrela-
tionship between popular spectacles and changing public taste, the
structural similarities between "twice-told actions" in disparate cultures.
Drieu also sees as axiomatic the political function of popular performances and the intimate connection between the audience's consciousness of social issues and the choice of entertainment.[14] His startling intuitions about the significance of contemporary ritual in the twenties,
however, are fundamentally painterly and poetic, rather than anthropo-
logical or productional. The dead meat on the stage and the disoriented
gaze of the bewildered spectator are his literary mirrors of the relationship between audience and performance, as well as of the more intan-
gible relationship between the audience and itself. By combining the
allusive and symbolic structures of poetry with a direct, practical analysis of stage forms, Drieu's text becomes a discursive, implicitly illustrated notebook, in many ways similar to Roland Barthes' critical essays
on popular arts but with a grave historical dimension added.[15]

The published account of Drieu's music hall experience created
something of a fuss among his friends. Impressed by his critical skill
and also vaguely offended by his display of aesthetic independence, they
began a new campaign, this time on behalf of the circus, proposed as
more "natural" and "simple" than the music hall and therefore a higher
form of popular art. The subsequent reviews of acrobats and circuses
mark the first appearance in Drieu's work of that complex fusion of visual mythology with polemics that would inform some of the most extraordinary scenes in *Gilles*, his major novel. Drieu had impressive visual models for his circus pieces, two striking treatments of the popular
nineteenth-century *parade* subject—a scene of a crowd of onlookers in
front of musicians or *saltimbanques*. In Honoré Daumier's *La Parade de
foire* (Fig. 1), a small watercolor drawing, the focus is on the grotesque
faces and three-quarter-length physical postures of performers on a
platform; the viewer stands in the place of the invisible spectators. In

14. See especially Altick, *Shows of London;* David Bradby, Louis James, and Bernard
Sharratt (eds.), *Performance and Politics in Popular Drama* (Cambridge, Eng., 1980); Richard Demarcy, *Eléments d'une sociologie du spectacle* (Paris, 1973); and Descotes, *Le Public
du théâtre et son histoire.*
15. Compare Drieu's analysis of the music hall with Roland Barthes' essay "Au music-
hall," in *Mythologies* (Paris, 1957), 199–201.

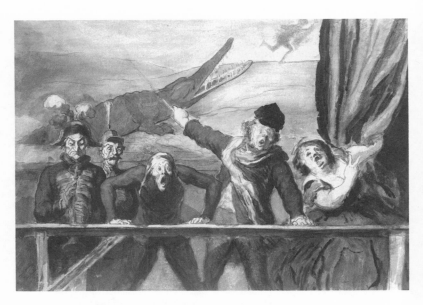

1. Honoré Daumier, *La Parade de foire. ca.* 1860. Watercolor, pen, and wash, 10½ × 14½ inches. Musée du Louvre, Cabinet de Dessins, Paris.
Photo: Réunion des Musées Nationaux.

2. Georges Seurat, *La Parade de cirque.* 1887–1888. Oil on canvas, 39¼ × 59 inches. Metropolitan Museum of Art, New York. Bequest of Stephen C. Clark, 1960.
Photo: Metropolitan Museum of Art.

Georges Seurat's monumental painting *La Parade de cirque* (Fig. 2), an ironic, "nocturnal" vision of the *parade*, the viewer's high gaze takes in the spectators' varied social classifications, then passes over their heads to the performers, who represent still another form of spectacle.[16] But in Seurat's treatment, the vast social-political implications of the subject take on a hieratic stature; for the moment captured in the picture, all motion and attention are fixed in an eternal stillness marked only by the unheard note the trombonist has just sounded. Drieu's reviews of two acrobatic performances, one at the Casino de Paris and the other at the circus, begin by focusing attention, in suitably "modern" fashion, on the sparsely decorated motions and forms of bodies in space, then gradually reverse the balance between subject and subtext, between the observation of visual phenomena and the submerged meditation on fashions in taste among artists. In a subtle work of demolition, the semiotics of acrobatic performance becomes a paradigm of the crisis of modernism. Behind the reviews of acrobats, the shadows of the surrealist movement trace a vast circus performance, sweeping aside in its imperial wake all bourgeois pretense, and then—in a muddled and ironic anticlimax—inadvertently encouraging empty and vulgar ritual.

Drieu's prelude to the acrobatic reviews is a textual meditation on modernism. Even the most striking new mythological forms, such as airplanes, movies, and skyscrapers, wear out their artistic effectiveness, he suggests. Cocteau, for example, has already moved away from novelty to return to the rose. Using poetry as a metaphor for all forms of writing, Drieu visualizes a ballet of natural and manufactured signs: "Ce qui importe, ce n'est pas que l'on parle des roses ou des machines, mais que le poème s'épanouisse selon le rythme doux de la rose ou se fragmente durement comme la machine à écrire"[17] 'What matters is not talking about roses or machines, but that the poem unfolds with the soft rhythm of the rose or falls harshly into fragments like the sound of the typewriter.' But the "young men with nothing to do" are tugging at his sleeve. "Ils deviennent plus difficiles. . . . Ils ne peuvent plus voir

16. For an extraordinary analysis of the tradition behind Seurat's *La Parade*, see Richard Thomson, *Seurat* (Oxford, 1985), 147–56. See also John Russell, *Seurat* (London, 1965), 214–19. In connection with Drieu's experience of the painting, Russell reminds us that Seurat's *La Parade* could still be seen in London through 1932, after which time it went to the Metropolitan in New York.

17. Pierre Drieu La Rochelle, "Chronique des spectacles," *Nouvelle Revue Française*, XXI (December, 1923), 732–33.

que les clowns ou les acrobates . . . des clowns et des acrobates aux abords précis, aux lointains vagues comme la mémoire." [18] 'They are getting more difficult. . . . They can no longer stand anything but clowns and acrobats . . . clowns and acrobats with precise contours and distant perspectives as imprecise as memory.'

The principal analysis of circus forms involves a featured acrobatic performance at the Casino de Paris. Drieu starts out relaxed, at ease with the clear cubist geometry of the set. There is nothing human visible:

> Le décor est dépouillé, c'est notre aveu désespéré, plus de lignes, plus de couleurs, plus rien—mais tout à l'heure les jeux purs de la lumière pris dans les derniers pièges indestructibles: un visage, un corps humain. Il y a un fond parce qu'il faut bien qu'il y ait un fond: un rideau gris, uni, à plis droits. Des appareils gymnastiques esquissent peut-être un premier plan: nickelés, si abstraits, si grêles, ce sont plutôt les entrailles du néant. [19]

> The decor is spare, our desperate declaration: no more lines, no more color, nothing. But in a little while the pure play of light caught in the last indestructible snares: a face, a human body. There is a background because there must be one: a gray curtain, of a single color, with straight folds. Some gymnastic bars sketch in the barest foreground: metallic, so abstract, so thin, they look like the bowels of nothingness.

Then a face dimly glimpsed becomes clearer as Barbette, the star performer, comes onstage. She is a visual and poetic sign, the mythical *Américaine* of the era, with bobbed hair and narrow hips. As she performs, her physical control is the visible text of a female type, the woman who is sufficient unto herself. The acrobatic display is a study in abstract will, "la domination lointaine, absolue, soudain brisée, sur n'importe qui ou n'importe quoi, par n'importe quel moyen," [20] 'a distanced domination of motion, absolute, then abruptly broken, on anyone or anything at hand, by whatever means.' Drieu reads the motions of the gymnastic performance as action idealized, reduced to its essence, so concentrated in its self-sufficiency, so indifferent to any objective that it becomes pure thought, the bodily turns and bends artistically controlled expressions of the need for variation and destruction.

18. Pierre Drieu La Rochelle, "Chronique des spectacles," *Nouvelle Revue Française*, XXII (January, 1924), 96–97.
19. *Ibid.*, 97.
20. *Ibid.*, 98.

The motions are not perfect, however; there are momentary flicker-
ings of gratuitous elements, an instant of less-than-perfect motion, a
small touch of self-indulgence. Is it Barbette's essential feminineness—
even stripped of the usual soft layers of fat and the normal beautiful
clumsiness—that creates lapses of art and essence in the performance?
Drieu begins to detach himself from his visual concentration, preparing
to form his reading. The performance ends; the audience breaks into
wild applause as Barbette moves to the footlights. She bows head all the
way down, then removes her wig. Her hair is cropped. There is a moment of existential wavering as Drieu waits for still another transformation, for the "third deceit" characteristic of the era—a woman pretending to be a man pretending to be a woman. But the show is over. The
beautiful American woman is a man. Drieu's shock, couched in the
jerky rhythms of his prose, mirrors a key theme of the text: the corrup-
tion of popular art forms by fundamental physical and moral deceits.

The realization grows that popular and elite audiences may share a
fascination with purely "showy" spectacles, with the accessories rather
than the substance of stage art. Clearly, Drieu is out of sympathy with
the witty and sometimes grossly sensual or deliberately epicene play-
fulness of much surrealist art. He does not share the sensibility we have
come to call "camp." After the Barbette incident, his critical voyage enters its roughest seas as he is forced to face the unfortunate resemblance
between Paris audiences at a popular sentimental play, gaping at the
elaborate historical costumes and titillated by the facile intrigue, and
his artist friends scurrying from one bad show to another. Beginning to
reach the limit of his tolerance for popular spectacles, Drieu looks
around him at the play. His evocation of the dreaming faces in the audience combines the signs of music hall, melodramas, and circuses:

> Il faut voir la tête des Parisiens . . . ils dodelinent de la tête: les femmes
> nues, les Fratellini, la grivoiserie et le doux cynisme des petits théâtres, les
> grands mélos pour femmes saoules, les otaries! Ils dorment et rêvent d'in-
> dustrie lourde.[21]

> The Parisians are something to behold. . . . They nod their heads ap-
> provingly at everything: naked women, the Fratellini brothers, the licen-
> tiousness and flabby cynicism of the small theaters, the grand melodramas

21. Pierre Drieu La Rochelle, "Chronique des spectacles," *Nouvelle Revue Française*,
XXII (February, 1924), 213.

for drunken women, the trained seals! And then they doze off and dream of heavy industry.

Drieu paints the audience as spectacle—a major theme of realist art, brilliantly captured by Daumier in *Le Cinquième acte à la Gaîeté* (Fig. 3)—subtly fusing the Parisian bourgeois of 1924, in pursuit of entertainment and nodding off at the theater, with a darker vision, with a languorous and sinister brother, Baudelaire's Ennui, smoking his hookah and dreaming of scaffolds.

The circus stage with its diverse nonverbal stunts constitutes a "return to nature," Drieu has been told. But what, indeed, is natural? Is anything we become accustomed to natural, be it margarine or a wig? What then happens to the distinction between artifice and art? "Je sens une défaillance qui gagne de proche en proche, de la laiterie à la littérature."[22] 'I sense a breakdown of contours that is spreading by degrees, moving from dairy products to literature.' Aragon, it appears, has been berating Drieu for criticizing popular spectacles too rigorously, maintaining that acrobatics and poetry have always been "arts d'exception," 'arts of exception,' and that different critical standards should apply. This quarrel, which involves divergent conceptions of the limits of art and the functions of criticism, deeply troubles Drieu. Musing on the underlying appeal of acrobatics, Drieu realizes that such a spectacle glorifies the spectators' idea of simple human ability. "Ces barres nettes, nickelées, ces quelques hommes . . . perpétuent encore pour l'étonnement oublieux et l'amusement niais des autres, les gestes de l'ancienne liberté de sa gloire physique."[23] 'These cleanly visible metallic bars, these few men . . . continue to perpetuate, for the forgetful astonishment and the foolish amusement of others, the gestures of man's ancient freedom, of his physical glory.' Day laborers, Drieu acerbically notes, enjoy seeing someone lift weights. Unfortunately, so do some writers.

The critical voyage reaches its climax at the circus, as Drieu sketches the signs of an acrobatic number. Text and subtext merge as circus performers and literary tumblers pass one another in a high-wire display:

Les trapézistes gambadent de branche en branche, par familles. Les jongleurs conquièrent leur dextérité, si vaine, en maniant le boomerang. Les équi-

22. Pierre Drieu La Rochelle, "Chronique des spectacles," *Nouvelle Revue Française,* XXII (March, 1924), 342.
23. *Ibid.,* 344.

3. Honoré Daumier, *Le Cinquième acte à La Gaîeté*. February 7, 1848. Lithograph, series *Tout ce qu'on voudra*, 8¼ × 10 inches. Bibliothèque Nationale, Paris.
Photo: Bibliothèque Nationale.

libristes traversent le pont de l'âne avec armes et bagages. Les acrobates rattrapent un instant le rythme de ce jeune homme vêtu de peaux qui errait dans les bois et qui . . . se trouvait aussi bien sur ses mains que sur ses pieds.[24]

The trapeze artists leap from branch to branch, in groups. The jugglers conquer their hollow dexterity by manipulating the boomerang. The tight-rope walkers nimbly cross the high wire. The acrobats recapture for an instant the rhythm of that young man dressed in animal skins who wandered

24. *Ibid.*, 343.

in the forest and who . . . was just as comfortable walking on his hands as on his feet.

The surrealists are wrong, Drieu concludes. Parisians come to the circus not in a naïve search for insight but "pour se débarrasser de l'Histoire et de sa pensée lente," 'to unburden themselves of History and its slow design.' The popular spectacles of Paris provide no art, only escape, oblivion, an acceptable way to achieve spiritual deadness. The subtext completely covers the text as Drieu finds himself overwhelmed by "le pernicieux mensonge du music-hall et du cirque," [25] 'the pernicious deceit of the music hall and the circus.' In romanticizing public taste his artist friends have become supremely and blindly condescending. Popular taste is not charmingly naïve and natural; it is grossly self-interested and wallows in the trivial.

The breadth and intensity of Drieu's experiment in criticism led inevitably to a theoretical and artistic dead end. The meticulous, savage attention he directed at popular shows would have exhausted all but the most serious and complex art forms. He was forced quickly to confront the dilemma facing "the serious intermittent critic," to use Renata Adler's term: to write authentic criticism the critic must have a sustained high level of art about which to write.[26] In five intense months Drieu literally wore out the enterprise of spectacle criticism, reducing the spectrum of performances observed to a handful of striking images. His visions of the contemporary music hall as a metaphor for French society and of the circus as a paradigm of the literary scene would reappear in his essays and novels.

Drieu was doubly disappointed. The reality of popular arts was not worth the critical effort. A more subtle discouragement came from his realization that the surrealists were betraying the ideal of art's freedom from constraint. Aragon in his drift toward a vague populism, others in their apolitical remoteness from the world outside their own esoteric circles not only romanticized the level of public taste; by defending the popular and the new for its own sake, they risked compromising themselves by all manner of dangerous engagements. The little quarrels with Aragon over the evening's entertainments became a larger disagree-

25. *Ibid.*, 345.

26. Renata Adler, "The Perils of Pauline," *New York Review of Books*, August 14, 1980, pp. 26–36.

ment over the issue of art's relation to society, presaging the imminent drift of the early surrealist movement into literary factionalism and practical politics.

In March, 1924, Drieu apologized to his readers for abandoning the series: "Vous comprendrez que je cesse cette chronique: je fuis la tristesse qui s'accumule pour le moment dans les lieux où les hommes s'assemblent."[27] 'You will understand why I am abandoning this chronicle: I am fleeing the gloom that is presently settling over the places where men gather together.' His passionate disavowal of the Paris rituals of the early twenties, the logical conclusion to a sustained dialogue between the writer-as-critic and the writer-as-spectator, functioned also as an exercise in literary self-definition, for as Drieu rejected, image by image and movement by movement, what had appeared to be the only still lively forms of contemporary French art besides painting, he cleared the terrain for a subsequent redefinition of literary genres within his own work. In a series of implied dialogues—between his own observations and the aesthetic judgments of his poet and painter friends, between contemporary French culture and the foreign influences that threatened it, between rituals and their spectators, between prose and poetry, gesture and painting—Drieu had recorded a unique critical adventure.

Drieu could not find in the casinos and music halls of Paris the noble primitive art his fellow surrealists chose to believe was there. In stagework with no content he sorely missed the play of the mind and of the passions. He expressed his impatience by criticizing the form of the productions, but his fundamental discontent was with a lack of meaning that extended to the very fabric of French life. Discouraged by the theater of rigorous spoken text, Drieu had hoped to find in less traditional popular spectacles the vivid emotions—the "blood"—of strong human intentionality. But his conception of the possibilities of theater was limited to things he already knew, to cubism, surrealism, and the innovations of Jean Cocteau. It would take Artaud, an early fellow surrealist with practical experience on and behind the stage, to elaborate a design to free French plays from their stifling naturalistic strictures.

The falling prose rhythms of Drieu's last spectacle review marked

27. Pierre Drieu La Rochelle, "Chronique des spectacles," *Nouvelle Revue Française*, XXII (March, 1924), 346.

the beginning of his inevitable break with the surrealists and sounded some of the opening notes of what would become the most complex and controversial part of his career, his work as a political journalist. Drieu's analysis of Parisians and their entertainments—one of the most striking confluences of literary art, cultural theory, and historical analysis to come out of the interwar years—culminated in a condemnation of the French national character. In his essays and in his novels, Drieu would continue to explore the links between public rituals and the iconology of modernist art. He would continue to walk through Paris, watching parades and observing their spectators, listening always for the sound of armies once again marching across Europe.

3

L'Homme couvert de femmes and the Demoiselles de Paris

"La vie, c'est si plastique," exclaims Gille, the hero of Drieu's dazzling and recalcitrant first novel, *L'Homme couvert de femmes*.[1] To translate his words appropriately is to enter the aesthetic ground between fiction and the visual arts: 'Life is so full of forms, so beautiful, so fit for modeling.' The novel's striking emblematic title evokes pictorial images of sylvan amours, of corporeal garlands, of cubist brothels, while its linguistic combination suggests a man protected by, hidden by, decorated with (as with scars and medals) women, as well as—at the simplest level—a man who has more women than he knows what to do with. Drieu's pictorialized tale of sexual license and its disillusionments in the twenties slyly acknowledges and satirizes some of the principal motifs of early surrealist prose—the *conte philosophique* on changing ideals of beauty, the prose epic of the "urban marvelous," the dialogic inquiry into contemporary *moeurs* (manners and morals)—and in several striking scenes with intertexts in cubist, surrealist, and traditional painting suggests and illustrates the fundamental relationship between physical desire and the iconology of the visual arts.

Drieu's early path toward fiction is paved with curious intergenre works. *Etat civil* (Vital statistics, 1921), an essay-memoir sometimes classed as a novel (Drieu did not consider it one), is loosely patterned after Joyce's *A Portrait of the Artist as a Young Man* but heavily dominated by the traditional codes of French confessional literature—Jean-Jacques Rousseau, Alain, the early André Gide.[2] In chronicling the cen-

---

1. Pierre Drieu La Rochelle, *L'Homme couvert de femmes* (Paris, 1925), 200. Hereafter cited in the text as *HCF*.
2. See Reck, "Drieu La Rochelle's *Etat civil.*"

tral psychological and intellectual lineaments of his first sixteen years, Drieu's scattered sketch of a French middle-class child and adolescent whose vision has yet to be expanded by the experiences of war and of experimental art displays many of the stylistic influences appropriate to its time—the symbolist legacy of Stéphane Mallarmé and his obsession with the "virgin page," a fair dose of reluctant Freudianism, and, on its final page, a striking futurist image of visual silence: "Une colonne de neige se lève au milieu des neiges infinies. Le monde est un tourbillon blanc."[3] 'A column of snow rises up in the midst of infinite snows. The world is a white whirlwind.' In *L'Homme couvert de femmes* Drieu began to fill, at times past the limits of its frame, the empty canvas he had prepared in 1921.

While surrealist painters such as Max Ernst began to explore the imagery of the struggle between the sexes in dreamlike anthropomorphic scenes, early surrealist literary treatments of sexual relations tended to remain heavily poeticized, didactically comic, or clumsily epicene.[4] As Drieu began in the early twenties to write his first brief short stories about male-female relationships, contemporary French fiction offered few methodologies adequate to his purposes. Drieu's 1921 *Nouvelle Revue Française* review of Aragon's first novel, *Anicet ou le panorama* (Anicet or the panorama), deliberately exaggerating the tale's shock value and setting up a convenient dichotomy between the private lives of the French and the English, served as a declaration of literary independence from taboos on subject matter:

> Les Français sont connus dans le monde pour le goût qu'ils ont de l'amour physique; eux seuls, dans les temps modernes, ont courageusement poussé à la fois l'aventure sentimentale et la quête du plaisir, et avoué dans leurs moeurs les conquêtes qui en ont résulté. Eh bien! ils n'en laissent rien passer dans leur littérature, ou si peu, ou d'une façon si dissimulée, si convenue, si hypocrite. Oui, les Français sont plus hypocrites que les Anglais, car sur ce chapitre les Anglais n'avaient rien à cacher, tandis que les Français avaient quelque chose à dévoiler.[5]

3. Pierre Drieu La Rochelle, *Etat civil* (Paris, 1921), 145.

4. For a detailed discussion of surrealist sexual themes, see Xavière Gauthier, *Surréalisme et sexualité* (Paris, 1971). For a full discussion of Aragon's early novels, see Rima Drell Reck, "Louis Aragon," *Dictionary of Literary Biography*, LXXII (1988), 3–25.

5. Drieu La Rochelle, "*Anicet ou le panorama*, par Louis Aragon."

The French are noted throughout the world for their taste for physical love; they alone, in modern times, have simultaneously and daringly explored the sentimental adventure and the search for pleasure, and integrated the results into their lives. Well, almost none of this has been visible in their literature, or only in a terribly disguised, conventionalized, hypocritical form. Yes, on this count the French are more hypocritical than the English, because the English had nothing to hide, while the French had something to unveil.

By using the word *dévoiler*, which connotes the undraping of a statue, Drieu suggested a text that exposes to the light the gestures, forms, and colors of physical love. A year after the Aragon review, scandal exploded over the sexual and scatological details in Joyce's *Ulysses*, to be surpassed in 1928 by even more intense outrage over Lawrence's *Lady Chatterley's Lover*. The disruption of traditional forms that characterized developments in the plastic arts was paralleled by a growing freedom in the use of language. Modernist writers such as Joyce, Lawrence, and Drieu used unconventional vocabulary and subject matter as much to restage the inner context of fiction as to outrage the public. Shocking words and explicit scenes became strikingly visible elements in a new plastic freedom related to the larger freedoms of a new age in art.

L'Homme couvert de femmes with its frank depiction of the games of sex and money in the twenties now appears comfortably at home among the novels of Fitzgerald, Hemingway, and Faulkner. However, in the France of 1925 Drieu's flamboyant transposition of the theme of idealism into jolting painterly images found no ready audience. Readers and critics were surprised, puzzled, or scandalized by the novel's odd juxtapositions of pictorial, confessional, and psychological elements and have largely tended to remain so for some sixty-odd years. Literary modernism's systematic disruptions of form and tone and its substitution of pattern, myth, and fragmentation for plot, theme, and analysis are now familiar to us. The most disturbing—and intriguing—offense to contemporary sensibility of Drieu's novel is its often awkward, at times ingratiating literary stance, somewhere between the brilliant extravagances of Aragon's "Le Passage de l'Opéra" (the first part of *Le Paysan de Paris*, completed in 1924) and the deliberate structural mannerisms of Hemingway's *In Our Time* (1925), some of which Drieu had read earlier in periodicals. In *L'Homme couvert de femmes* Gille

Gambier, the hero Drieu continued to model over the years in two later novels and several short stories, makes his debut, here twenty-seven years old, on the move between Paris and the south of France, on the active prowl with women, an alternatingly sullen and long-winded seeker of the physical and painted world of ideal forms.

The plot is simple. Gille arrives at the country house of Luc, a cultured homosexual friend, and Finette, Luc's wealthy widowed sister. Piqued by Finette's obvious interest, Gille postpones a potentially advantageous liaison by successively allowing two female visitors, Molly and Françoise, to seduce him. He also briefly considers taking to bed the sculpturally bejeweled Englishwoman Lady Hyacinthia, but finds her vague internationalist pronouncements an anaphrodisiac. Soon depressed by the shallow sexuality of all these women who move so quickly from one man's bed to another, Gille escapes for a few days to Paris, where he makes a frantic tour of bars and brothels. On returning to the country he begins—after an initial fiasco induced by total exhaustion—an affair with Finette that offers physical pleasure and potential financial security. Increasingly attached to Gille, Finette nevertheless remains hesitant to commit herself emotionally. The arrival of Jacqueline, a woman Gille had loved intensely and idyllically during the war, accompanied by her blind pianist husband, raises complex questions about Gille's memories of the past. Refusing to believe in the possibility of more than one great love, Gille manages to reduce his remembered experience with Jacqueline to a mere illusion. Wanting more out of his emotional life, he also begins to reject the ironic Finette. After a long, meditative despair, further fueled by Luc's haunting admonition that both he and Gille are looking for impossible perfect unions, Gille packs, throws his bags into the car, and flees.

Contradicting its printed division into two parts, the novel's eighteen chapters clearly fall into three segments, forming an odd asymmetrical triptych: on the left, Gille's arrival and brief stay at Finette's (60 pages); at the center the Paris interlude (18 pages); on the right Gille's return to Finette's and his stay over several months (130 pages). In this secular altarpiece, the middle panel dominates; the first section sets the basic aural and dramatic context; the third, least successful part attempts to understand the roots of Gille's character and of his aesthetic-moral vision of life. In the last part Drieu's struggle to disentangle and illustrate Gille's inner nature results in a visible hesitation between a traditional confessional structure and objective narration of interactions among the characters. Gille threatens to usurp almost all of the narrative space with loudly staged self-analyses, an extensive written *histoire sentimentale* addressed to Finette, and several windy philosophical meditations. With its long chunks of prose, startling stylistic shifts, and several unconvincing interior monologues in the minds of the women, the third part appears disjointed rather than deliberately fragmented. Lively dialogues connected by formal transitions alternate with abruptly offset recollection sequences studded with pictorial effects. The dichotomy between visual and aural narrative focus remains largely unfruitful in the third part, although some of the abrupt juxtapositions barely miss being exciting. What Drieu appears to be seeking—and what he will adopt in several later works—is a version of literary collage, a conscious juxtaposition of diverse linguistic and plastic elements. This early novel's groupings and shifts of scene also hint, awkwardly, at the picture gallery structure that will shape several of the later novels.

As the novel opens, brief lines of dialogue present Finette and two female visitors discussing the newly arrived Gille approaching them across the lawn. These initial pages have both the look and sound of some of Hemingway's dialogues, something of a feat in French. Gille first appears as a body with a few lightly sketched plastic qualities:

> —Gille . . . comment dites-vous?
> —Gille, cela suffit.
> —Qu'est-ce que c'est?
> —Il a un corps convenable et une frimousse qui peut être attrayante pour certaines. (*HCF* 11)

> —Gille . . . what?
> —Gille, that's enough.
> —What's a Gille?
> —He has a pretty good body and a little mug that some women find attractive.

This almost pure, distanced dialogue gradually becomes more strongly visual. Approaching Finette's group, Gille and Luc see an unfinished, Poussin-like composition, "trois femmes claires, assises sur le perron bas, devant la façade assez noble de cet ancien rendez-vous de chasse" (*HCF* 12), 'three light-colored women, seated on the low outer steps, in front of the rather noble facade of the ancient hunting lodge.' As Gille is introduced to the women, he begins to fill in their empty outlines with small perceived physical details, while his attention, always *en passage* (in motion), continues to flit and flicker. Immediately finding Gille's obvious distraction attractive, the women instinctively angle and shift to fall within his range of vision. Finette briefly turns the conversation to a guest expected in a few months, a Madame de B., whom she describes as a vast outline to be filled in. "Elle a un visage et des bras! La pire littérature devient possible; vous savez, tous les grands mots" (*HCF* 14). 'What a face, what arms! The worst literature becomes possible; you know what I mean, all the grand words.' Mme de B. instantly becomes the never seen, strangely familiar symbol of ideal beauty (and Drieu's ironic counterpart of Aragon's Mirabelle in *Anicet*), whose form Gille will "compose" and embellish at intervals throughout the novel.

Drieu's variable use of dialogue is almost cavalier. After its initial appearance as a visual sign of stylishly aural fiction, the dialogue becomes largely a plastic element. Characters fence and position themselves through verbal exchanges. Gossip is described as a sacrificial ritual that scatters little imaginary mummies emptied of blood and meaning and arranges them at grotesque angles. In some of the novel's more awkward exchanges, Drieu overtly conceives dialogue as a form of illustration, presenting characters as passing verbal sketches around the pictorial space. Most of the scattershot experiments with dialogue appear to be part of a deliberate effort to modernize and disrupt the traditional geometry of the French seventeenth-century *récit*. One oddity stands out strikingly, a scene of unspoken dialogue in which Gille sings his thoughts silently to himself over the drowsy heads of a group of dope addicts. The resemblance to the voice parts in the "Nighttown" episode of Joyce's *Ulysses* is clear, but Drieu introduces an element that is peculiarly his own, an odd visual-theatrical configuration combining the broad strokes of caricature with the audience-oriented forward stance of the music hall or comic opera. This small, curious touch, barely developed and crammed in among the novel's eclectic assemblage of literary forms, will reappear exploited to maximum advantage in *Drôle de voyage* as musical and comedic arrangements of dialogue.

The fundamental pictorial conception of *L'Homme couvert de femmes* is easily read in its substitution of pattern for plot and of fragments for wholes (breasts for women, a few stars for the sky) and in its odd visual

4. Pablo Picasso, *Les Demoiselles d'Avignon.* 1907. Oil on canvas, 96 × 92 inches. Collection, The Museum of Modern Art, New York, Acquired through the Lillie P. Bliss Bequest. Copyright 1990 ARS N.Y./SPADEM.
Photo: Museum of Modern Art.

conception of dialogue. With the Paris interlude, however, Drieu's pell-mell exploration of the residues of classical and romantic iconology, his juxtaposition of views and viewers, his frequently jarring shifts of style, his depiction of the man covered with women as an artistic transforming mirror all converge and point to the presence of a crucial interartistic metaphor—of an icon that illustrates, explains, and rereads the novel, and is itself in turn reread by the text. The icon of Drieu's pictorial brothel novel is clearly the most extraordinary brothel picture of all time, Picasso's *Les Demoiselles d'Avignon* (Fig. 4). The novel's struggle with the disintegration of forms is defined against Drieu's reading of the most significant and unsettling painting of the early modernist era.

Drieu first saw the untitled painting around 1917 at Picasso's studio, in the company of Louis Aragon, at the time his closest friend and soon after literary adviser to collector Jacques Doucet, who bought the painting from Picasso around 1920. (Aragon is one of those sometimes credited with giving the canvas its name.) The painting lived a private but influential life, visited and admired by writers and artists for some thirty years after its completion in 1907, first in Picasso's studio and then in a kind of altar Doucet built for it in his Paris home.[6] Reproduced for the first time in the magazine *La Révolution Surréaliste* in July, 1925, and first exhibited publicly at the Petit Palais during the Paris World's Fair of 1937, the painting was an intimate part of Drieu's surrealist years in "le délicieux Paris de bordels," 'delicious Paris of the brothels,' that reached their high point in 1925 with the publication of *L'Homme couvert de femmes*, dedicated to Aragon.

The fame of Picasso's huge painting (eight feet high by seven feet eight inches wide) as the first work to explore the possibilities of cubism has tended to obscure some of its other, equally revolutionary qualities.[7] As Leo Steinberg has brilliantly and exhaustively demonstrated, Picasso's careful elaboration of his project through numerous sketches and studies to its final form raises two important issues.[8] The first is a direct challenge to the long-standing view of the painting as "a battlefield of trial and experiment," to use Alfred H. Barr, Jr.'s, phrase, with Picasso adding and changing elements over a long and discontinuous period of time, putting in the faces resembling African masks as a gratuitous, artistically encyclopedic, last touch late in 1907, some time

6. For details on the housing and ultimate exhibition of the painting, and on the likely source of its name, see William Rubin, *Picasso in the Collection of the Museum of Modern Art* (New York, 1972), 197, nn. 9, 10, 12. For an exhaustive examination of the development and historical and iconographical context of the painting, see the catalogue of the exhibition recently held at the Musée Picasso, *Les Demoiselles d'Avignon* (2 vols.; Paris, 1988).

7. For a traditional view, see Alfred H. Barr, Jr., *Picasso: Fifty Years of His Art* (New York, 1946), 54–57.

8. Leo Steinberg, "Picasso's Philosophical Brothel," Part 1, *Art News*, CXXI (September, 1972), 20–29; Steinberg, "Picasso's Philosophical Brothel," Part 2, *Art News*, CXXI (October, 1972), 38–47.

after the rest of the painting was finished.[9] In fact, primitive sculpture could be viewed in Paris earlier than 1907 and Picasso doubtless felt its impact before he began his composition. The encyclopedic quality of the work is indeed striking, but no less so than an earlier compendium painting (my term) such as *L'Enseigne de Gersaint* (*Gersaint's Shopsign*) by Watteau (1720–1721), a two-part work showing the interior of an art gallery with dozens of paintings hung four deep on the walls. What is radically memorable about Picasso's compendium painting is its startling juxtaposition within single figures of disparate historical elements and diverse pictorial styles. Each of the female figures is disturbingly encyclopedic, while the works in Watteau's painting are all quietly contained within their frames. Picasso made *Les Demoiselles* jarring on purpose.

The second issue raised by Steinberg's study concerns the extraordinary intensity of the painting, its sheer *presence*, which is only minimally explained by the cubist elements. Our growing familiarity with cubism has in no way served to diminish the work's overwhelming physical impact on the viewer. Its effect on a literary imagination such as Drieu's is as much, indeed, more directly related to the issue of the painting's effect than to its radical historical importance. As Steinberg's study makes clear, the painting went through numerous conceptual alterations, each shifting still another element, changing another proportion of parts, a visual editing process that culminated in a gravely and deliberately startling composition. The rotation and compression of space, the deliberate assault on narrative painting, the cruel barbarism of two of the faces, and the violence of the forward-jutting planes make the entire painting an immense, encyclopedic metaphor for early modernist art in its most explosive and erotic form. Equally important for Drieu, the painting is intensely theatrical, a vivid and deliberate staging of the acts of making love and of making art that at every turn questions its own conception. In a 1924 critical piece, Drieu wrote, "Puisque notre visage ne peut être qu'un masque, portons la main sur ce masque." [10] 'Since our face can only be a mask, let us strike at that mask.' This remark, oddly similar to Roland Barthes' description some forty

9. Alfred H. Barr, Jr., *Picasso: Forty Years of His Art* (New York, 1939), 60.
10. Drieu La Rochelle, "Chronique des spectacles," *Nouvelle Revue Française*, XXII (February, 1924), 211.

years later of modern literature as "un masque qui se montre du doigt," 'a mask that points to itself,' underlines Drieu's interest in exploiting the theatricality of art.[11]

Picasso's painting is monumentally theatrical, with its two areas of deliberately parted curtains, its three pairs of eyes staring directly out at the viewer, the seemingly tipped surface of the table with fruit that juts out past the picture plane at the lower edge. The three central figures are seen from differing viewing perspectives: *la gisante* (second from the left) is lying down and seen from above; the caryatid figure at the center is standing upright; the butterflied, crouching woman at the lower right is viewed from above and is ambiguously on her back or on her knees. His earlier studies for the painting reveal Picasso's successive elimination of two male figures, one originally depicted as entering from the left, the other seated at the table in the center. Art historians have largely concurred in seeing these narrative simplifications as part of Picasso's discovery of a new pictorial focus, as a development away from his initial vision of a brothel scene as a partially didactic, partially variational composition to a vision whose center of pictorial and emotional gravity is in a radically new location—out *in front of the painting*, in the rapidly closing space between the viewer and what he sees.[12] This forward motion results in a sense of the viewer *being seen* by the painting. The radical suppression of the traditional "safe" viewing space creates a relationship between painting and viewer that seemed to Drieu—already inclined by his childhood sense of participation in book illustrations, by his direct immersion in violently moving forms and images during battle, and by his persistent identification of physical love with artistic vision—a bold confirmation of his own sense of *walking into pictures*.

The final version of *Les Demoiselles*—the only one Drieu knew—is a painting conceived as a huge "closet" stage that includes the viewer and makes him a performer in the play. (Genet's *Le Balcon* is a more recent and far more elaborate, and obvious, illustration of the same fundamental performance-participation metaphor.) The relentless staginess of Picasso's brothel, which loses none of its original immediacy seen at greater distance in a gallery, also provided Drieu with a visual confir-

11. Roland Barthes, *Essais critiques* (Paris, 1964), 107.
12. Among them are Robert Rosenblum, Leo Steinberg, and Roger Fry.

mation of the intimate connection between satire and modern painting. The multifaceted, cool-eyed women who fill most of the pictural space are constructed of elements from traditional studies of nudes, from Iberian sculpture, from African art; they are, in fact, *illustrations of illustrations*, composites of diverse layers of culture, big brutal exemplars of the wild cultural eclecticism that had made Drieu call the Paris spectacles of 1923 "ce Théâtre-Babel des Champs-Elysées," 'this Theater of Babel on the Champs-Elysées,' and that would lead him over the years to refer to Picasso as "a great painter of ruins." [13] For Drieu, Picasso's "philosophical brothel" (the phrase is Steinberg's) was many things at once: an intimate and unsettling view of a familiar place, a vast door opening onto new plastic possibilities in narrative, and a disturbing artistic vision that demanded refuting.

A lifelong pilgrim of "gallery pictures" (paintings too large to be viewed comfortably outside of specially designed settings such as museums), Drieu continued to brood on the commanding visions he found in the major canvases of his life—*Les Demoiselles d'Avignon*, Watteau's *Gilles*, Delacroix's *La Liberté guidant le peuple*, Manet's *Olympia*—and to compare them with the other source of monumental images, of "dream food" for his time, the movies. (When characters in his short stories are not employed in art galleries, they are art critics, cultural journalists, or work in films.) The ultimate structure of *Gilles* (1939), Drieu's most ambitious novel, would follow the scenic and conceptual principles of a museum trip. In 1925, recently emerged from almost six years in the army, resonating to the promises of surrealism, hearing the brilliant, negative voices of Eliot and Joyce, Drieu had in his first novel to deal with Picasso's painting.

The Gille of *L'Homme couvert de femmes* is an artist without portfolio, an explorer of the plasticity of the visible world whose field of vision is filled with female forms. Gille's images of the first two women he beds down are incomplete, a small harvest of pleasing traits he adds to his ongoing portrait of Mme de B. Molly provides "a big behind silhouetted against the moonlight," the literary cartoon *châtelaine* (country squiress) Françoise a delightful smell of grass and woods. The emotionally elusive Finette, who plans to wait Gille out after his return

---

13. Drieu La Rochelle, "Chronique des spectacles," *Nouvelle Revue Française*, XXI (December, 1923), 729.

from the Paris orgy, remains an unfinished form, an irregular sequence of elusive images that psychologically and physically disarm Gille in their first close contact.

> Dans une maison isolée, on l'avait attiré dans un guet-apens. Prisonnier d'une femme en allait-il oublier la foule des femmes? Cette image de Finette . . . prise dans un jeu de glaces, elle était partout et nulle part. N'allait-elle pas s'asseoir au milieu de ces glaces et à force d'immobilité, de réalité, lasser leur machination infinie, les faire tomber en miettes? (*HCF* 91)

> He had been ambushed in an isolated house. One woman's prisoner, was he going to forget the crowd of women? And this image of Finette . . . seen in a play of mirrors, she was everywhere and nowhere. Was she going to sit down among all these mirrors and with her stillness, her solid presence, exhaust their infinite interplay and shatter them into myriad fragments?

As in surrealist films, in Drieu's novel mirrors create multiple, artistically elusive images that suggest an unseen world of magic.[14] Finette vanishes into her reflection; Gille cannot quite fix his own image in the glass. The moving, fragmented portraits reflected in the swinging doors of a mirrored armoire create a dizzying disturbance of perception. Gille prefers Mme de B., the composite painterly creature of his imagination. For the reality of forms he can reach, touch, and model, he seeks out the painted and staged world of the brothel.

An extended analysis of the Paris brothel sequence brings into high relief the mythology and iconology of a 1925 urban *musée imaginaire*. In restaurants and bars Gille observes the elaborate rituals of idleness; in the streets and music halls he meets an assault of erotic imagery in posters, signs, and nude entertainers; in the rolling, enclosed spaces of Paris taxis he seeks out brief spiritual retreats. The textures, images, and themes of the novel's central panel provide a striking dramatic text of Paris in the twenties, with Gille's breathless tour of "les îles perdues des femmes," 'the lost islands of women,' making visible the inner core of Drieu's tale—the mode of intersection between the world as seen and as experienced. The world of brothels is in potentiality the world of art and freedom, a vast repository of forms that can quickly obliterate Gille's memories of Finette's largely empty world of mirrors.

14. A useful discussion of this technique appears in Herbert S. Gershman, *The Surrealist Revolution in France* (Ann Arbor, 1969), 30–34.

As Gille arrives in Paris after dark, the smells and sounds of the city arouse his senses:

> Les bouffées imaginaires de la ville ameutèrent dans son âme une populace de forces énervées. Comme un voyageur qui revient des solitudes, en s'approchant de ce vieux mystère éventré, bien que son nez fût fatigué de l'odeur séculaire de toute cette tripe cent fois repliée sur elle-même, il s'échauffa encore. (*HCF* 73)

> The invisible exhalations of the city revived in his soul an army of enervated powers. Like a traveler coming back from deserted places, as he got closer to this ancient disemboweled mystery, even though his nose was weary of the secular odor of all this tripe a hundred times folded in upon itself, it inflamed him once again.

The decaying presence of Paris is the first Baudelairean note of Gille's richly inflected urban odyssey. Eager to cleanse himself of the sticky-sweet peace of the countryside, he heads for a bar, drinks a great deal, and mentally devours the painted faces around him, looking forward to "une volupté sauvage," 'a savage voluptuousness.' No luck. All the women present are already in hand for the night. Waking quite late the next day, he listens to the sound of the city in motion, then prepares for his sortie, dressing with the care of an actor going onstage. During lunch at a crowded businessmen's restaurant, Gille mentally groups and classifies the other patrons, whose day is half over when his own begins, then turns his painterly eye to the successive still lifes formed on his table by the courses of his meal, the last a cheese "with streaks of death in it." Wandering the streets, he immerses his gaze in the waves of passing faces that break over him. At last arrived on the "sidewalk of the prostitutes," he prolongs anticipation by first entering an art gallery and gorging himself "on volumes . . . thighs, backsides, breasts . . . the full figure of a nude silhouetted against stars" (*HCF* 77).

Back on the street, Gille sees a big woman, "ce grand bateau. . . . Faces multipliées: la chair, tourne sur elle-même et fait face à tous les points du monde. Ce fard, cette hanche. Ce sourire, ce bas. Dans Gille, il y a une avalanche, un effondrement. Il est heurté par une belle épaule, par un quartier de roc" (*HCF* 77). 'Like a big boat. . . . Multiple surfaces: flesh, that turns on itself and billows in all directions. Makeup, hip. Smile, stocking. Inside Gille, an avalanche, a cave-in. He is struck by a big shoulder, by a huge side of rock.' The quick, jerky rhythms of

Gille's perceptions recall Bloom's cubistically arranged thoughts as he watches the rich white stockings flash on Grafton Street in *Ulysses*. Hesitating for a minute because he is reluctant to give up all the other forms on the sidewalk, Gille once again takes in the full picture of the huge figure: "Sa croupe et sa poitrine, c'était sur le bitume ondulé déjà comme sur le flot des draps, surchargés de feu et de nuages, l'épaisse coque du vaisseau de ligne en plein combat" (*HCF* 78). 'Her rump and bosom already looked against the uneven asphalt as they would against the waves of the sheets, full of fire and clouds, like the thick hull of a battleship in full combat.' He follows the big woman into a hotel.

Nude, she is a huge white treasure chest, a model bigger and more beautiful than those in paintings, with fine small wrists and ankles, high calves "artistically worked," knees like "precision pieces." She looks like a Matisse, a Rubens, a Fragonard nude; Gille is proud of his conquest. But topping this huge, glorious, painterly body with its fine joints is a jarringly disparate head:

> Si le corps était resté à l'abri des coups, [la tête] en était meurtrie, et de la mauvaise peinture sur une peau livide, et des cheveux hachés sur la nuque. Mais un oeil immobile comme la mer qui noie en soi-même ses tempêtes: et l'ivoire des dents où l'or est un ornement barbare, comme nourri de la puissance continentale d'un éléphant. Du reste, cette tête, Gille la trancha quand d'abord il la baisa au cou, les lèvres retroussées, avec ses dents, pour marquer la limite supérieure de ses caresses, et elle roula dans l'abîme. (*HCF* 79)

> While the body had remained unmarked, the head was badly bruised, with bad painting on the pale skin and hair hacked off at the neck. An eye as immobile as the sea that swallows its own storms: and the ivory of her teeth where gold makes a barbaric ornament, like the foreign spoils of an elephant. Gille separated this head from the rest when he first kissed her on the neck, his lips drawn back, with his teeth, to mark the upper limit of his caresses, and the head fell off and disappeared into space.

Gille rejects the head—a Picassoesque neoprimitive with a single eye, seen like a *symboliste* woman underwater—posed on the ravishing, generously undulating volumes of the body. Unlike Picasso's sturdily constructed women with their angular breasts, savagely pointy elbows, and direct stares, Gille's *demoiselle de Paris* is a conveniently detachable composite. Gille carries out an artistic excision, a curious painterly barbarism of his own, by mentally biting off the jarring head and throwing it away. (The striking rhythms and skillful word order transpositions of the French text lose their tom-tom beat in translation.) The Baude-lairean *voyage sensuel* that follows silhouettes Gille over the girl like "a god" against the sky. But Gille cannot keep his model from growing back together, from insidiously challenging his mastery of his medium. As they chat briefly after making love, the girl reveals that she is bisex-ual but prefers a man when he knows what he's doing.

After a fitful rest back in his room, Gille ventures out again, select-ing a house from his mental directory of brothels, which includes "des maisons calmes où des femmes vivent nues comme des poissons dans l'eau," 'quiet houses where the women live nude, like fish in water,' others where the girls sew and extend familylike friendship, "like nuns receiving in their convent," and offer refreshments to friends (*HCF* 83). In "a house of savory silence" Gille is suddenly presented with a room-ful of choices. Unable to organize and select, he faces an extraordinary multiple, composite female figure, and drowns in colors and forms:

> Des portes s'ouvrent à deux battants. Gille se trouve devant la merveille du monde. Il n'y a qu'un grand corps féminin, modulé infiniment comme une seule parole solitaire. Il n'est qu'une chair pour tant de seins et tant de hanches, il y pousse des cheveux multicolores, des ongles comme des co-quillages et par là-dessus s'étendent des grandes taches de fard. Il ne voit rien. (*HCF* 84)

> Both doors opened wide. Gille was immersed in the world's greatest mir-acle. Just one big female body, infinitely modulated like a single word. One flesh for so many breasts and so many buttocks, multicolored hair growing, fingernails like mollusk shells, and on top big splotches of makeup. He is blinded.

Confused and unmanned by the hallucinating surrealist vision, he picks a girl at random; she is the wrong one—her breasts lack form. All the same, he undresses for the third time that day (another costume change), thinking ahead to dinner.

During the hours still to be spent before evening comes, Gille re-joins the rituals of Paris, touring the bars, devouring his newspaper, reading all the *texts* that pass before his eyes. "Il lit tous les visages, tous les articles, les alcools de toutes les couleurs. Il grandit, il élargit, il déploie ce lieu d'une main magnanime" (*HCF* 85). 'He reads all the faces, all the articles, all the many-colored alcohols. He makes longer, wider, he unfolds the scene with a magnanimous hand.' With Gille mildly drunk and a trifle lonely, the Baudelairean voyage takes on a cinematic touch as he typecasts the characters coming into the bar, then briefly runs a silent western film through his mind:

> Il sait d'où ils viennent tous ceux qui entrent ici: ceux qui ont reçu l'argent tout bonnement et ceux qui l'ont arraché d'un geste délicat; ceux qui n'ont rien fait, qui ont dormi; et ceux qui ont maigri dans une salle de boxe.
>
> Pourquoi regretter des Far-West de légende, quand ici on est au milieu d'une bande qui écume, rafle et a toujours son plein. Gille tâte leur secret naïf: le monde n'existe pas, mais il y a un coin plein de bonnes choses: fourrures et boutons de manchettes, personne n'en veut, c'est pour nous. (HCF 85–86)

> He knows where they all come from: those who have earned their money and those who have stolen it with a delicate gesture; those who have done nothing but sleep; and those who have grown slim in a boxing gym.
>
> Why long for a legendary Far West, when right here one is surrounded by a gang mounted on frothing horses, a band that makes its raids and always gets a haul, outlaws, with a sack of treasures: furs and cufflinks, belonging to no one, they're ours.

Gille's sense of being surrounded by an empire of human signs, by an album of physiognomic types in the streets of Paris, perpetuates the traditions of nineteenth-century caricature, which served to classify the city's crowds into comprehensible groupings, into collections of qualities, *métiers*, and masks.[15] Gille walks, dreams awake, organizes the vast world of women, "les bourgeoises, les mères de famille, les femmes du monde, le faubourg, le gratin, les jeunes filles" (HCF 86), 'the bourgeoises, the mothers, the women of high society, of the Faubourg Saint-Germain, the elites, the proper young ladies,' and continues to seek the transfiguring artistic experience that can give form to his day.

As the streets fill up with prostitutes out for the evening, Gille once again enters a brothel. In the novel's most lavish, extended physical scene, Gille makes love to a redhead named Gaby and at last succeeds in completing and becoming part of the painting he has been seeking all day:

> Gaby est blanche, rousse, verte. Elle a une dent verte. Gaby a une stature admirable. Mille hélices tournantes composent ses volumes éblouissants:

15. See Judith Wechsler, *A Human Comedy: Physiognomy and Caricature in 19th Century Paris* (Chicago, 1982).

belles coques et belles conques. Des cheveux de rouille et des yeux, comme sous l'eau, des pièces de cuivre perdues. Gille en sait long sur la pourriture des rousses, ce lait près de tourner de leur peau fleurie de toutes parts de traces roses et cette puissante pigmentation: lisières fétides, franges fumeuses, lits de feuilles mortes, cressons délavés.

Gille s'émerveille bientôt devant un brasier mouvant de beaux membres emflammés. Il reporte la main sur le monde dont il a semblé s'écarter un instant. Et c'est d'une main lourde, douce, qui, pelotant la pâte, ajoute singulièrement à l'oeuvre de Dieu. (*HCF* 87)

Gaby is white, red, green. She has a green tooth. She is large. A thousand turning helices compose her dazzling volumes: beautiful hulls, beautiful conchs. Hair like rust and eyes, as if under water, pieces of lost copper. Gille knows all about the decay of redheads, the milky skin just on the verge of spoiling, flowered all over with pink spots and the powerful pigmentation: fetid groves, steaming clumps of hair, beds of dead leaves, washed-down bunches of greens.

Gille is in total wonderment before this moving mass of limbs on fire. He reaches out for the world he couldn't grasp a moment ago. And with a heavy hand, a soft hand, molding the clay, he adds something new to the work of God.

Like a painter, a sculptor, he creates Gaby as he makes love to her. This *demoiselle de Paris* is a triumph of composite artistic vision, a brilliant, vivid, compliant mass of fragrant volumes and recesses, a painting become *drame*, a Venetian nude—an ecstatic late Titian figure (Fig. 5), the "Natural Venus" in her lush, tangible, Parisian environment—a Rubens he can touch and grasp hold of.[16] As the text shifts to the imagery of a violent ride through a burning village, a hybrid of romantic painting and narrative, Gille rides like a conqueror through a devastated landscape, with his redhead as booty slung over his saddle. He becomes a high romantic artist, an outlaw, a novelist, then once again a modernist painter, a "creator of ruins." Dismantling Gaby like a surrealist dummy, he pulls her left arm back over her head and imagines a seam opening, like a dark stroke in a painting, from her armpit to her flank, "an immense plain split open." At last exhausted, he draws back to admire his composition, but it has already changed, as the girl reassembles herself, shaking off the flames, a surrounded prey become quiet

16. For a discussion of the Natural Venus and her birth in Venetian art, as well as of the tradition of the "Ecstatic" nude, see Kenneth Clark, *The Nude: A Study in Ideal Form* (Princeton, 1956), 118, 294–95.

5. Titian, *Bacchanal. ca.* 1658. Oil on canvas, 69 × 76 inches. Prado, Madrid.
Photo: Warren Gravois.

and virginal. Gille's extraordinary painting remains fixed on his retina
as he leaves the brothel. Disrupting his plastic reverie, the madame asks
if he is pleased; he thinks to himself, "What more could he ask of his
gods?" Sinking into a taxi, Gille rolls home through the infernal streets
of Paris.

Gille's visual sentimental education is the central motif of the novel's
third part. During his restorative retreat to the countryside Gille explains the origins of his obsession with the painted world of the brothel.
First introduced to the Folies-Bergère as an adolescent by a lascivious
old uncle, Gille remained illumined by "un paradis rouge, plein de
grandes viandes," 'a red paradise, full of huge pieces of meat,' that followed him through "l'immense machine à illusions de la ville," 'the
great dream factory of the city.' Unable to escape the assault of imagery

in posters, sidewalk silhouettes, in the figures of women plying their
trade on the streets, Gille continually saw "sur les murs, dans le ruisseau,
d'incessantes théories de femmes peintes" (*HCF* 117), 'on the walls, in
the river, endless processions of painted women.' His highest religious
memory was not of a spiritual smile but "of a breast with a cynical expression." Under his eyelids prostitutes imprinted their "gluey forms."
A Baudelairean *mendiant* (beggar) of Manichean visions of beauty, a
more spiritual Don Juan who sits in a bar writing the names of women
he has known on the back of a playing card, Gille has continued his
imaginary journey to distant isles in search of "un grand corps blanc,"
'a big white torso.' The iconology of his epic quest for ideal beauty has
been eclectic and encyclopedic, ranging from Greek statues and high
Renaissance nudes through dusky Baudelairean temptresses to his present tour of the museum of contemporary women, with the headless silhouette of Molly, the mirrored faces of Finette, and the cubist "ruined
beauties" of Picasso's *Demoiselles.*

Drieu's early preference for pictorially conceived fiction was vividly
highlighted in one of his first critical pieces, a 1920 review of Paul
Adam's historical novels. Contrasting Adam's colorful tales with "the
French nineteenth-century *chansons de geste*" of Maurice Barrès, Charles
Péguy, and Charles Maurras, Drieu noted that these "moralists for the
generation of 1890"—that is, Drieu's own—wrote largely colorless
philosophical epics of the great street battles of 1830, 1848, 1871, of the
Dreyfus Affair. "Their work narrates but does not evoke history. Their
meditation makes all these struggles part of the permanent reality of
human thought." They lacked Adam's striking visual sense, his "naïveté
and robustness, the daring of a medieval juggler . . . intoxicated with all
the accidents of color, sound, all the gestures that affect the substance of
things." Identifying the early iconological influences on his own sense
of fiction, Drieu cited the picture books he loved at the age of five,
the illustrated battle tales of his seventh year, and the novels of Paul
Adam he discovered at fifteen. These were Drieu's equivalent of Don
Quixote's books of chivalry. With the hand and the eye of a Flemish or
Spanish painter, Adam adored ideas and "made us feel their presence
sensually as in a Rubens painting, where one sees allegory captured,
sunk into the flesh."[17]

17. Pierre Drieu La Rochelle, "Paul Adam," *Nouvelle Revue Française*, XIV (April,
1920), 577–79.

In *L'Homme couvert de femmes*, his own youthful allegory of the early twenties, Drieu "sank" his quest for ideal beauty into the illuminated text of the brothel. By means of one major analogue, Picasso's painting, and hundreds of lesser ones, Drieu depicted his hero Gille as a pilgrim of the streets and pleasure houses of Paris, as a secular saint whose retreat in the wilderness is a Louis XIV chateau in the south of France, being ruined by time and by the introduction of modern plumbing. Depressed by the degradation of beautiful structures, by the destruction of forms mirrored in the activities of the band of men and women gathered at Finette's and in the decor of their lives, Gille obsessively hears the end of the world not as a whimper, but as water slipping through pipes.

> On entend l'eau courir dans cette vieille solide bâtisse Louis XIV—Finette est si fière de l'avoir percée d'une tuyauterie compliquée—l'eau court et ces hommes et ces femmes se lavent sans cesse, ces femmes qui se sont arraché les oeufs du ventre, ces hommes qui répandent leur sémence comme Onan. Cette maison se ruine, je sens ses pierres se carier comme mes os. . . . Ce temps est celui des substitutions: chaque chose est remplacée par son faux. . . . Tout d'un coup cela s'abattra. (*HCF* 210)

> You can hear water running in this solid old Louis XIV building—Finette is so proud to have pierced it with complicated plumbing—the water runs and these women and these men keep on washing themselves, these women who have made themselves sterile, these men who scatter their seed like Onan. This house is crumbling, I feel its stones becoming porous like my bones. . . . This is the time of substitutions: everything is replaced by its counterfeit. . . . All at once everything will cave in.

Animated by a vision of fiction as a peculiar form of painting, Drieu's first novel relentlessly flies apart at the seams. In his eagerness to represent pictorially the hidden links between order and disorder, between art and desire, Drieu tosses in a vast number of striking but often ludicrously incongruous images. Gille thinks to himself that, unlike the people he sees around him, he never really "loses his head" to desire. "Toujours dans les tourbillons, dans le choquement des genoux, il a perçu à travers la guirlande des corps, les fortes attaches, les grandes serrures d'airain qui tiennent les choses unies" (*HCF* 65). 'Always, even in the emotional storms, in the shock of knees, he could make out, across the garlands of bodies, the strong joints, the great bronze locks that hold things together.' Surveying images of human bodies in the act

6. Pablo Picasso, *Bathers*. 1918. Graphite on cream wove paper, 9¼ × 8¼ inches. Fogg Art Museum, Harvard University, Cambridge, Mass., Bequest of Paul J. Sachs, Class of 1900: A testimonial to my friend W. G. Russell Allen. Copyright ARS N.Y./SPADEM.
Photo: Fogg Art Museum.

of love, Gille invokes a vast tangle of images—the visual tradition of Renaissance *blasons d'amour* (emblems of love), the decorative shapes of sylvan amours, the neoclassical "garlands of bodies" of Picasso's postcubist sketches (Fig. 6)—in order to signal, beyond the skin and sweat and grimaces, the "strong hinges" and "bronze locks" that imply a higher unity. Gille sorely lacks ironic self-awareness and often contradicts himself, one minute seeing passion as a means of access to another world, the next as an obstacle; he remains unshakably, and unjustifiably, convinced that he alone is not self-absorbed. The novel's huge jumble of Baudelaire, Picasso, a touch of Eliot, and a soupçon of Hemingway lacks the notes of acidic etching that its subject seems to cry out for. Some of what Drieu characterized as Joyce's "comic despair" would have improved *L'Homme couvert de femmes* considerably. On balance, however, this lopsided triptych is a striking debut, a work that disturbs and overwhelms with a wealth of plastic detail that Drieu would not again approach until the thirties. Most notably, this first novel establishes—with a mass of visual detail and a striking degree of theatricality—Drieu's search for a mode of fiction as vivid and memorable as the world of painted forms. When friends began in the late twenties to call Drieu "the man covered with women" they were acknowledging the emergence of an original fictional iconology.

4

Blèche, Le Feu follet: In the Paris Wasteland

PARIS IN THE TWENTIES: SURREALISM, URBAN ATOMISM

The artistic context of *Blèche* (1928) and *Le Feu follet* (1931) was marked by major areas of intersection and change. As political issues increasingly intruded into literature, as the high visibility of cubism and futurism began to dim before newly pronounced strains of surrealist and narrative-expressive painting, as the revelations of Eliot and Joyce began fully to penetrate Drieu's consciousness, his alienation from the avant-garde of the immediate postwar years deepened. The poor critical reception of *L'Homme couvert de femmes* coincided with a noisy public quarrel with the surrealists. In the summer of 1925 a group of surrealist writers and painters headed by Breton and Aragon publicly condemned poet-ambassador Paul Claudel for supporting French colonial policy in Morocco and declared their sympathy with the communists, maintaining that "the light comes from the East." Drieu's open letter in the August, 1925, issue of the *Nouvelle Revue Française* expressed intense disappointment with the surrealists' betrayal of their artistic independence. To prefer the Russian over the surrealist revolution, he wrote, was to expose fully the incurably bourgeois temperament already hinted at by the priggish strategies of Breton's 1924 surrealist manifesto, which had spelled out "a solid, detailed position, amply supplied with doctrines, examples, precedents, authority, disciples, hawkers, all the modern conveniences." Given half a chance, the Chinese and the Russians would become as stuffy as the contemporary French avant-garde. "All the Russians and Chinese want is typewriters, futurist painting, taximeters, a definitive edition of the complete works of Anatole France, and gunpowder and bullets . . . so they can create a little regional, temperate nationalism. And in literature it's pretty much the same as in politics. All you surrealists are doing is picking up old cigarette butts: images, Freud, Einstein, Caligari, literary painters, *poètes maudits*, the whole rationalist mysticism—and now neo-orientalism."[1] Asserting his right to choose neither communism nor fascism, Drieu underlined his contempt for the "Montparnasse revolutionaries" whose biggest accomplishment was to stage riots at banquets.[2]

Despite deteriorating relations with Aragon, in his third and final open letter to the surrealists Drieu deplored the stony critical silence that had greeted the 1926 publication of *Le Paysan de Paris*. He seemed unaware that the surrealists themselves, in particular Breton, were also ignoring Aragon's surrealist masterpiece because of theoretical opposition to the genre of the novel.[3] As the politicization of avant-garde literature continued, a number of surrealists officially joined the Communist party, Antonin Artaud and Philippe Soupault were expelled from the movement for pursuing "the stupid literary adventure," and Drieu commenced his slow drift to the right. From the heart of the surrealist vision he retained his attachment to the Aragon of *Le Libertinage* and *Le Paysan*, to some lines of Paul Eluard, to the quality of Breton's prose, and to a few impressive "moments" in Soupault's novels. Among the painters, he was drawn to Giorgio de Chirico, some of Max Ernst, and René Magritte. The "found art" assemblages of Marcel Duchamp and the dreamlike, slippery-looking blobs of Yves Tanguy, like the literary products of automatic writing, struck him as trivial and lacking the essential element of human passion. Surrealist art, Drieu noted in his third letter to the surrealists, is "exquisite . . . the supreme phase of decadence, and thus, the most likely to call forth the destruction of this declining civilization."[4]

Drieu remained indelibly marked by some of the major insights of surrealist painting, by its emphasis on startling visual framing, on dramatic selection and amplification of small detail, by its free distortion of proportions and inherent theatricality. Most of the plays Drieu wrote

1. Drieu La Rochelle, "La Véritable erreur des surréalistes," 168–69.
2. For an account of the July, 1925, banquet for symbolist poet Saint-Pol-Roux at the Closerie des Lilas, see Roger Shattuck, *The Banquet Years* (New York, 1968), 359–60.
3. For a fuller discussion of Aragon's difficulties with the surrealist ban on the novel, see Reck, "Louis Aragon."
4. Drieu La Rochelle, "Troisième lettre aux surréalistes," 15.

beginning in 1930 were stiff, talky, and hopelessly abstract, but his ideas for their staging reveal a strong sense of scene and of dramatic framing. Several mirror his conscious desire to transfer to the stage the chiaroscuro, ambiguities of vision, and geometric stances of mannerist painting, to reread the talking bodies of classical tragedy in the light of surrealism's intuitions about spatial relations. Drieu's inability to visualize the practical use of theatrical space made it difficult for some of the most imaginative directors of the time to animate his peculiar theater of ideas.[5] Only in the novel—in the perceptions of Gilles, for example— would Drieu find it possible to express the degree of heightened sensibility he experienced when confronted with Agnolo Bronzino through a canvas by Magritte. Drieu's eclectic pictorial preferences and borrowings extended to collage, the major discovery of synthetic cubism.[6] This facet of his visual taste was slow to resolve itself, however, largely because gratuitously ugly decoration struck him as a waste of time. Drieu was fond of saying that one could tell instantly when Picasso was having a bad day from the sardine can stuck on the canvas. Seeking a way of reconciling disparate narrative modes, Drieu began to observe with skeptical but informed interest, as did his friends Malraux and Borges, the increasing methodological sophistication of filmed narrative and to experiment with deliberately fragmented texts.[7]

Along with surrealism and cubism, another major intertextual layer concerns us here, the influence of Eliot and Joyce as refracted (Harry Levin's excellent term) back into French literature. *Blèche* and *Le Feu follet*, Drieu's most rigorous, controlled, and pessimistic novels, illustrate a dark vision of Paris in the twenties, covered by the huge, dusty cloud of "urban atomism that floats over the capitals of Europe."[8] The commanding visions of the writers Drieu referred to as the "Anglo-Saxon" masters of modernism provided a new iconological layer for

5. For a detailed study of Drieu's published and unpublished theater, see Lansard, *Drieu La Rochelle*.
6. Useful discussions of the origins of collage appear in Edward Fry, *Cubism* (New York, n.d.); Sariane Alexandrian, *Surrealist Art* (New York, 1985); and Patrick Waldberg, *Surrealism* (New York, n.d.).
7. For a basic survey of the relationship between film and narrative, see John L. Fell, *Film and the Narrative Tradition* (Norman, Okla., 1974).
8. Pierre Drieu La Rochelle, "*La Condition humaine* en 1933," *La Nación* (Buenos Aires), 1933, rpr. in Drieu La Rochelle, *Sur les écrivains*, ed. Frédéric Grover (Paris: Gallimard, 1966), 287.

his art. An excellent knowledge of English and keen interest in new modalities in literature made Drieu an ideal French—always intensely French—reader of *Ulysses* and *The Waste Land*. Although his references to Joyce's novel are more specific than those to Eliot's poem, both works were more important *as images* than as texts for Drieu's own reading of his world. An emblematic photograph appears in a recent study of Sylvia Beach and literary Paris in the twenties; it shows Drieu among a group of prominent *Nouvelle Revue Française* writers posed in front of Shakespeare and Company, the bookshop that published *Ulysses*.[9] In addition to their bold use of literary fragmentation, of collage or literary cubism, these two defining modernist works magnetized Drieu by the intensely specular light—a superb instance of *mise en abyme*—they cast on two of his French literary masters. In Joyce's rereading of Flaubert and Eliot's rereading of Baudelaire Drieu found new ironic pigments for his own portrait of contemporary France. By their independent existence in a language other than French, *Ulysses* and *The Waste Land* assumed in even greater measure than contemporary French works the iconicity that drew him to painting.

Blaquans of *Blèche* and Alain of *Le Feu follet* inhabit the Paris wasteland of the twenties. In *Blèche*, a mannerist literary self-portrait of a political journalist, and in *Le Feu follet*, a cubist-surrealist visualization of nothingness inspired by the 1929 suicide of surrealist Jacques Rigaut, Drieu deliberately abandoned the loose pictorialism of his first novel, *L'Homme couvert de femmes*. The family resemblances between these two subsequent novels, the first largely unknown, the second one of Drieu's best-known and most widely read works, are striking. Both are set entirely in Paris and rely on severely restricted narrative viewpoints. Both integrate the mannerisms of French classical forms—the psychological *récit*, the Racinian tragedy—with the iconology of cubism and surrealism. *Blèche* earned Drieu the grudging admiration of contemporaries who had despaired of seeing the author of *L'Homme couvert de femmes* write "real novels."[10] The formal rigor and pictorial intensity of *Le Feu follet*, as well as its subject matter—drug addiction—profoundly shocked Drieu's contemporaries and added to his reputation as a demonic personality. The mythological force of *Le Feu follet* continues to

9. Noel Riley Fitch, *Sylvia Beach and the Lost Generation: A History of Literary Paris in the Twenties and Thirties* (New York, 1983).

10. Ramon Fernandez, "*Blèche*, par Drieu La Rochelle," *Nouvelle Revue Française*, XXXI (December, 1928), 868.

fascinate and mislead critics, who overread the strains of classical tragedy and ignore the pictorial conception. It is significant that these two novels, more than any of Drieu's others, influenced Sartre and Albert Camus in the forties and fifties. Sartre's fictional portraits of *le salaud* (the man of bad faith) clearly draw on the intensely ironic self-narration of *Blèche*, while his striking depictions of the horrors of physical contact show strong resemblances to that novel's key pictorial scenes. The first part of Camus' *L'Etranger* is a striking rereading of the cubistic psychological portraiture of *Le Feu follet*. For the major fictional moralists of a subsequent literary generation, the special qualities of Drieu's two most restrained and selective novels showcased the rich narrative possibilities of voice and vision in skillful combination—the purely aural effect of Dostoyevsky's *Notes from the Underground*, for example, combined with a controlled pictorialization of French classicism, nineteenth-century caricature, and modernist iconology. Drieu's inclination to fuse artistic modes from fiction, spectacle, and painting, at times overwhelming in *L'Homme couvert de femmes*, works to striking advantage in *Blèche* and *Le Feu follet*.

Drieu's interim experiments with odd forms of fiction included "L'Automate" (The automaton), published in the *Revue Européenne* in 1926, a fragmented, neosurrealistic text in which an unidentified first-person narrator who appears to be a Parisian journalist floats through the city, reading the rituals of theatergoers, observing women applying their makeup, and watching embracing couples silhouetted against posters depicting staged or filmed love scenes. This "automatic man" is a twenties cultural critic, a contemporary "painter of modern life" (Baudelaire's appellation for painter Constantin Guys), whose fragments appear to be "printed prophecies" several days old, slightly crumpled pieces of newsprint drifting along a city street. "L'Automate"'s ironic comparison between white-gloved gentlemen descending in an elevator and mineworkers going down in search of coal, his final fragment tersely and objectively describing a suicide in the Seine suggest a form of ironic pictorial fiction that Drieu would later develop within the painterly consciousnesses of his most striking central characters, Gilles and Dirk Raspe. The most intriguing fragment in "L'Automate" depicts a crowd watching a boxing match:

> Perché dans le cintre du cirque, dans une ombre céleste, je regarde le combat du boxe. En bas, sur le plateau, deux petits hommes se cognent. La

foule massive et sombre les enveloppe. Les projecteurs, qui tiennent cruel-
lement dans leur lumière ce drame minuscule, sont les vingt yeux d'un mon-
strueux savant nocturne. La foule énorme, lubrique, se penche sur son
microscope. Son sang s'échauffe, elle voit deux armées.[11]

Perched in the gallery of the arena, in a celestial darkness, I watch the
boxing match. Down below, on the canvas, two tiny men strike one another.
The massive dark crowd envelops them. The projectors that fix this tiny
drama cruelly in their beams are the twenty eyes of a monstrous nocturnal
savant. The enormous crowd, lustful, leans over its microscope. Its blood
aroused, it sees two armies.

The sense of multiple vision that animated the "Chronique des spectacles" in 1923–1924 reappears here in the steep angle of spectatorship,
while Drieu's rapidly drawn portrait of a bloodthirsty crowd achieves
the visual and psychological force communicated by the enhanced colors, exaggerated facial gestures, and emblematic theatricality of paintings by German expressionist George Grosz, a contemporary whose
work he admired.

Le Jeune Européen (The young European, 1927) provides the bridge
between Drieu's growing attraction to political journalism and his
ongoing exploration of narrative stances. Critics have long assumed, on
the basis of Le Jeune Européen's odd admixture of tones and angles of
approach, that it was originally conceived as a novel. In fact, nothing
supports this view. In retrospect this essay, published in the same year
that Drieu first met André Malraux, seems totally consistent with the
tradition of intergenre works typified by Malraux's La Tentation de l'Occident and Antimémoires. Drieu's text uses a life story very loosely resembling his own as a literary myth. As the young European recounts
his basic biography in the opening section, he becomes a modern René
who has survived the war, traveled through the world, made some
money, and returned disillusioned to live in Paris. The second part
traces his choice between "blood and ink" and the difficult birth of his
literary vocation. The intensely personal, self-critical tone of this section, which led a contemporary critic to deplore Drieu's "unacceptable
mixture of the moi and the world,"[12] is a carefully managed parody of

11. Pierre Drieu La Rochelle, "L'Automate," La Revue Européenne, XXXV (January,
1926), 14.
12. Benjamin Crémieux, "La Suite dans les idées; Le Jeune Européen; Les Dernier Jours,
par P. Drieu La Rochelle," Nouvelle Revue Française, XXIX (November, 1927), 671–76.

romanticism and of subsequent approaches to confessional literature. In "Blood and Ink" Drieu plays a series of roles: a wiser Musset, a more cynical Stendhal, Flaubert preparing to write a twenties *Bouvard et Pécuchet*, Gide with more practical experience of life, the Joyce of *Ulysses* at once indulgent and critical of Stephen Dedalus's literary ambitions. The final section, "Le Music-Hall," bears an epigraph from Aragon's *Le Paysan de Paris*—"There is a form of modern tragedy: it's a kind of huge steering wheel that turns and that no hand controls."[13] In an imagined visit to the Casino de Paris Drieu reworks several key elements from the "Chronique des spectacles" into a grand cultural-mythological meditation. Unfortunately, the visit to the music hall lacks color and detail, remaining vague, generalized, and overloaded with lists and summaries. Aware of its failings, Drieu several years later tried unsuccessfully to have Gallimard reissue "Le Music-Hall" as a separate volume illustrated by Grosz.

THE HOLLOW PORTRAIT: BRONZINO, MAGRITTE

Blèche and *Le Feu follet* are forms of the hollow portrait, the psychological *récit* reconceived as visualization of an absence. The term *hollow portrait*—my own—requires a bit of explanation. In examining the two types of paintings that illuminate the narrative strategies of Drieu's striking 1928 and 1931 novels, Bronzino's mannerist portraits and Magritte's images of opaque, hatted forms seen from the back or with their faces obscured by large, free-floating objects, in distinguishing what connects them with each other and with the self-portrait in *Blèche* and the disappearing portrait in *Le Feu follet*, one sees emerge a startling vision of the human presence. The figure in the paintings is impenetrable, compacted, withdrawn, a form striking most of all for its capacity simultaneously to magnetize and deflect the viewer's gaze. The sitter stares with averted, opaque, or somehow distracted gaze out of the Bronzino canvas at something he or she alone sees, holding the background, foreground, and invading look of the viewer suspended. The black silhouette in a Magritte canvas organizes the surrounding pictorial space and the objects there displayed, suggesting possibilities for a reading, but itself remaining infinitely *thirsty*, appropriating all poten-

13. Pierre Drieu La Rochelle, *Le Jeune Européen* (Paris, 1927), 66.

tial meaning into itself. The figures by Bronzino and Magritte are hollow portraits that subsume and contain what surrounds them. The viewer may become absorbed in them, may even by an act of vision enter and be contained by them, but can never fill them up.

In Bronzino's *Ugolino Martelli* (Fig. 7) one is struck immediately by the self-absorbed stillness and impenetrable interiority of the sitter, briefly distracted from his reading by having to pose for the painter. A finger of his right hand marks a line in his text and also directs the eye to the uncovered corner of the table at which he sits; the point of the table marks the forefront of the pictorial space. The draped wrist of Martelli's left hand holds up at an oblique angle on his upper thigh a second, closed book. His stylized "natural" pose, constructed of opposing twists and turns of the body, focuses our attention first on his hands, then on his face, then back into what Charles McCorquodale aptly calls "the vertiginous perspectival lines" of foreground table and background architecture.[14] The figure of the sitter forms an elongated oval seen slightly flattened, as a silhouette placed a bit behind and at a lightly oblique angle to the picture plane. It appears that Martelli, a noted literary figure of his time, has been reading Homer's *Iliad* and that his off-canvas hours include the book perched on his knee by contemporary humanist Cardinal Bembo. The architectural setting has been identified as the courtyard of Martelli's *palazzo*, with a statue of David with Goliath's head between his feet against the far wall to the left.

The decor here serves, as in Bronzino's other portraits, as visual context, pure surrounding, an abstract space, a function of the figure and its presence. In the Martelli canvas the decoration is architectural and sculptural; in portraits painted a few years later Bronzino's decor becomes a dark, undefined background with—at the most—a few dim panels, as in the Louvre's *Youth with a Statuette*, or a suggestive arch as in the Uffizi's *Lucrezia Panciatichi*, the model for Henry James's Milly Theale in *The Wings of the Dove*.[15] The painter's intense sense of scene, his conception of portraiture as quintessentially *stagy*, fortified by his early work in theatrical decorations—highly praised in his time but now lost to us—is here made fully visible. The Bronzino mannerist portrait is a play, an illusion painted as an illusion, a subtle subversion of

14. Charles McCorquodale, *Bronzino* (New York, 1981), 52.
15. See Meyers, *Painting and the Novel*, 19–30; and Tintner, *Museum World of Henry James*, 96, 99, 121, 211.

7. Agnolo Bronzino, *Ugolino Martelli. ca.* 1535–1536. Oil on panel, 40 × 33½ inches. Gemäldegalerie, Staatliche Museen Preussischer Kulturbesitz, Berlin (West).
Photo: Jörg P. Anders, Berlin.

the classical solidity on which it is based. From the muscular, moving masses of Leonardo and Michelangelo to the stilled and slightly flattened figures of Bronzino's portraits is a noticeable step toward painting conceived as surface rather than depth. Bronzino, who is known to have said, "As everyone knows, art works only on the surface," moves toward the modern vision of paint on canvas as a dialogue between the artist's materials and his inner vision, as painting about painting.[16]

Magritte's *Le Grand Siècle* (Fig. 8) is a characteristic rereading of the traditional portrait by one of the most unsettling surrealist painters of the century. The composition immediately raises a number of un-answered questions. Which is the primary subject, the silhouetted man seen from the back or the landscape he appears to be looking at? Does the title suggest an unexpanded narrative relationship between the clas-sical chateau seen in the far distance and the dense receding *coulisses* of trees on either side? What about the stamped tin sky marked with ar-rows pointing back toward the viewer? Where can the viewer's eye come to rest? Which frame is the significant one, the edges of the painting, the margins of the middle distance, or the rough stone blocks—the tra-ditional portrait parapet reread by heavy industry—that form the fore-ground barrier and compress the viewing space up against the ceiling / sky? Or indeed the frame formed by the viewer's presence as enclosed and put to the question by the mysterious featureless sitter / stander who looks away, at the odd scene or at something we cannot see? Many of the ambiguities of Bronzino's *Ugolino Martelli* dog us once again: an enclosed, opaque presence set in ambiguous relationship to a symbolic-architectural decor; an image of the human presence that fascinates and rejects the invading gaze; a psychological and visual conundrum that challenges the relationship of painting to the seen world. This again is a form of the hollow portrait.

Magritte's deliberately ambiguous restaging in *Le Grand Siècle* of the figure-ground relationship common to modern portraiture since Rem-brandt recalls the *portraits-paysages*, the portrait-landscapes of Henri Rousseau, but with a critical difference. Rousseau's serene narrative combinations express a delighted refusal to separate the person and the objects that surround him, a denial that Roger Shattuck sees as the hall-mark of a "primitive" sensibility and that Kenneth Clark interprets as Rousseau's instinctive return to the art of four hundred years before his time.[17] In deliberately subverting both the portrait and the landscape, Magritte is at once wisely primitive and devilishly civilized. In facing

16. Bronzino's remark is quoted in McCorquodale, *Bronzino*, 45, and related to its original context on pp. 161–63.
17. Shattuck, *Banquet Years*, 89; Kenneth Clark, *Landscape into Art* (Boston, 1961), 136–37.

8. René Magritte, *Le Grand Siècle*. 1954. Oil on canvas, 20 × 24 inches. Städtisches Museum Gelsenkirchen, Gelsenkirchen (Federal Republic of Germany). Copyright 1990 C. Herscovici/ARS N.Y.
Photo: Städtisches Museum Gelsenkirchen.

away from the viewer, the posed figure creates a viewing space inside the picture. (Several other Magrittes show a view seen through a cutout shaped like the figure in *Grand Siècle*.) The landscape seen in deep perspective seems to be losing its battle with the heavy foreground bulwark of the low stone wall and with the stamped tin ceiling/sky. We have then a portrait that is not a portrait and a landscape—being annihilated by what encompasses it—that is not a landscape; both elements of the painting suggest their own imminent absence. In a rare explanation of his methodology, Magritte described continually sifting through "the appearance of things, until from the process they acquired an emblematic value." [18]

18. Patrick Waldberg, *René Magritte*, trans. Austyn Wainhouse (Brussels, 1965), 197.

Magritte's portrait-and-landscape is the symbolic confrontation of two familiar emblems, a painterly construct more radical in its reconception of representation than the decor or reflecting eyes in Bronzino. Magritte's painting is visually and geometrically closed, with the traditional foreground definitional element—the point of the table in *Ugolino Martelli*—transformed into a wall of concrete blocks. The figure is *partially* decentered; he is thus almost a viewer, but still the central subject. Without the traditional visual trajectory markers of the mannerist portrait that guide the viewer's gaze to, through, behind, and back again to the face, however, the Magritte portrait figure disorients and disturbs with his opacity, with the fact that we cannot see his eyes and therefore lack any focus on his character. Eyes are frequently obscured in Magritte's work, or portrayed as apertures on other views (*Le Faux Miroir*), or closed (*Je ne vois pas la [femme] cachée dans la forêt*, a painting frequently shown framed by photos of famous surrealists all with their own eyes closed). With the eyes obscured or subverted, we have a mask, an effigy, a silhouette—or a mysterious or blind portrait. Although René Magritte preferred the peaceable isolation of his native Belgium to the dramatic folderol of the Paris surrealist milieu, where he spent only three years (1927–1930), his unique pictorial conceptions early became an intimate part of the French visual context, with frequent illustrations and reproductions appearing in surrealist periodicals and with works in shows—in the company of Jean Arp, Salvador Dali, and Yves Tanguy—at Camille Camoens' gallery on the rue de Seine, which closed in 1930 shortly after its important first collective showing of collages. Drieu saw Bronzino's paintings regularly at the Louvre and on trips to Germany, Italy, and Spain. In the narrative methodologies of *Blèche* and *Le Feu follet* Drieu reflects the fundamental shifts in the artistic perception of character suggested by Bronzino and Magritte.

BLÈCHE: MANNERIST PORTRAITS, VEGETABLE LOVES

Blaquans, the first-person narrator of *Blèche*, is an almost invisible subject. His retrospective account of a recent disturbance in his life, structured in three parts—the discovery of a theft from his apartment, a flashback to six years and to a year earlier, and the crisis of his relationship with his secretary, Blèche—is a triumph of narrative subversion. The care he devotes to modeling and positioning the theft and the figure of Blèche within the context of his self-portrait becomes a *mise en abyme* of the arts of portraiture and of storytelling. A veteran of the war and an influential political editorialist for the conservative newspaper *Le Catholique*, married and the father of three children, Blaquans lives alone in a bachelor apartment on the rue Chanoinesse, "at the dead point of the Ile de la Cité, under the flank of the Notre-Dame Cathedral, in the shadow of a shadow." [19] In the slightly grandiose, measured cadences of his first words Blaquans appears as an opaque form externalized into the details of his decor, a sparely and carefully appointed room that is a classic grisaille, a painting executed entirely in shades of gray. "J'avais ouvert les yeux et partout l'unité de mon âme, l'harmonie de ma solitude: rien que des murs de soie grise. Qu'est-ce qui ressemble plus à ma vie monochrome que cette teinte de cendre chaude qui s'étend partout?" (*BL* 11). 'I opened my eyes and all about me, the unity of my soul, the harmony of my solitude: nothing but walls of gray silk. What is more like my monochromatic life than this shade of warm ashes that covers everything?' Six years earlier he had stumbled upon the recently vacant room in space-hungry postwar Paris and had instantly conceived it as the defining center of a newly constructed life. His initial visit had been a spatial revelation of framing, rectangles, volumes within volumes. Through the door appeared the interior of a perfect cube, with a single window, a high ceiling, the "ideal antechamber for a Racinian play, or one of those interchangeable and anonymous places, evenly bathed in the scented breath of beautiful souls, traversed by Stendhal's heroes and heroines" (*BL* 100). The centered door directly faced the only window. On one side wall was a fine mantelpiece in black marble topped by a tall mirror, facing it a radiator "like an organ stripped of its flesh," flat and pure enough not to jar. The polished inlaid wood floor through the slowly opening door was a quiet riffling of geometric forms, a premonition of pages thumbed in the hand. Here in a world of depth enclosed, of vision forced in upon itself, Blaquans planned to perfect the fleshless literary voice that would form his contact with the world.

With the discovery that an expensive pair of earrings his wife has given him to finance a solitary journalistic trip to America and Russia

---

19. Pierre Drieu La Rochelle, *Blèche* (Paris, 1928), 15. Hereafter cited in the text as *BL*.

has disappeared, a play of splintered light pierces the visual field. The clarity of Blaquans' relationship to the church, of his memories of the war, of his stable distance from his wife, Marie-Laure, and their three noisy children, of his contempt for the public and contemporary culture becomes blurred. His initial search focuses on three symbolic locations. When the small, strapped and clasped lined coffer where he remembers placing the earrings appears empty, he shakes it violently, trying to make the vacant space yield up the bottomless glints of invisible faceted forms. As he next searches one volume at a time behind the visual fortress of a lavishly bound four-volume set of Montaigne, with its "army of atoms" of grained calfskin catching the room's muted light and its dark printed letters on the pages inside looking like strangely shaped "arms against the void" (*BL* 18), Blaquans reveals his vision of literature as an armorial display, a museum of outmoded but physically durable artifacts. As he carefully displaces and repositions the geometric segments of his setting, the grisaille is disturbed and afterimages of absence remain burned into his vision. The final possible cache is wholly symbolic, the table holding neat stacks of manuscripts that cannot possibly conceal anything and the "black rock" of the typewriter (an odd shading on the rock as a traditional iconographic figure of the church) standing metallic and empty for the moment. In this small world of order, there seems to be nowhere to misplace anything. Someone has deliberately taken the earrings. With this realization, Blaquans sees the carefully grouped forms of the decor waver, and he fights off physical nausea watching a faint fall of fragments.

Narrating his fitful effort to discover the thief with sudden flits and stops, selecting details and modulating shadows for a nuanced self-portrait of the political journalist as an olympian figure out of reach of the physical world of other people, Blaquans gradually sketches a profession of evasion. His treasured authors, Saint Augustine, Montaigne, the Pascal of *Les Provinciales*, are, in his eyes, immortal journalists. His own duty as a writer is to throw light "on a narrow range of things" (*BL* 12–13), to concern himself only with "the great phantoms, France, the Church, Communism" (*BL* 91); his ambition is to somehow collect and refine his daily (the French word is *journaliers*) columns into the durable stuff of literature. How is a man of his detached, farsighted vision to deal with the practical complexities of tracking down a thief? Applying the methodologies of his journalism, Blaquans casts an eye on the sustaining mythologies of his life. Everywhere visual flaws appear. His journalistic writing lacks the density and luster of literature. His perfect wife has a harelip and appears most of all as the visible symbol of his decision, after being wounded in the war and suffering from periodic bouts of sexual excess, to shut out the impure world of the flesh. His three sons are a sticky mass he frankly prefers to avoid. He knows nothing about the vague loyal reading public to whom he feeds evanescent words on "big subjects." Vannier, his powerful boss at *Le Catholique*, is a repulsive, tentacled monster swiveling on a padded chair in front of a Louis XV desk, sucking money out of the petty enterprise of Parisian journalism. Questioning his faithful housekeeper Amélie, a figure out of nineteenth-century illustration, listening to her pretentious servilities and looking at her robust, buxom form and the menacingly starched folds of her apron, Blaquans is overcome with a physical horror and spiritual malaise much in the manner of Roquentin in *La Nausée* facing the gnarled tree roots in Bouville's public park. The perfect room begins to appear ever so faintly flawed by little signs of wear, of disarrangement, almost imperceptible notes of color that disturb its muted compositional perfection.

Blaquans' suspicion settles inevitably on his young typist Blèche, who volunteered a year earlier to type manuscripts for him after her workday at *Le Catholique*, and whose presence he has thus far largely screened from his consciousness. Reviewing their evenings together, remembering Blèche's unusual interest in his writing, wondering about her offer on first hearing of the theft to give him a pearl necklace, goaded by hints from housekeeper Amélie, Blaquans begins to focus on the visible signs of Blèche in his life. Stepping back to survey his own self-portrait with its carefully distributed mannerist chiaroscuro and a spatial decor marked by the few emblems of his profession—stacks of papers, a typewriter, a few carefully selected books in the single bookcase to one side of the window—including *Les Provinciales* by Pascal, identified by Drieu as the author of the novel's epigraph, "Une jolie demoiselle pleine de miroirs et de chaines," 'A pretty young woman full of mirrors and chains'—Blaquans begins to notice the presence in the room of other pictures. The most striking is a rival portrait in oil of a glowingly redheaded typist with skin so blindingly pale it appears marked by green flecks, with a full, glistening lower lip, and damp-looking eyes like the women in Flemish paintings. Much of the time Blèche has seemed totally absorbed by her work, a silent instrument whose swift fingers on the keys taking dictation have been transforming Blaquans into a "writer" while she has been *une Pythie*, a Delphic priestess transmitting the truth. Occasionally over the past year, however, Blaquans has noticed her appear to change form and become an icon out of contemporary fashion illustrations, a siren with bobbed hair, blue-shadowed eyelids decorated with "myriad painted looks" (*BL* 110), endless cigarettes, and clothes that look like costumes over the pronounced angle of her hip-tilted slouch. Her silhouette on the stairs in a belted coat has been a poster come to life. Her hands typing have looked like an image out of *le modern style* (art nouveau) with long, thin fingers like the spokes of a paper fan or the exploring legs of a strange insect. Blèche has been a series of incomplete transformations, an unfinished figure waiting to be released from her "chrysalis of the badly brought up young girl" (*BL* 233) and shaped into an image in art. In the person of Blèche a degraded contemporary mythology has saturated the enclosed air of Blaquans' decor with a damp, moody presence. She has rearranged his papers, borrowed a book and returned it spotted with tear stains and marked by an intimate ribbon. She has consumed endless sandwiches, smoked constantly, lapped port, flung herself on the divan after a strenuous bout of work. She has spoken of her shadowy painter-lover and the sorrows of her life in accents copied from boulevard theater and bad novels. She has dramatized her sordid life between a divorced, loose-living mother and an indecisive, art critic father; she has shared her longing to devote herself to a man with an important mission in life. She has spent more and more time in Blaquans' room after her work is done, lying on the divan looking dreamy and strange. "Une Blèche envahisseuse" (*BL* 67), 'an invading Blèche,' has brought into the very air of the room the textures of her presence, with its moisture, color, and slipperiness, with its debris of lemon rinds and crumbs and small objects left out of place.

Disturbed by a rising perception of encroaching disorder and growingly ambivalent about Blèche and her relationship to the theft, Blaquans hires a private detective, Mordaque—the previous occupant of the room—to investigate. The former policeman in the French colonial army, with "cheeks emblazoned with dark blood" (*BL* 68) and a dyed mustache, turns out to be a heraldic figure out of popular mythology and Blaquans' lower-class double. A failed journalist who briefly and unsuccessfully published a magazine for retired policemen, Mordaque now lives in a greasy, narrow, untidy room with underwater lighting cast by a single bare bulb hanging from the high ceiling. Facing Mordaque, Blaquans is forced to reremember the room on the rue Chanoinesse as it appeared the first time he saw it, cluttered with piles of folders and loose papers on the floor, marred by a jumble of mass-produced furniture set off by a ghastly Louis XV divan, its walls covered with cheap, elaborately decorated wallpaper, lit by an ugly wrought-iron lamp. The concierge had supplied the final detail, her recollection of Mordaque's installation, for his journalistic enterprise, of a red-headed typist. As Mordaque eagerly agrees to investigate Blèche, Blaquans tries to imagine the detective's conception of his task. "Il allait mettre le nez dans les affaires de celui qui, en reprenant son bail, était entré dans son enfer, il allait voir cette autre sirène qui s'était haussée, le buste en avant, sur le roc noir et pailleté de l'Underwood" (*BL* 86). 'He was going to peer into the affairs of the man who, by taking over his lease, had walked into his inferno. He was going to see that other siren who had risen up, her torso curved forward, on the black spangled reef of the Underwood.'

With the "rock" of the typewriter suddenly invaded by a twenties siren and turned into a dark metallic shoal, with the ambiguous figure of Mordaque hovering in his mind, Blaquans' hollow portrait of himself is subverted. The carefully framed image of a writer with vast dim subjects, neatly surrounded by the figures and emblems of his profession, appears shadowed and rippled, as if by bulges from beneath the canvas caused by unseen stirring forms. Blaquans, who has avoided being *un visuel*, feels himself menaced by the physical presence of others (the *existents* of Sartre's vocabulary) and most of all by their *looks*. The room with no pictures and almost no color has been the precarious decor of a protective ritual, his journalistic enterprise a form of abstract magic, a way of conjuring away with words and *formules* the too-real world of people who walk and ooze, who talk and eat, who disgustingly exist. Blaquans, who eats almost nothing, cooking a little rice in his bathroom, taking an occasional piece of fruit, like Sartre's heroes finding

most food distasteful to the eye, the palate, and the spirit, suddenly con-
fonts a thickening perception of instability.[20] Novelist Colette, the only
one of Drieu's contemporaries to comment on *Blèche*'s remarkable visual patterns, called it "something of a masterpiece, where the lights
and shadows are distributed with a painter's touch, a novel full of de-
tours and anxiety, that one cannot put down. It [has] the unstable color
of an era and a generation."[21] The look of "unstable color" to which
Colette referred, a function of the text's numerous antitheses—strong
color against gray, words against silence, density against emptiness, motion against stasis—reflects the hallucinating impression that everything in Blaquans' world is threatening to become its own opposite.
The Racinian antechamber on the rue Chanoinesse is on the verge of
becoming the mystery cube-room of a Magritte interior, with its objects transformed, their proportions strangely revised, their arrangement mysterious, their textures unnatural and unsettling.

The unstable multiple faces and shapes of Blèche, the leering fan-
tasies of Mordaque, seem to have set loose and propelled into motion
the swarming life barely concealed behind Blaquans' carefully arranged
surfaces. His thick veil of words in the conservative Catholic press have
insulated him in a world of phantoms; some, like the mythical Marie-
Laure, a "Virgin of the soldier's world," he has totally assimilated;
others, like the dimly perceived reading public, he has addressed only
from a distant pulpit. Paris has been the "comfortable bed of his spirit"
(*BL* 12), an abstract stage set for nocturnal meditational strolls. He has
walked in the city looking at no one, almost blind to the impressionist
pink of an evening sky, unaware of brief arcs of summer lightning, listening only to the sound of the asphalt under his feet and the sensation
of telephone fibers vibrating far below the street. Planning to force her
into a confession by warning her of Mordaque's impending researches,
Blaquans phones Blèche to come to his apartment on a Sunday, then,
awaiting her arrival, goes out for a daylight walk. His walk is silhouetted against the memory of his first meeting with Blèche a year

20. For a strikingly detailed analysis of Sartre's literary treatment of food, see Catharine Savage Brosman, "Les Nourritures Sartriennes," in Ronald W. Tobin (ed.), *Littérature et gastronomie: Huit études réunies et préfacées par Ronald W. Tobin* (Tübingen, 1985),
229–63.
21. Colette, *Le Journal*, November 25, 1934, quoted in Frédéric Grover, *Drieu La
Rochelle* (Paris, 1979), 219–20.

earlier, when she had offered him a lift to the Bois in her old Citroën 5 cv., then shared with him her interest in his writing and her desire to help him collect his articles into a book. This afternoon "the grave Paris with wide perspectives for meditation" (*BL* 111) of a year ago has become a scene of urban carnage:

> C'était encore le Paris des vacances, quand des promeneurs espacés flottent dans le vêtement trop large que leur fait la rue vide: un grand labyrinthe désabusé de son bruyant secret, et qui gît, tout ouvert, tout détendu, comme une bête abandonnée qui épanche ses entrailles et son odeur morte. Sur ce cadavre découragé, un orage poussif était vautré depuis plusieurs jours et ne parvenait pas à se soulager par des coups de tonnerre onctueux et de faibles pluies tièdes. Notre-Dame semblait une vieille forêt desséchée, auprès d'un arroyo de plomb, bordé de factoreries maussades: l'Hôtel-Dieu, la Préfecture. Je songeais aux fins de civilisations quand on voit les broussailles apparaître en ordre serré au bout des rues et s'effondrer les casernes vides,—dans une chambrée, il reste une vieille bougie attachée à une planche par sa cire sale. Cela sentait, sous le ciel bas, l'automne, la maladie de foie, le dessous de bois équatorial, la décadence. (*BL* 162)

> It was still the Paris of vacation time, with scattered strollers lost in the oversized garment of empty streets: a huge labyrinth stripped of its noisy secret, lying open, limp, like an abandoned animal with its entrails spilling out and its smell of death. Over this sad corpse, a wheezy storm had been sprawling for several days, unable to relieve itself with oily streaks of lightning and weak warm rains. Notre Dame looked like an old, dried-out forest, next to a lead canyon bordered by sullen commercial establishments: the Hôtel Dieu [hospital], the Prefecture of Police. I thought of the end of civilizations, when one sees weeds appear in thick ranks at the ends of streets and empty army garrisons crumble to the ground—and in a barracks, all that remains is an old candle stuck to a plank with its dirty wax. All of this smelled, under the heavy sky, of autumn, of liver disease, of the underside of equatorial wood, of decadence.

Blaquans' vision of Paris of the end of the world, of the twenties wasteland, is a striking fusion of Baudelaire, Eliot, Ernst, and Magritte. The city appears as a desultorily assembled theatrical decor, an untended, overgrown urban garden at the very edge of the habitable world, a labyrinth stripped open to the view and strewn with debris, unevenly lit and almost dark in daylight, warm, sticky, odorous, the decaying stage set of a dying world whose prophet Blaquans aspires to be.

His subsequent meeting with Blèche, set off and narrated with the same meticulous verbal touch earlier applied to his self-portrait, becomes a study in conflicting narrative impulses. Blèche arrives damp from the rain, at once awkward and shamefully graceful, an oddly familiar monster from the past. Blaquans confronts both the beauty and the horror of the scene as *La Femme*, banned from his life since his marriage, emerges from a tangle of images, a panoply of styles.

> Quand Blèche entra chez moi, je crus voir une Hollandaise, née à Java: cette rousse languide. Elle avait le teint colonial de tous les Parisiens, ce jour-là: les reflets de jade de sa peau tournaient au vert-de-gris.
>
> Sur le divan où elle s'était affalée, elle émergea d'un manteau imperméable, reptile, les cuisses lourdes et liées, le buste errant dans un pâle crêpe de Chine, ici trop plaqué, ici trop mou. Sur sa poitrine et sur ses épaules, d'où tombait la lingerie pâmée, une légère onction moite recouvrait le satin de la peau: un oignon entr'ouvrant ses voiles . . . une mèche était plaquée sur sa tempe comme une liane détrempée. (*BL* 162–63)
>
> When Blèche arrived at my apartment, she looked like a Dutchwoman born in Java, a deeply languid redhead. She had the colonial complexion of all Parisians that day: the jade highlights of her skin were turning grayish-green.
>
> On the divan where she had collapsed, she emerged from a raincoat, reptilian, her thighs heavy and close together, her torso floating in a pale crepe de chine, here stuck to her, there falling loose. On her chest and on her shoulders, where the limp fabric was falling away, a light damp oiliness covered the smooth skin: a tulip bulb half opening its veils . . . a lock of hair was stuck to her temple like a damp tendril.

The faintly corroded redhead beached on his divan appears as a siren, an art nouveau figure emerging from her chrysalis, a hybrid Flemish painting filling up the visual space of Blaquans' room with her watery presence. He finds himself unable to communicate with her. Her patent inattention and indifference to his oversubtle and awkward explanations for asking her to come that afternoon exacerbate his sense of being literally at sea. "My words did me a disservice. . . . They breathed banality, worse, vulgarity" (*BL* 164). His words are thick, as if spoken underwater. He stops speaking and feels himself drowning in the thick, damp silence. "La présence de Blèche se faisait de plus en plus opaque, bornait et bouchait ma vue. . . . Tout était à la rousseur: septembre, les six heures du soir, l'orage aux rampements soufrés sur les toits éffondrés. Cette longue fille pâle, renversée parmi mes coussins, maçérait dans son élément" (*BL* 164–65). 'The presence of Blèche was becoming more and more opaque, narrowing and blocking my vision. . . . Everything was bathed in the reddishness: September, six o'clock in the evening, the sulfury storm gusts on the battered rooftops. This long, pale girl, lying back among my cushions, was macerating in her element.'

The text of the physical seduction is a massive hybrid of arts and styles, at once a mythological visual encounter, with all the drama and color of centuries of love scenes portrayed in paintings—mystical ecstasies, violent rapes, delicate pastoral dalliances, surrealist woman-plants eating their lovers—and a slightly mannered nightmare scene of literary murder, with recognizable corpses floating up out of a vast collective fund of damsels despoiled, led by the drowned Ophelia. Waves of fear, vengeance, and confused motivations wrench Blaquans' narrative loose from any semblance of textual "pact" with either himself or the potential reader of his tale. He reveals himself as fairly adept at manipulating prose rhythms and visually literate within a narrow range of painterly subjects. Clearly, his tastes run to autobiographical writing tinged with oratorical tones, elevated forms of journalism, classical drama, and young women either actually virginal—as was Marie-Laure when she nursed him during the war—or, like Blèche, with their mature forms still unexpanded. The almost disjointed curves and decoratively flowing clothes of the epicene women in paintings by Gustave Moreau and Odilon Redon and in posters by Alphonse Mucha reappear in Blaquans' visual rendering of Blèche with her clothes slipping unaided from her body, with her closed eyes turning the usually unsettling intrusion of her heavy-lidded gaze into a mercifully unreadable inward stare. When Blaquans makes love to Blèche, he literally sees himself murdering her, in a heavy-handed play on the sexual connotation of the word *mourir*, to die. But his satisfaction, literary and artistic as well as physical, is miserably short-lived. Blèche reapplies her lipstick, puts on her clothes, and leaves without saying a word. Blaquans has not "touched her heart," and his adventure in creating durable literary or plastic form out of slippery matter sputters to extinction.

When Blaquans learns at the *Catholique* office the next day that Mlle Chardin (Blèche) has tried to commit suicide, he reads her action as a proof of love. His musings during a taxi ride to the hospital are a triumph of literary pretensions. Looking out at the city from the dirty little padded enclosure with its gnawing meter, he imagines the events of his former life "painted on the stones; here Chimène, under the gaslight, having fixed her lipstick, promised to be faithful; here Horace said farewell to Curiace and revving his Bugatti. . . ." (*BL* 189). Through the cab window, Paris seems a tawdry Venice of memories, some personal, some literary, a deceptive network of texts. His first visit to the still unconscious girl lying on her hospital bed offers him a beautiful, pale death mask, a perfected Blèche who is indeed his own creation, drained of her color, still, no longer threatening, an effigy stripped of its ephemeral connotations. She now has style, as "l'habile dormeuse qui avait su attirer l'ombre de la mort dans le creux de son oreiller" (*BL* 197), 'the skillful sleeping figure who had known how to entice the shadow of death into the hollow of her pillow.' By his second visit (Blaquans has learned that Blèche is innocent of the theft), Blaquans is desperate to know the girl's feelings for him, to put what he considers "honesty" into their relationship. Reviving, she evades his questions and begins to degrade and mythologize her suicide attempt, speaking of it in the past tense, "When I killed myself," referring to the seduction with a particularly repulsive phrase, "Quand vous m'avez prise," 'When you took me,' that reeks of cheap fiction.

Before Blaquans' eyes the beautiful image of the dead Blèche, "shaped by death, sleep, and my inner turmoil" (*BL* 225), dies, revealing the suicide attempt as a pitiful sham, the gesture of "a young girl stuffed with literary memories of the lowest possible quality" (*BL* 229). The passionate love scene in the gray room slips into a banal adventure that Blaquans is laboriously recasting into a rambling, self-justifying reminiscence, an inconclusive piece of not-quite-literature with a hollow ending. Blèche disappears, then later sends a card from Liverpool with her best wishes and the information that she has accepted a job with a Franco-American fashion house in New York. Popular mythology in its crudest form strips Blaquans' world of its brief, disturbing encounter with a colored, pulsating world of forms. He returns to his journalism, his world of "spiritual mannerism" (*BL* 202), the daily production of thick, colorless words for a deaf and blind world, and to his carefully hung but now eternally unfinished self-portrait.

LE FEU FOLLET: CUBIST VISIONS, SURREALIST ROOMS

Le Feu follet, the darkest and most rigorously limited of Drieu's novels, is an illustrated satire combining cubist and surrealist elements with the idiom of nineteenth-century caricature. A radically compacted hybrid of abstraction and anger, the novel works as a kind of "literary painting," to apply the term first used pejoratively by early critics of surrealist paintings and collages and later adopted proudly by Aragon to identify nonrepresentational plastic art. Born of the interartistic context of the twenties, conceived as a bitter farewell to an era destroyed by its own insufficiencies, Drieu's brilliantly written 192-page pictorialization of the last three days in the life of a drug addict carries an emotional charge as intense as the two capstone war novels of 1929, Hemingway's *Farewell to Arms* and Erich Maria Remarque's *All Quiet on the Western Front*, while maintaining the deliberate silence about the war commonly agreed on by the surrealists.[22] Major fiction dealing directly with the war arrived a bit later in France than in America or Germany, with Céline's *Voyage au bout de la nuit* in 1932 and Drieu's *La Comédie de Charleroi* in 1934. *Le Feu follet*, written in 1930 and published in 1931, is in fact an *obverse* novel about the war. The hero Alain, the will-o'-the-wisp or *ignis fatum* of the novel's title—a brief light or temporary fire fed by the gases given off by decomposing matter—appears as an evanescent, almost transparent icon moving through a physical setting undermined by the artistic modes of decomposition and negative form—cubism and surrealism. The narration of his extinction is an apocalyptic variation on the hollow portrait, on the Magritte portrait-and-landscape in which an ambiguous figure gazes at the emblematic essence of a strange landscape under a cool, gray, shadowless light. The world of dissociation, of proportions transformed, of meticulously rendered objects superimposed over one another represented in the novel is illuminated by the passionate residue of a dialogue on the plastic arts of the twenties.

The novel's admitted source is the much rehearsed and carefully staged suicide in November, 1929, of surrealist Jacques Rigaut, the model for Gonzague in Drieu's 1924 short story "La Valise vide" (The empty suitcase). Drieu's shock at Rigaut's death—shared by other members of the original crew of *Littérature*—was compounded by his guilt at having ignored Rigaut's clear need for emotional support and read too lightly his literary apologies for suicide. The second, more deeply hidden but more significant source of the novel is a deep-rooted

22. For an extended analysis of this pact, see Daix, *Aragon*.

early quarrel between Drieu and Aragon over directions in contemporary painting that came to light—many years after Drieu's death—with the publication in 1981 of Aragon's collected writings on modern art. The Aragon volume includes a long essay on Max Ernst written in 1975 for a major retrospective of the painter's collages at the Grand Palais and originally published in a limited edition. Tracing his lifelong attachment to Ernst's work, Aragon describes a memorable dialogue with Drieu following the first Paris exhibit of Ernst collages in 1921. "I remember one of the first arguments I had with a friend I then considered a close friend, Pierre Drieu La Rochelle. He had a superb mind and was gifted with incredible self-assurance on matters of art. He told me—I hadn't asked—that the surrealists (meaning the literary surrealists) had no luck with *their* painters, that they *really* didn't have the painters they deserved." [23] Aragon describes burying his anger over the remark until March, 1930, the date of the historic collective show of collages at the Galerie Goemans, 49, rue de Seine, for which he wrote *La Peinture au défi* (Painting takes up the challenge). Aragon's brilliant polemic proclaiming the social and historical significance of collage was a direct challenge to Drieu's attack on its triviality. Drieu responded in turn by writing, in three tightly revised drafts, a stinging countertext on the destructive effects of experimental art—*Le Feu follet*.

Alain is a fictional illustration of *le point blanc*, a term Aragon uses in his text on collage to connote the daub of white that marks a highlight on a colored object in an oil painting and that serves as a visual point of reference for the elements in the picture and ultimately for the viewer's gaze. Alain, Drieu's visual and moral point of reference, appears in the novel as a fleeting light that marks the highlight of decay and will leave nothing behind. Another central idea developed in *La Peinture au défi*, and shared in conversations between Drieu and Aragon earlier in the twenties, builds on what Aragon identifies as the inherent theatricality of collage. He suggests collages all of whose elements would be painted or repainted and imagines them grouped or massed "in arbitrary succession" to form an entire stage landscape, an immense *décor* made of pictures. [24] Several key scenes in *Le Feu follet*—among them the trip to Falet's photography gallery and the visit with the drug addicts—illus-

23. Louis Aragon, "L'Essai Max Ernst," in *Ecrits sur l'art moderne* (Paris, 1981), 317–18.
24. Louis Aragon, *La Peinture au défi*, rpr. in *Les Collages* (Paris, 1965), 58, 62.

trate this idea by using descriptive elements that look like surrealist paintings, collages, and photographs to create the entire visual context. Their passionate quarrel over plastic forms would expand into an eternal separation over diverging political extremisms, but Drieu and Aragon would continue—each on his own side and with occasional stated references to the other—the dialogue in other forms over the years.

Thirty-year-old Alain, with his still handsome but increasingly deathlike face that looks like a wax mask and his abundant but false-looking hair, is the effigy of a generation gone astray.[25] By contrast with the subtle modeling, careful shadings, and fine sensuous detail that surround Blaquans' mannerist self-portrait, the depiction of Alain relies on flat colors, heavy charcoal outlines, crudely colored captioned cartoons, sparely used geometric shapes, starkly angled planes, figures that look like fragments of plaster statues. The thing-world through which Alain moves has a cheap solidity, the density of concrete rather than marble; interior spaces tend to press down from above and walls lean menacingly inward. The ritualistically arranged emblems of Alain's room at the sanitorium where he is attempting a last drug cure include small stacks of common things—cigarette and match boxes, cheap novels (detective, pornographic), magazines (American illustrated, avant-garde)—and on the mantelpiece a spare surrealist assemblage, two disparate and equally useless *objets*, "a highly subtle instrument, a perfectly flat platinum chronometer, and a horrible little colored plaster statuette of incredible vulgarity, bought at a fair" (*FF* 35). The mantelpiece mirror, a giant collage of photos and pieces of newspaper, displays prominently two grotesquely posed close-up photographic portraits, with nostrils, mouths, foreheads, a mustache appearing like fragments of a monumental landscape (a biting recreation of Man Ray's work), flanking an insignificant newspaper clipping pasted up with four postage stamps—"the human spirit reduced to two dimensions" (*FF* 35–36).

Alain's room is deliberately enclosed, with the blinds always drawn and daylight rarely visible, a vision of shrinking, abstract space. "A little box inside a slightly larger box. A mirror, a window, a door. The door and window opened on nothing. The mirror opened only on itself" (*FF* 36). Alain, Drieu affirms, is not a primitive who would be moved by the soul, the palpitation of objects, for whom a tree or a stone would hold

25. Pierre Drieu La Rochelle, *Le Feu follet* (Paris, 1931), 18. Hereafter cited in the text as *FF*.

the power of suggestion of a lover's body. "For Alain's imagination, objects were not points of departure; they were dead places where his exhausted imagination had come to rest after a brief, useless trip through the world. Through aridity of heart and irony, he avoided having any ideas about the world. Philosophy, art, politics, or morality, all systems appeared to him as impossible rodomontades. . . . The world was so lacking in consistency that there was nothing he could lean on. In his eyes, only solid objects retained their form" (*FF* 37–38). Apart from his cubist collage-room, Alain is most comfortable in deliberately anonymous, depthless, neutral public places—bars, cafés, dingy hotel rooms—or spaces like drug addict Praline's living room that look like sets about to be dismantled. "The walls were bare, the sparse furniture composed of a few roughly drawn lines. It was like being in a storage room filled with packing crates" (*FF* 129).

Where the opaque first-person narrator of *Blèche* attempts consciously to dominate or shut out the world he moves through, Alain exists as an empty space within the visible world, a barely seen and rapidly disappearing shape briefly silhouetted against a series of props, present as a querulous voice and an unaccountably disturbing presence within scenes of failed human encounters. He takes taxis from one place to another, even for short distances, avoiding visual encounters with the living presence of the city. "Abstract stations: once again in a taxi, he looked at nothing, neither right nor left. Of the city that rose up and dipped down again on the right and on the left all he perceived were a few dim evocations, some personal memories. Alain had never seen the sky nor the facades of houses, nor wood floors, the things that throb; he had never looked at a river or a forest; he lived in the empty rooms of morality: 'The world is imperfect, the world is bad. I disapprove, I condemn, I annihilate the world.' . . . His spirit was an empty carcass scoured clean by the vultures that circle over great empty cities" (*FF* 126–27). Alain feeds on the world, creating a void around himself. He sees other human beings as portraits, clowns, dummies, talking heads whose voices and words are less significant than the colors of their faces or the texture of the fabric that covers their furniture. Lydia, the wealthy American with whom he makes love in a grisly hotel room as the novel opens, paints "on her dead face a strange caricature of life. White on white, red, black" (*FF* 18). The text evokes a Paris dawn that Alain ignores, a scene with the same gray, damp, metaphysical look as

Eliot's London and some of its infernal structure. "The morning slid over the night like a damp rag on a dirty windowpane. They walked down the rue Blanche, between the garbage cans, filled with offerings." Alain watches Lydia walk "on ankles of clay" like a crumbling idol, her makeup pasting an irregularly moving feverish spot on the grisaille of dawn. Taxies roll down streets like out-of-control billiard balls (*FF* 20–21). The apartment of his friend Dubourg, who has taken refuge in ethnology and a bestially placid marriage, is painted white, with a cream-colored carpet, soft to the eye except for the stronger color notes supplied by book bindings, a few flowers, some primitive upholstery fabrics, a few fragments of Coptic embroidery. As Alain "sits among the hieroglyphs" (*FF* 90) and listens to Dubourg arguing for Alain's rehabilitation, he judges still another mythology to be mediocre. Progressively, Alain's form of negative vision corrupts the most solid objects of his world, the very stones of the city, which appear to be disintegrating. "La rivière coulait grise, sous un ciel gris, entre les maisons grises. . . . Les pierres carrées s'amollissaient dans l'air humide" (*FF* 110). 'The river ran gray, under a gray sky, between the gray houses. . . . The solid stones were turning soft in the humid air.'

The severest assault on Alain's guarded visual state is Dr. Barbinais' suburban sanitorium, where the hallway, salon, and dining room walls are "tapestried with literature," covered with portraits of famous nineteenth- and twentieth-century writers (the former have solid faces, the latter "effaced features") admired and displayed solely for their neurotic ailments (*FF* 24). Alain, who hates literature and makes a point of avoiding museums of any kind, tries not to look at the sick famous faces. At dinner the assorted *pensionnaires* (none is truly mad but the doctor's wife—the rest are simply weak) make up an album of crudely colored satirical drawings (*FF* 25–33), a text on contemporary society, Balzac as reread through Freud. "These communal meals seemed to Alain the most incredible moments of his stay in this place that combined all the most horrible features of the sanitorium and the family pension" (*FF* 25). This sweeping critical commentary, a highly literate, intertextual reading of European society in the twenties, contrasted throughout the novel with the mythology of America—as represented by Lydia's check for ten thousand francs, by the ship *Leviathan* that is taking her back home, by a description of New York as "a frank atrocity"—highlights the novel's most notable narrative flaw, Drieu's difficulty incorporating his own condemnation of the Paris wasteland into the "empty room" of Alain's restricted consciousness. Drieu's tendentious assertions, out of character with Alain's explicitly antiliterary and antivisual way of perceiving the world, creates a troubling duality of tone and signals the inevitable problems highly intelligent, intensely visual novelists have with deliberately limited characters. (Henry James's insoluble dilemma with the restricted central consciousness of Hyacinth Robinson in *The Princess Casamassima* made him abandon such an approach in subsequent works.) Alain, as much a visual object lesson as a character—certainly not a tragic hero, being too weak, too little self-conscious to qualify for that role [26]—is himself something like the cheap literary portraits at Dr. Barbinais', minus the literary talent. Indeed, Barbinais, a collector of people, values Alain as "a splenetic dandy in the tradition of Messieurs Chateaubriand and Constant, as well as a closely observable specimen of mysterious contemporary youth" (*FF* 46).

Drieu's satirical vision, easily integrated into the narrative in *Blèche*, in *Le Feu follet* becomes a hovering authorial presence that combines with the apparent subject of drug addition to create a disturbing and recalcitrant novel that is difficult to forget and—it appears—difficult to forgive. Received with open hostility or stony silence in 1931, *Le Feu follet* has continued to be regarded as a scandalous or frightening tale and to invite bowdlerization in adaptations into other media.[27] Louis Malle's 1963 film changed Alain into an alcoholic and explained away Lydia's gift to him of ten thousand francs as partial repayment of a debt. Such defensive rereadings underline the novel's genuinely wrenching effect without identifying the source of its destructive energy, of the almost electrical charge that comes not from the specific identification of drug addition or from the often angry, metaphysically slanted authorial intrusions, on which novelist John Updike focused when he wrote of "things thin with the thinness that implies a background of immense loss."[28] The profound shock of *Le Feu follet* is rooted in its vivid and bitter creation of a terrifying negative world—a world distorted, unstable, incomprehensible, and filled with menace, a world that threatens

26. For a well-argued exposition of the "classical" interpretation, see Thiher, "*Le Feu follet.*"

27. See Frédéric Grover, "*Le Feu follet:* Un roman qui fait encore peur," *Magazine Littéraire*, No. 143 (December, 1978), 28–31.

28. John Updike, "Death's Heads," in *Picked-Up Pieces* (New York, 1975), 260–69.

the viewer and refuses to look back at him, a place where mirrors reveal no reflections, where solid objects cast no shadows—or if they do, shadows of the wrong shape. It is Ernst's world, Magritte's world without the humor or sense of fantasy, a world of nightmare uncontained.

Alain's vision is filled with a collection of disparate secondhand representations, of degraded *things*—the fraying vestiges of a fine dandy's wardrobe bought with the quickly exhausted legacy of his estranged American wife Dorothy, now figured only by an unanswered telegram; the paper fetish of Lydia's check; the heroin syringe and the revolver side by side in the nightstand. In a description of Alain's one dim fantasy of ambition Drieu angrily parodies the dada-surrealist taste for "camp." Alain's dream of opening in Paris or New York a boutique specializing in "all the outmoded, ugly, or absurd objects spawned by popular industry over the last fifty years . . . objects that became the rage in the twenties with 'persons of taste' who aped and extended the passing whims of a few artists, and of selling at an enormous profit a heterogeneous bazaar: flea carousels, collections of sentimental or smutty postcards, popular illustrations, glass paperweights, ships in bottles, wax figures, etc." (*FF* 57—58) is the feeble fantasy of an exhausted imagination. When his friend Dubourg abandons him at a minuscule photography boutique "dilated by a crude light" and presided over by Falet, the fashionable photographer, who appears painfully thin, with "a high arched spine over which little shoulders form a feeble circumflex accent . . . above this, a bit of gray skin, false teeth, eyes like a sardine . . . a fetus born dead and revived by a serpent's bite that had left him its venom" (*FF* 113–14), Alain finds himself in a "museum of horrors." The walls are covered with portraits distorted and stripped of any semblance of reality. Eva Canning, a woman Falet supplies with drugs, looks to Alain like "a statue gone astray. Formed by the hands of a Pygmalion who only knew how to copy, she had the beauty of replicas. Her shoulders, her thighs had the weak excess, the redundancy of low era sculpture" (*FF* 117). Stripped down to smoke her opium, Eva becomes a magnificent, bloodless form in plaster. "For [Alain], the world was filled with empty forms. Enough to make you scream, enough to make you die" (*FF* 119). Taking his last heroin shot, he watches the naked Eva reclining on her fur coat. "One of her shoulders, hard and polished, gleamed in the light from a small lamp. This fragment of a broken statue rolled in a desert with no top and no bottom, came to rest in a warm, lapping abyss" (*FF* 121). Alain is literally inside a surrealist painting, unable to find the walls, floor, or ceiling. He flees and enters a staircase, where he finds an endless series of steps that appear covered with bodies ascending and descending in the superimposed flickers of motion of the nude in Duchamp's painting or the figures in an Italian futurist scene (*FF* 122).

As Alain moves in smaller and smaller concentric circles toward his predictable end, his field of consciousness defines the identifiable contents of an illustrated small world of Paris, a "Paris Room" or intimate gallery of the twenties hung with drawings, set and costume design sketches, a full wall of caricatures, a group of fashionably ugly photographs, a few primitive prints and patches of fabric. Sculpture is represented by an abbreviated collection of grotesquely grouped *objets* and a few chunks of broken statuary randomly arranged. The narrative text functions as a catalogue raisonné of Alain's world of contemporary art, enhanced by a commentary on the obtaining mythologies of the collection as embodied in a sequence of failed human contacts with Lydia, Barbinais, Dubourg, the addicts, the wealthy Lavauxs. The final outdoor scene, a night walk through Paris with Milou, a young *raté* who models himself after Alain, reaches its climax in a brief dialogue on the Champs-Elysées with a horrible-looking prostitute whose brilliant particolored rags provide the novel's brightest visual note and establish its iconographic links with the Parisian imagery of Eugène Delacroix, Victor Hugo, Charles Baudelaire, and Emile Zola.

The final scene, in which Alain prepares for his suicide by arranging himself carefully on his pillows, arching and baring his chest, and taking the revolver in his hand, is a striking echo of the visual composition of Man Ray's 1922 photographic portrait of Jacques Rigaut (Fig. 9), who is shown from the rear in a three-quarter view lying on a neatly made bed, with his head tipped back and his masklike pallor accentuated by slicked-down hair, a formal dark suit, and a meticulously knotted tie. In the right foreground, a small, dark, hinged paper doll of a male figure with joints marked by white rivets stands on the tightly stretched sheet, casting a spidery shadow cut off by the photo's right edge. Rigaut stares dreamily at the doll. Despite all the elaborate preparation, the novel's finale is shocking when it comes. After a penultimate scene in which Alain refuses further human contact by rejecting an invitation to lunch with the beautiful Solange Lavaux, who is trying to head off the suicide,

9. Man Ray, *Portrait de Jacques Rigaut*. 1922. Photograph. Man Ray Trust, Paris.
Copyright 1990 ARS N.Y. / ADAGP.
Photo: Man Ray Trust, print from the original negative.

the text's last two lines, with their rigorous, broken rhythm, jolting repetition, and tight encapsulation of the novel's central visual iconology, are far more effective than Alain's earlier quoted musings of moral despair: "Un revolver, c'est solide, c'est en acier. C'est un objet. Se heurter enfin à l'objet" (*FF* 192). 'A revolver, it's solid, it's steel. It's an object. To finally strike up against an object.'

Drieu's second and last wasteland novel, a brilliant *texte-objet*, at once embodies and attacks the tradition it represents—the spare, hard, American-style novel—by presenting the war as seen from behind the panels of a surrealist exhibit. The spaces of Drieu's subsequent fiction would open out and restore the art displaced by the avant-garde extremes of the twenties. With Malraux and Céline, Drieu would reach for a unifying vision of contemporary life in the rich iconology of premodernist plastic arts. The bitter look of a Paris without Delacroix, of a gray stone landscape turning soft with the *alcools* of drugs and liquor, would send Drieu back to the clarity of vision he had remembered from the war, to the infinite moments of creative possibility glimpsed on the verge of death, and to the "heart-rending play of politics" that would periodically pull him back to the world. He would move from the blind object-world of *Le Feu follet* to the re-vision of the war years in texts that would allow him to unite the techniques of the Americans, the Paris of the late teens and twenties, and the apocalyptic-creative visions of the army years. Ahead lay the mirror stories of *La Comédie de Charleroi*, the turbulent heart of the thirties, and *Gilles*.

5

Gilles, I: Finding the Center

NOVELISTS, PAINTERS, THE CONTEXT
OF THE THIRTIES

La Comédie de Charleroi established Drieu as a master of short fiction
precisely at the point in his career when he most began to crave "big"
solutions—in his personal life, in politics, in literary form. Having mas-
tered the lapidary dialogues of the American modernists, having forged
a practical rhetoric out of Céline's raging ocean of poetic slang, Drieu
entered on what he would later call—with a characteristic admixture of
pride and irony—his "descent into a political destiny." The February,
1934, Stavisky riots in Paris, in which leftists and rightists faced one
another and the police in protest over a major government scandal,
seemed to Drieu a failed revolution that missed toppling the weak and
corrupt Third Republic. Later that year he declared himself a fascist,
saw his political play *Le Chef* run for only five performances, introduced
and cotranslated D. H. Lawrence's last novel, and began a series of
newspaper articles tracing an evolving semiotics of national salvation in
Rome, Prague, and Budapest. In 1935 he traveled to Nuremberg,
Berlin, and Moscow and began a long-lived liaison with Christiane Renault, wife of the French industrialist. Playing out the role of historian-
philosopher who compensates for his too-comfortable creative life by
active involvement in politics, Drieu lived the political watershed of the
thirties by writing on all fronts at once—as journalist, novelist, play-
wright, and critic. In the novels of fellow modernists Malraux, Huxley,
Céline, and Lawrence, Drieu assessed—with a remarkable ability to
penetrate and sympathetically comprehend work quite different from
his own—a range of solutions to the problem of form in an extended
narrative.

81

Drieu's 1930 *Nouvelle Revue Française* review of *Les Conquérants* (1928) and *La Voie royale* (1930) captured as well as has ever been done since the brilliances and weak points of Malraux's fiction. Calling the younger writer *l'homme nouveau* (the new man), Drieu set into high relief the oddly choppy, visually haunting quality of these early Malraux novels, the impression they convey of insight rapidly and incompletely embodied, of a writer too busy to be "literary" in the traditional way. Describing Malraux's striking style as "la griffe," 'the signature mark,' of a feverish, restless imagination impatient with subtleties and interested only in "eternal man . . . facing his eternal problems: action, sex, death," Drieu identified Malraux's elliptical discourse, the peculiar concision that turns to obscurity, as his greatest flaw. "He's a novelist, but seems to lack some of the skills of a novelist . . . the skills of a storyteller. His novels are rapid narratives, sweeping, bewitching, but narrow and unilinear." Drieu felt that Malraux was limited by his concentration on solitary mythological heroes, by what was perhaps a characteristically French lack of inventiveness. "[Malraux] will have to move beyond his present method, which is to show us a hero, always alone, moving out of a dark corridor toward a blinding end. There is no progression, no conflict between this self and other selves. Malraux's universe is the universe of a solitary man separated from the immobility of death only by some precipitous adventure." Moved most of all by its "two or three grand scenes . . . an adventure isolated against nature," Drieu captured in a startling architectural image the flawed formal structure of *Les Conquérants:* "a solid novel, standing on a firm base, but narrow, built straight up. Compact, with holes. Firm at the base, wavering at the top."[1] Drieu's second essay on Malraux, published in Argentina in 1933, viewed *La Condition humaine* (1933), Malraux's first long novel, as a brilliant but troubling illustration of the narrative difficulties involved in sustaining the reader's interest through four hundred pages "in something that is beginning to disintegrate at the beginning of the book and continues to decline. . . . This absence of conflict, this disappointing and irreducible parallelism of individual destinies, strikes me as the very form of tragedy in our era. This same characteristic also leaves its mark on the two other major collective novels of our era,

1. Pierre Drieu La Rochelle, "Malraux, l'homme nouveau," *Nouvelle Revue Française*, XXXV (December, 1930), 879–85.

Gide's *Les Faux-Monnayeurs* and Huxley's *Counterpoint*." [2] By 1933 Drieu was also becoming somewhat impatient with Malraux's persistent choice of exotic settings, with his broadly cinematic effects, and with what appeared to be a growing emphasis on leftist political causes. But alone among French novels recently published in Paris, Malraux's and Céline's *Voyage au bout de la nuit* struck Drieu as works "with human dimensions."

In a painstakingly detailed review of Huxley's *Point Counter Point*, Drieu described the "multiple, slow skating motions, with no violent conflicts . . . the bundle of rectilinear tales" that made it "a bad novel, but an important book." [3] Huxley's vast, talky structure struck Drieu as the inevitable result of an overintellectualized milieu, the product of a world of young *littérateurs* swimming against a tide of complex, intricately structured nineteenth-century fictional masterpieces based in an extinct world of certainties. By contrast, Drieu's preface to the first French translation of *Farewell to Arms* communicated his admiration for, as well as his sense of remoteness from, Hemingway's world, "a solid universe one can touch with the hand, with no intellectual implications, a place with the suggestive power of things, of art objects." [4] When confronted with the heavy symbolism of D. H. Lawrence's *The Man Who Died*, which he prefaced and cotranslated, Drieu admitted the superiority of *Sons and Lovers*, *Women in Love*, and *The Rainbow* but read the British modernist's last work before his death as a notable effort to create a viable mythology of passion in the face of a hostile contemporary world.

Drieu's admiration for Céline, whose *Voyage au bout de la nuit* he defended privately in the early thirties and publicly in the *Nouvelle Revue Française* in 1941, was based on a complex admixture of sympathy and natural revulsion. To regard the novel that landed on the French literary scene in 1932 like a bombshell as a deeply traditional, indeed old-fashioned work, to perceive immediately its affinity with the French medieval tradition and the lineage of Rabelais, to admire it most of all for its revolutionary linguistic innovations and rich plastic detail, to *not*

2. Drieu La Rochelle, "*La Condition humaine*," 286–87.
3. Pierre Drieu La Rochelle, "A propos d'un roman anglais," *Nouvelle Revue Française*, XXXV (November, 1930), 721–31.
4. Pierre Drieu La Rochelle, "Préface à *L'Adieu aux armes*, d'Ernest Hemingway" (Paris, 1931), rpr. in *Sur les écrivains*, ed. Grover, 105–108.

mistake it for a work of specific social protest as did some, and to make these judgments on the spot—these were Drieu's notable critical accomplishments. He recognized Céline as a realist sprung from the most profound layers of French art, as a writer with an overwhelming "sense of the real such as one finds squirming at the bottom of a sack, or in the smaller sculpted areas of cathedrals, and in more recent times in the work of Daumier, Gavarni, Guys, Toulouse-Lautrec."[5] Recognizing here a striking, if almost uncontrolled, response to the modernist dilemma, Drieu wrote in the 1942 preface to *Gilles*, "Céline s'est jeté à corps perdu dans le seul chemin qui s'offrait . . . cracher, seulement cracher, mais mettre au moins tout le Niagara dans cette salivation."[6] 'Céline threw himself headlong into the only road open to him . . . to spit, only to spit, but to put all of Niagara Falls into that gesture.' Less impressed by *Mort à crédit* (1936) than by *Voyage*, Drieu continued to marvel at Céline's artistic handling of popular speech, comparing it to the use of impasto, the thick application of paint on canvas that leaves visible the marks of the brush or palette knife. In making his linguistic method part of the textural richness of the work, Drieu noted, "Céline makes use of Célinism in the same way that recent painters have made use of fauvism or cubism."[7]

In a series of brilliantly conceived and elegantly written literary letters to Victoria Ocampo, editor of the influential Argentinian literary magazine *Sur* (and for a few years one of his lovers), Drieu defined his emerging private canon. To the names of Joyce, Huxley, Malraux, and Céline, he added Faulkner. When the aristocratic Ocampo complained of finding Céline unreadable, Drieu urged her to come out of her lavishly appointed, somewhat provincial literary cocoon and to try to understand the fundamental dilemmas facing the European literary modernists of 1934:

> I saw Huxley in Paris. He's written a play and wants to go on a tour around the world. *Counterpoint* drained him completely and he has no idea what to do. It's strange, these people who have nothing to say, who run out of things to say. . . . At bottom, he's attached to nothing. We're all a bit like that, we

5. Pierre Drieu La Rochelle, "Un Homme, une femme," *Nouvelle Revue Française*, LIV (May, 1941), 721.

6. Pierre Drieu La Rochelle, *Gilles* (1942; rpr. Paris, 1969), 10. Hereafter cited in the text as *G*.

7. Drieu La Rochelle, "Un Homme, une femme," 723.

bourgeois writers, because the civilization we're attached to is empty. Gone are the Christian Middle Ages, gone is the rational Renaissance, instead it's mass production and sale of anything at all. . . .

Willed Christians like Claudel or willed communists like Middleton Murry or Aragon surround us. But the mass is you and me and Huxley. . . . The only real ones are the big terrible *skeptics* such as Joyce, Valéry, Gide.

If I don't become a socialist or a communist, I'll croak. . . . But I'll arrive at socialism too late, like Gide. The difficulty is that, to become a communist, one must be a materialist. No way. . . . That's why my novels are so bad when they're not negative. The only good things today are negative (including Lawrence).

We writers are as sick as our mass-produced things. Some write on a production line. Art for art. Or when we are sincere, we cry *merde* (*Le Jeune Européen, Ulysses, Counterpoint*, Lawrence's critical pages, *Monsieur Teste*, Gide the "communist").[8]

While working on the stories of *La Comédie de Charleroi*, Drieu had completed and published *Drôle de voyage* (1933), an intergenre novel that reintroduced Gille Gambier, now a few years older than in *L'Homme couvert de femmes* and employed in a vague diplomatic post. On a visit to the Pyrenees home of wealthy friends, Gille becomes fitfully involved with Béatrix Owen, the virginal daughter of wealthy English aristocrats. As the novel's four clearly separated parts move rhythmically between the south of France, southern Spain, and Paris, Drieu's fluid, at times confused, conception of his subject—somewhere between a play for reading and a series of set and costume drawings—becomes obvious: he is satirizing his own earlier Gille novel, as well as Gide's *Les Caves du Vatican*. Jean Lansard's detailed study of Drieu's theater, revealing the existence of the unpublished play *Gille* (1931), has shed considerable light on the weaknesses of *Drôle de voyage*.[9] Another version of Drieu's unpublished play, the 1933 novel is a painterly, dramatic, and musical text woven of vignettes and caricatures, plays within plays, and vocal arrangements, a tale over which hangs a heavy cloud of theatricality, as rooms, houses, and natural scenery look like stage sets about to vanish when the curtain falls, while characters woodenly act out costumed

8. Pierre Drieu La Rochelle, letter to Victoria Ocampo, December, 1934, quoted in *Sur les écrivains*, ed. Grover, 150–52. References to several other of Drieu's most interesting letters to Ocampo appear in Andreu and Grover, *Drieu La Rochelle*, 219ff.

9. See Lansard, *Drieu La Rochelle*.

roles. Drieu had no illusions about the merits of his second Gille novel, but the critics, put somewhat at their ease by its similarity to Gide and by the reappearance of themes and characters from Drieu's earlier works, found themselves able to praise it. To critic Edmond Jaloux, a dissenter who had complained of the hero's inability to make up his mind, Drieu clarified in a letter the mixed interartistic motivations behind the novel, explaining that Gille was "not an indecisive man. He knows from the beginning that it all will not work, but makes believe. . . . I wanted to write a comedy like those of Watteau and Marivaux and Couperin . . . where a French audience knows how the ballet will end." [10]

In the thirties Drieu published several articles on painting in *Formes* and *L'Europe Nouvelle* that show him asking the same questions about form, passion, and representation posed in his critical essays, following some of the same arguments about what is modern, and—as in his odd 1929–1931 discourse-by-novel with Aragon about surrealist painting—taking a strong position on art and showing an acute awareness of current art historical issues. After visiting a major exhibition of Goya's drawings at the Bibliothèque Nationale, Drieu argued with Eugenio d'Ors's monolithic view of Goya as a "baroque" painter and recreated the Spanish painter from a different vantage point, that of a modernist writer looking for counterbalancing figures in the carpet. "Yes, Goya is baroque, because his anxious, hasty, uncombed grace already announces all the romantic and impressionist complaisances. But he is also still classical; the seriousness of his craft [*le sérieux de son métier*] is still in harmony with his spontaneous expression in art of the seriousness of his soul. This is not the difficult and trembling reconquest of craft and vision of a Cézanne. Goya remains complete: draftsman and colorist. He remains beyond those quarrels that will forever divide art between line and color, between Ingres and Delacroix." [11] Drieu admits that Goya occasionally "trembles" when he begins to oscillate between academicism and caricature, thus predicting Manet, Degas, and Picasso. For Drieu's own generation, however, the notion that art must shake off

10. Pierre Drieu La Rochelle, unpublished letter of July 15, 1933, to Edmond Jaloux, quoted in Lansard, *Drieu La Rochelle*, I, 310.

11. Pierre Drieu La Rochelle, "Goya," *L'Europe Nouvelle*, XVIII (May 11, 1935), rpr. in *Drieu La Rochelle*, ed. Hanrez, 69.

"the yoke of beauty and perfection" is axiomatic; for them completeness is no longer possible. Drieu recognizes that Malraux is exciting *because* he is incomplete, elliptical, too much in a hurry to perfect *the art of the novel*, and that Céline's genius consists in having looked into the swarming sack, in having faced the *décadence* of the contemporary world and chosen to announce it with an apocalyptic torrent of language.

Nevertheless, old loves die hard. Drieu made one sustained, almost despairing attempt to write a traditional novel. The result was *Rêveuse bourgeoisie* (1937), a long family saga, "a vast machine" (Drieu's phrase) based on the lives of his grandparents and parents around the turn of the century, that reconceived the fictional world of Balzac and Zola through Barrès and Freud; with it Drieu hoped at last to convince critics and readers that he could write a "real novel." His effort quite eclipsed by the critical success of Aragon's *Les Beaux Quartiers* (1936, the second volume of *Le Monde réel* series), Drieu turned with a clear sense of relief away from his recent active involvement with rightist politics and traditionally structured fiction and started work on what would be his most daring and complex novel.[12]

As Drieu began his novel on January 25, 1937, increasingly detaching himself from the political world and taking stock of his artistic vocation, he found that he frankly preferred the solitude and personal freedom of art to the world of action. Increasingly, he revisited the Louvre and attended art shows. The massive exhibition at the Petit Palais (some fifteen hundred works) of "Les Maîtres de l'art indépendant, 1895–1937," provided him with a vast survey of nonacademic French painting during the decades dealt with in *Gilles*, from Matisse's orientalism and Marcel Gromaire's war icons to huge etiolated panels in the manner of Pierre Puvis de Chavannes and a vast stream of often derivative compositions marked by cubism.[13] The emphasis at the Petit Palais show was on figurative painting, with Pierre Bonnard, Braque, André Derain, Raoul Dufy, Matisse, Picasso, Georges Rouault, André

12. For a detailed account of Drieu's political involvements in the thirties and their relationship to his fiction, see Reck, "Pierre Drieu La Rochelle."

13. The brilliant 1987 recreation of the original exhibition, much of it drawn from the museum's permanent collection, accompanied by an excellent critical preface, is chronicled in the exhibition catalogue, *Paris 1937, L'Art indépendant* (Paris, 1987). See also Rima Drell Reck, review of *Paris 1937, L'Art indépendant*, *French Review*, LXI (May, 1988), 998–99.

Dunoyer de Segonzac, Maurice Utrillo, and Edouard Vuillard the artists most prominently displayed. Cubism was deemphasized and surrealism largely excluded, reflecting the taste of organizer and Petit Palais curator Raymond Escholier, a decorated veteran of the 1914 war and author of books on Delacroix, Daumier, and Matisse, who wanted to assemble, by means of a government-sponsored display held in conjunction with the Exposition Universelle of 1937, the basis for a permanent collection of modern French art to be housed at the new Palais de Tokio (now the Musée d'Art Moderne de la Ville de Paris). Picasso's *Guernica*, hung in the summer of 1937 at the Spanish pavilion of the exposition, confronted Drieu with still another monumental image of the Spanish painter's great negative genius. Here was the disintegrating world of Europe immortalized in a frescolike canvas incorporating the whole history of Western painting and bearing the marks of every contemporary "disease" Drieu was rejecting—surrealism, journalism, and leftism.[14] From June through October of 1937, an important Van Gogh exhibit—226 works—held at the Palais de Tokio began to stimulate Drieu's intense admiration for the Dutch painter whose work was attracting increasing attention in art historical circles. The first International Surrealist Exhibition to be held in Paris opened on January 17, 1938, at the Galerie des Beaux-Arts. There Drieu found what he considered visible proof of the movement's creative impoverishment; from it he returned, his spirit of satire reinvigorated, to the second part of his novel in progress depicting the surrealists in the first years of their decline.[15]

Turning away from the world even more determinedly, Drieu plunged back into his novel, completing the first draft in August, 1938, just before the Munich accords betrayed Czechoslovakia and temporarily averted war. He then resigned formally from the Parti Populaire

14. The most useful studies of the genesis of Picasso's painting are Rudolph Arnheim, *The Genesis of a Painting: Picasso's "Guernica"* (Berkeley, 1962); and Santiago Sebastien Lopez, *El Guernica y otras obras de Picasso: Contextos Iconográficos* (Murcia, 1984). A particularly striking early reading of the painting, stimulated by its first London showing and printed in an exhibition pamphlet published by the New Burlington Galleries, is Herbert Read, *Picasso's Guernica* (London, 1938), 6. For a history of the painting's return to Spain, see the exhibition catalogue *Guernica-Legado Picasso* (Madrid, 1981).

15. For Drieu's immediate reaction to the Surrealist Exhibition, see the excerpt from his article "Au temps des surréalistes," *Je Suis Partout*, March 11, 1938, rpr. in *Sur les écrivains*, ed. Grover, 314–17.

Français and, working harder than he had ever done before, proceeded with the massive rewriting.[16] As he worked, he put some of his hopes for the novel into letters to Christiane: "Let the book resemble a bit the paintings we have loved, those powerful, seemingly excessive landscapes by Van Gogh that are in fact so well seen, so closely observed, along with—in the corners—certain of the *shocking delicacies* of Manet." [17] Always, when tired or discouraged, or simply for the special light his paintings shed on the contemporary world, Drieu turned to Watteau. "Yes, looking at Watteau, I knew not only that this is everything, but that it's nothing." [18] This note of hope and despair fused—everything expressed with the tone of ironic passion that casts its glow over all of Drieu's work—is central to the vision he was creating in *Gilles*. I have elsewhere identified this special note as *l'accent Drieutique*, that modest-acidic-idealistic-despairing sound which is specifically his. A letter written immediately after completing the correction of proofs of *Gilles* in August, 1939, expressed Drieu's intense sense of disorientation on emerging from his work: "The writing has really unsettled me. . . . Literature is a terribly dangerous game." [19]

Sensing that his novel required some sort of introduction to its public, Drieu published "Le Héros de roman," subtitled "de Fabrice à Gilles," on December 16, 1939, in *Les Nouvelles Littéraires*, just as Gallimard was releasing *Gilles*, situating his fictional hero squarely within the tradition from which he sprang:

> The fictional hero . . . is that marvelous realm where observation and creation, memory and dream, realism and idealism, regret and hope, illusion and cold objectivity come together. . . . The man . . . he is in his own eyes and the figure others see. . . . The creature glorifying himself before a mirror and the lesser being born of his words and actions. . . . Lucien Leuwen can still become a soldier, a financier, a diplomat, a politician, or a political figure. Fabrice del Dongo can still become, like Julien Sorel, a priest or a

16. In conversations with the author (March, 1986, and May, 1987), Marc Hanrez confirmed vigorously that the manuscript of *Gilles* shows the most massive reworking of any of Drieu's texts.

17. Pierre Drieu La Rochelle, unpublished letter, quoted in Desanti, *Drieu La Rochelle*, 345.

18. Pierre Drieu La Rochelle, unpublished journal, entry of October 16, 1939, quoted in Lansard, *Drieu La Rochelle*, I, 23.

19. Pierre Drieu La Rochelle, unpublished letter of August, 1939, quoted in Desanti, *Drieu La Rochelle*, 346.

soldier. Mosca, on the other hand, can no longer be anything but a man of politics. . . . Only a young man can embody action and dream, love and ambition, spirituality and sensuality. . . . A young man who happens to be rich or poor is neither a poor man nor a rich man. . . . But a man of forty wears poverty or wealth like a stigma. . . . At the end of his youth, Frédéric of *L'Education sentimentale* is no longer anything but a rentier.[20]

In linking his novel to Stendhal and Flaubert, Drieu was trying at once to identify his potential readers and to prepare a simplified backdrop for his outrageous, ironic dramatization of a still unchronicled period in French life. Such an artistic ploy depended in large part for its success on the reasonable expectation of a commonality of literary background and also on a personal schematization of French regional temperaments that few of his potential readers understood. Drieu's vision of Stendhal as the last eighteenth-century man to live into the nineteenth, his vision of Flaubert as a fellow Norman, a writer threatened by the same "great shadow of monotony" that hung to a lesser degree over other fellow Normans such as dramatist Pierre Corneille and painter Nicolas Poussin, were not to become clear, or public, until the little-read *Notes pour comprendre le siècle*, published in 1941. The example of Flaubert, a novelist seeking an impossible equilibrium for a tendency toward lyric prose, a natural worshiper without a religion, was critical to Drieu's own fiction. Finding no great visions, Flaubert had "at least evoked great absences." By dint of situating "the disease of rationalism in its decor," he had also created the first great paralyzed hero of the nineteenth century—Frédéric Moreau.[21] Flaubert was in fact Drieu's great negative model. Drieu, however, a veteran of battle and an ardent admirer of the early eighteenth century, preferred to think of himself as a Stendhal, that is, as a middle-aged writer still illumined by the glow of a pre-rationalist sensibility who at worst risked facing a long delay in literary reputation.

THE PICTURE GALLERY NOVEL

Drieu's neohistorical, picaresque modernist work, published in a censored edition in December, 1939, then reissued under the occupation in

20. Pierre Drieu La Rochelle, "Le Héros de roman: De Fabrice à Gilles," *Nouvelles Littéraires*, December 16, 1939, p. 1.
21. Pierre Drieu La Rochelle, "Naturalisme et symbolisme," from *Notes pour comprendre le siècle* (Paris, 1941), rpr. in *Sur les écrivains*, ed. Grover, 225–32.

complete form with a newly added author's preface in July, 1942, has had a troubled but persistent life over the decades since its initial appearance, recurring in histories of the twentieth-century French novel as an important but blurrily defined point of reference and being invoked as a symptom of bad political choices. Republished in France in 1962, it has been translated into German, Spanish, Italian, and Japanese but to date remains unavailable in English. A riveting and unforgettable novel, *Gilles* combines brilliant visual detail, striking satire, varied prose rhythms, and complex modulations of narrative tone that merge into a vast, disturbingly disjointed dramatization of the interwar years in Paris. The novel's undulled verve continues to unhinge ideological critics, while many of its satirical portraits continue to occupy source hunters reading it as a roman à clef. The objections of traditionalist critics of fiction, who condemn the dismembered chronology and diagnose the peculiar juxtapositions of rhetorical modes as a symptom of Drieu's lack of skill, recall many of those first raised to novels by Joyce, Woolf, and Faulkner.

The 1942 preface, a fascinating *défense et illustration* of experimental realism, shows the effects on Drieu of his novel's chilly reception and disastrous historical timing. In place of the exhilarated and exhausted but still hopeful novelist of the 1939 letters, who had just completed the most demanding literary effort of his career, in 1942 Drieu appears the older master—the Flaubert of *L'Education sentimentale* facing perhaps a hundred years of hostility to his most complex and significant work— trying to predict what place literary history will assign to his text. Surveying his own earlier novels with an unsparing critical eye, he addresses repeated criticisms that he had devoted too much attention to politics in his writings: "I devoted a lot of attention to many things, including politics . . . because there is a lot of politics in human existence (there always has been) and politics is intimately tied up with all the rest. Name me a single great artist of the past . . . who was not gripped by politics, even when he was by nature drawn to the most private mysticism" (*G* 9). His most important readers—fellow writers— had missed the art of his novel. François Mauriac admired "La Permission," the first part, but appears to have read no further. André Malraux, waiting over the years for *le Drieu* (the big Drieu novel), after perusing the text of *Gilles* privately pronounced it *encore un Drieu* (just another failed Drieu novel) and kept silent about it to his friend. Jean Paulhan admired the novel but soon found himself quarreling with

Drieu about Aragon's participation (Aragon was now a doctrinaire communist) on the *Nouvelle Revue Française*. Gaston Gallimard, ever the faithful friend and publisher, ran a well-placed ad on the back cover of the February, 1940, *Nouvelle Revue Française*, stressing the novel's deceptive traditionalism: "La Vie d'un homme de 1917 à 1937, n'est-ce pas la première fois qu'un romancier traite ce grand sujet?" 'The life of a man from 1917 to 1937. This is the first time a novelist has dealt with this important subject.' But *Gilles* was a tough novel for its time and seems to remain a tough novel for our own.

When Jean-Paul Sartre in 1948 called *Gilles* "un roman doré et crasseux," 'a golden and dirty novel,' he vividly suggested at once the beauty and the subversive power of Drieu's passionate modernist text.[22] Drieu's complex, violent recombination of the iconology of the nineteenth century with the rhetoric of twentieth-century political extremisms, his passionate rejection of the Third Republic, his massive savaging of the surrealist movement, and his vivid depictions of interpenetrating passions—love, money, politics, and art—for a long time placed the novel beyond rational critical examination. Over the years *Gilles* has been read as a "document," a confession, a myth, even a fluke—the work of an accidental novelist, a political writer who happened to dabble in fiction. Aware quite early that a context seemed to be lacking, Drieu tried in his 1942 preface to explain what he had done, to set his striking and complex novel into the fabric that surrounded it. "Je me situe entre Céline et Montherlant et Malraux" (*G* 10). 'I place myself among Céline and Montherlant and Malraux.' Drieu's usage of the word *entre* (between, among) points to the dynamic network, the *réseau* of French modernism that he was attempting to map. The passage merits full quotation:

> I place myself between Céline and Montherlant and Malraux.
>
> I have strictly spoken what I saw like Montherlant in *Les Célibataires*, but with a tendency toward diatribe like Céline; however, this tendency was confined within narrow limits, because, although I am a great lover and defender of a kind of excess in the history of French literature, in practical terms I am a Norman, and like all Normans scrupulously subject to the disciplines of the Seine and the Loire. I also had an inclination to step outside the bounds of France like Malraux, but was too much in the grip of Paris to

22. Jean-Paul Sartre, "Qu'est-ce que la littérature?" in *Situations, II* (Paris, 1948), 228.

go abroad; I went to Spain and Germany and Russia only to verify ideas about France.

I have often laughed bitterly thinking of the narrow, the minuscule scope of the dramas I have put under the microscope in *Gilles*, in comparison with the breadth of themes in Malraux, in Giono, a breadth for which I feel I was born.

But France is a nation of painters where Daumier represents a fundamental necessity as much as does Delacroix. (*G* 10)

Decorated, rich, contradictory, self-referential, intensely visual, rhetorically diverse, a recognizably modernist novel, an interartistic fiction about fiction, *Gilles* is a mythology of the years between the wars featuring a hero named after the figure in a painting by Watteau. Like all long, irregularly structured, dense novels—*La Chartreuse de Parme*, *L'Education sentimentale*, and *Ulysses*—Drieu's novel secretes its own environment, demanding a form of reading and rereading that results in a spatially detached concentration, in an overview that takes it in in a single look, or in a group of single looks. *Gilles* stays in the mind and in the visual imagination like a splendid overcrowded museum—like the Louvre, where Drieu spent so many hours. Visiting and revisiting the text, one begins to notice groupings of pictures, walls of frescoes, rooms of decorative arts and of drawings. Images and plastic constructions from literature and painting—the picaresque novel, the cartoons of Goya, the sensual history pictures of Delacroix, Daumier's Paris and Parisians, the cubist canvases of Picasso and Braque, landscapes and cityscapes and portraits, some of them doubled by Flaubert's pictures of narrative checkmate and Stendhal's comic opera scenes, the confrontational compositions of Manet, the immemorial nightmare of *Guernica*—come together, glowing scenes of visual beauty crowded in with jolting sequences of vituperation and awkward swatches of traditional storytelling, in a huge modernist canvas that defies comfortable classification. The unintegrated perceptual psychology, discontinuous chronology, multiple levels of narrative reference, and peculiar narrative perspective in which the hero Gilles exists in a visual plane distinct from that of other characters in the novel, all now seem far more familiar to initiated readers of Joyce, Hemingway, Woolf, and Faulkner, of Malraux and Céline, than they did to readers in the early forties. Drieu's use of montage, cartoons, and the rhetorical rhythms of journalism as part of the novel's visual and textual iconography can now be understood as an integral part of the transitional modernism of the thirties, the era that saw the creation of Picasso's *Guernica* and that ended with the publication of *Gilles* and of *Finnegan's Wake*.

While the four parts of *Gilles* suggest a chronological structure—moving from 1917 ("La Permission"), to 1925 ("L'Elysée"), to the late twenties and early thirties ("L'Apocalypse"), to 1937 ("L'Epilogue")—on closer inspection, they do not in fact trace a history; instead, they form a series of "studies" that embed the figure of Gilles within discrete situations along a fragmented time line. Each part shows Gilles perceiving the picture of a place, then seeking to become part of that picture by accommodating to its formal patterns. The configuration of each part follows a similar pattern—a picture or grouping of pictures with, at the center of each, larger than the other figures, Gilles, variously attired, and in the background some oddly costumed secondary characters who appear to look up at him. Gilles is seen life-size, standing facing forward, as if on an invisible platform, like Watteau's *Gilles* (Fig. 10) in his white clown suit with its pleated ruff. In the enigmatic portrait of Watteau's late career Drieu found a painted analogue for his conception of his novel and its central character—the clown in unstable repose, as author of his own comedy and also its primary actor. In the novel the painted icon stands behind the narrative, creating multiple mirrors of the central character. Gilles seems to float through the segmented narrative time, appearing successively as Gilles the soldier on leave, Gilles the petty diplomat and friend of the surrealists, Gilles the political journalist and prophet of revolution, Gilles the exile about to die. All the Gilles figures coexist, illustrations of phases in a life visually perceived but not causally narrated or made coherent, making it possible to read individual parts of the novel in any order at all, to compare and relocate them, with no significant effect on the individual portraits.

Drieu's depiction of the twenty years between 1917 and 1937 has the same fractionalized, encyclopedic, ultimately nonreferential and anti-synthesizing look and feel as Joyce's twenty-four hours in Dublin in *Ulysses*. Stephen Dedalus meditates on history, but, grasping only images and fragments, he experiences an antihistorical world. The archetypal patterns behind *Ulysses*—Greek myths, Homer's epic, the myths of Shakespeare the writer and of Hamlet, the evolutionary record of the development of a language—are flexible and detached from historical time. Within twenty-four hours of a single day, Joyce creates a poetic

10. Antoine Watteau, *Gilles*. 1718–1719. Oil on canvas, 184½ × 149½ inches. Musée du Louvre, Paris.
Photo: Réunion des Musées Nationaux.

modernist history, a series of fragments musically arranged. Drieu's narrative, stretching over twenty years, also collects fragments, pictures, and scenes, but, unlike Joyce's, its disparate elements lack the contagious enlargement imparted by ancient myths. Instead, Drieu turns to a pictorial context, constructing a synchronic museum of *Gilles*, a modernist prose epic in the tradition of *Don Quixote*, a satire on its own genre using the new aesthetic discoveries in vision and language to replace the realistic narrative posited on the belief in a developmental or cyclical theory of history.

Drieu's choice of Watteau's *Gilles* (recently renamed *Pierrot, dit autrefois Gilles* [formerly called Gilles] by the Louvre) as the principal icon of his novel reflects a dazzling fictional conception that would seem impossible to ignore. But, apart from recalling an occasional remark by one of Drieu's friends puzzled by his intense if often obliquely expressed attachment to the painting, apart from some superficial comments about the rounded nose shared by Drieu, Gilles, and the figure in the painting, critics have largely ignored the intimate relationship between the novel and the painting.[23] In his preface to the *Cahiers de l'Herne* volume on Drieu, Marc Hanrez has suggested in passing that two of Drieu's novels, *Gilles* and *Mémoires de Dirk Raspe*, relate to painting in some way.[24] The matter has rested there. Drieu's preface to *Gilles*, however, his repeated references to Watteau in letters, his conscious identification with Diderot and Baudelaire as critics of art,[25] and his early association with Aragon and the Paris milieu of the twenties point, as I have earlier suggested, to more complex interrelationships, to elective affinities with unique painterly conceptions, and—in the case of Watteau and several other artists—to the influence of specific paintings. Drieu's complex imaginative and physical relationship to the world of painting appears in its most palpable, organic form in the imagery and conception of *Gilles*, in the novel's unique integration of the world of French painting, beneath the flesh and the costumes, into the very bones of Gilles' world. Surrounded by portraits, landscapes, and historical scenes, by drawings and caricatures, by decorative detail, by pictorialized visions of the theater, Drieu's hero is himself a picture, a series of pictures, a creature who lives—as he himself says—by images, a painted figure in a painted world.

---

23. Dominique Desanti cites Emmanuel Berl's oral recollection of Drieu's "peculiar" attachment to Watteau's painting and on the back cover of her book notes and illustrates what she calls "an undeniable facial resemblance" between Drieu and Watteau's figure (*Drieu La Rochelle*, 158, back cover).

24. Hanrez, Preface to *Drieu La Rochelle*, 2.

25. For a careful analysis of both as art critics, see Gita May, *Diderot et Baudelaire, critiques d'art* (Geneva, 1957).

In his remarkable essay "What Have Modernists Looked At?" art historian Charles H. Roeder, Jr., has pointed out that "the opportunity to look carefully and frequently at a particular painting" has often been as important a factor in the development of individual artists as the material objects of their external world.[26] Like many of the painters whose work he admired, Drieu was himself influenced by the experience of museums, looking "carefully and frequently" at a great many paintings in the course of his life, at the Louvre and the Uffizi and the Prado and the Schloss Charlottenburg in Berlin, at the *capitale*'s myriad art galleries, in art books and periodicals. *L'Art au XXe Siècle*, the illustrated review edited by a character in one of Drieu's short stories, is closely modeled after an actual periodical. Himself owning very little art—a Rouault, a few drawings—Drieu loved to visit museums, whose special spaces and configurations were an essential part of his visual experience. Letters from his teen years record vivid reactions to paintings in museums in London and Oxford, while a note from April, 1914, suggests the museum in Munich as a fine setting for a novel. Of a writer with no sense of aesthetics, Drieu says that he has "l'esprit d'un gardien de musée," 'the mind of a museum guard.' (I have never been able to forget that phrase when visiting museums myself.) In every city or town he passed through, Drieu visited the museum if there was one, lending an additional ironic layer, for example, to his choice in the 1942 preface to *Gilles* of Carpentras in the Vaucluse as the prototypical small town far from Paris where a contemporary novel can be read "sanely." Carpentras has a museum that houses a brilliant Hyacinth Rigaud portrait of the Abbé de Rancé.

Everywhere one looks in Drieu, there are paintings and museums, or places with that specular quality particular to museums, places where everything appears part of a collection—framed, set off, on view. In a fragment written in 1940, Drieu describes a visit, in the company of a friend recently returned from the front, to an exhibition at a Paris art gallery of sixteenth-century paintings from the Ecole de Fontainebleau. In his friend's eyes Drieu sees reflected first the beautiful painted nude forms, then superimposed over them the silhouettes of German sol-

26. George H. Roeder, Jr., "What Have Modernists Looked At? Experiential Roots of Twentieth-Century American Painting," *American Quarterly*, XXXIX (Spring, 1987), 56–83.

diers carrying guns from American films.[27] This is the kind of literary vision that leads into the picture gallery novel. As a function of the general critical indifference to the presence of painting in Drieu's work, critics have glossed over the many painters' names that appear in the letters, novels, stories, and essays as just words. But if a writer loves Manet and puts his name into a letter, that name is more than just a word—it is a *sign* for a great many other things, visual, emotional, social, historical, literary. To say *Manet* is to suggest an image, a series of images, a network of associations. Clearly, when Drieu called his novel *Gilles*, he was openly inviting intertextual readings; he was pointing directly—as his novel points, in typical modernist fashion—to ways of reading it. As it happened, for half a century politics and personal reactions to satire outweighed aesthetic considerations; but works of art change in time. Oil paintings darken and flake or are cleaned in line with new theories of their original color values, textures, and conceptions of space. These "colored muds in a sticky substance" (the words are master restorer John M. Brealey's) resist remaining what they were when first painted.[28] Novels also change. Our vision of them changes; the resonances of words flatten out or become more pronounced; highlights become visible that were formerly obscure. What looked distorted fifty years ago may now seem merely difficult, or satirical, or even—most ironically for an experimental work of art—"true." Drieu's politics, his spasms of literary anti-Semitism, and some of his attitudes toward women remain exceedingly difficult to accept. His extended attack on the surrealists, capped by an evocation of the grotesque gathering that Roger Shattuck later called the "last banquet," is still at moments funny but far less complex and stylistically satisfying than his portrayal of the 1929 Radical Congress.

Drieu's *Gilles* is a brilliant, ironic, modernist master text, more complex, richer, wilder than *La Comédie de Charleroi*, indeed one of the few major literary works to come directly out of the French experience of World War I and one of the few to portray what the French call *l'entre-deux-guerres* (the period between the wars) in its light. Literary historians and critics have often applied the medieval doctrine of prefiguration to reading interwar fiction, seeing it purely as pointing forward to

27. Pierre Drieu La Rochelle, "L'Ami du front," in *Drieu La Rochelle*, ed. Hanrez, 109. This previously unpublished piece was originally written for *Le Figaro* in 1940.

28. For a profile of John M. Brealey, see Calvin Tomkins, "Colored Muds in a Sticky Substance," *New Yorker*, March 16, 1987, pp. 44–70.

the work of the writers Sartre called the "third generation." There is in fact a vast gap in our efforts at synthesis, sometimes a jump directly from surrealism to Sartre (I borrow this magisterial ellipsis from Roland Barthes, who in an interview spoke of "viewing surrealism, Sartre, Brecht, la littérature 'abstraite,' and even structuralism, as so many *modes* of the same idea"[29]), that fails to take account of *transitional modernism*, a period that includes Drieu, Céline, the early Aragon as novelist, Malraux before the art histories. Such a grouping calls for a study of the watershed of the thirties in the light of what preceded it rather than solely as prelude to what it led to after the war. A bit of backward-looking? Perhaps. But as Paul Fussell has convincingly shown in *The Great War and Modern Memory*, much English literature dealing with World War II was shaped by the literary experience of World War I rather than by the actual events of 1940 to 1945. It can similarly be demonstrated that—despite their long sojourn in the limbo of literary pariahs—Drieu and Céline had much the same effect in France. An intelligent rereading of Drieu can help bring light to our still incomplete understanding of what the "European War" (the Library of Congress's significant new classification for World War I) meant to those who saw it from the inside.

My approach in the preceding chapters has been eclectic, flexible, geared to the configurations of the individual texts. With *Gilles*, this eclecticism expands further to include some of the exciting new insights that have emerged from intense contemporary interdisciplinary ferment in art history and spectacle criticism. Recent art historical readings of several of the painters most important to Drieu—Watteau, Bronzino, Jean-Auguste-Dominique Ingres, François Millet, Daumier, Manet, Seurat, Van Gogh, Henri Rousseau—have intensified my attention to details, iconographic layers, visual-social and literary-painterly interactions and have illumined and brought new plays of "modeling" to my multiple rereadings of the novel. This vein of inquiry has also helped to explain some of Drieu's own more puzzling comments on his text, his odd spatial explanations of fictional structure, his allusions to his characters as "sketches" of the same subjects executed over a long time span, his marked emphasis on comparisons with the iconology and the methodologies of painting.

In *Gilles* Drieu constructed what I call the picture gallery novel, a

29. Barthes, *Essais critiques*, 263.

special frame for his literary purpose, an airy, fluid, changeable written structure, in which he could write as he pleased, by scenes, by leaps, by rushes of careful modeling and segments of bare canvas, by intensely visualized scenes punctuated with rapidly sketched, linked icons. He could communicate Gilles' peculiar hunger for life, for "le séduisant mouvement de hanche de la vie charnelle," 'the seductive hip swing of the carnal life,' he could evoke Gilles' incredible aesthetic appetite and his inexpressible desire to take in the world *as image* with a roll call of "les biens du monde," 'the riches of the world,' that reads quite simply: "les livres, les jardins, les musées, les rues" (*G* 38), 'books, gardens, museums, streets,' or—more specific and more charged with historic and plastic resonances—"le Louvre, la place de la Concorde, les Champs-Elysées, Versailles" (*G* 78). Such a novel lives on architectonic surprises, as canvases discourse with one another and with the spectator—the character, the novelist, the reader—in a structure that becomes an artistic object in its own right. As in a museum, the walls, the ceilings, the doorways and windows and staircases become part of the visual experience. Paris apartment walls and offices, the "perspective" of the river, monuments and building facades themselves previously inscribed—with dates, names, with scenes from earlier novels—become "notes" in the compositions that depict them and in the fictional scenes that contain them. Everything is multiple and seems constantly in motion. Images come to the surface, are briefly visible—iridescent and on the verge of vanishing—then once again submerge. This impression of movement contained within a frame, this conception of story as picture, reflects a constant in Drieu's fiction. "La comédie des formes," 'the comedy of forms,' was Drieu's term for this theatrical interplay of human desires, actions, and social structures with the visible world of nature and art. His phrase brings to mind Balzac and Zola, Daumier and Manet; it also brings to mind the techniques of plastic deformation and confrontational composition that characterize early modernist painting and its attempt to render Paris as spectacle, to read—as T. J. Clark has suggested—what was with modernization becoming illegible.[30]

Drieu, however—unlike Manet and the impressionists who largely concentrated on urban or idealized rural subjects—incorporated into

30. See Clark, *Painting of Modern Life,* esp. 23–78.

his novel a dense network of references to the great, heavy, rich and dull, ambiguously regarded and ambivalently depicted chunk of France referred to *en bloc* to this day as *la province*, all that is not Paris and its environs. For in the interplay between city and country, between urban modernization and the gradual restructuring of society in the provincial capitals by the outer edges of revolutionary shock waves throughout the nineteenth century, in the common calvary of World War I visible on the war monument of every town in France ("on a wall, a long list of war dead, bigger than the town," *G* 357),[31] in the expansion of the *musées de province*—whose continued existence and often significant if limited holdings continue to resist the efflorescence of new major museums in *la capitale*—is to be found the agonizing and fruitful dichotomy that Drieu lived and played with and wrote about. When strangers attempt to identify Gilles at the funeral of his second wife, Pauline, the dialogue provides in sure, quick strokes a summation of the issue:

> A l'enterrement de Pauline, Gilles entreaperçut le petit nombre de ses amis qui le regardaient avec curiosité comme ne l'ayant jamais vu.
>
> Un très vieux prêtre, qui avait été son professeur au collège, murmura à quelqu'un qui l'interrogeait: "Monsieur, je n'ose vous répondre, car il se peut que des parties entières de Gilles Gambier m'échappent, mais je lui retrouve le même regard que sur les bancs de ma classe de philosophie, c'est un homme de nos provinces de l'Ouest perdu dans votre terrible Paris."
>
> "Mais non, s'exclama un écrivain catholique, monsieur l'abbé, c'est le plus pervers des Parisiens.
>
> —L'un n'empêche pas l'autre." (*G* 441)

At Pauline's funeral, Gilles half noticed that the few of his friends present were staring at him curiously, as if they'd never seen him before.

An elderly priest who had been his teacher in secondary school murmured in reply to someone who was questioning him, "Monsieur, I hesitate to answer you, since there may be whole sides of Gilles Gambier that escape me, but I find he has the same look he had in my philosophy class: he's a man from our Western provinces lost in your terrible Paris."

"Oh no," exclaimed a Catholic writer, "Monsieur l'Abbé, he's the most perverse of Parisians."

"One does not exclude the other."

31. For an immensely suggestive and informative analysis of the symbolism of World War I monuments, see Maurice Agulhon, "Politics, Images, and Symbols in Post-Revolutionary France," in *Rites of Power: Symbolism, Ritual, and Politics Since the Middle Ages*, ed. Sean Wilentz (Philadelphia, 1985), 177–205.

Few French novelists since Balzac have caught better than Drieu the plastic and psychological polarities between Paris and the provinces and the long shadows these polarities cast in the imaginations of their heroes. Flaubert approached the subject in *L'Education sentimentale*, but his total negativity toward the country rendered all of Frédéric's rural visions except the privileged scene in the Forêt de Fontainebleau pictures of total despair. Drieu's Gilles, shaped by the landscapes of Poussin and Watteau and by his experience of the country as battle site, thrives away from Paris and is in fact something of an expert on the provinces. From Drieu's own easy familiarity with the *musées de province* and his peripatetic writing habits comes Gilles' ability to move around naturally in the less inhabited reaches of Normandy, Brittany, the southwest, and the Midi as a man at ease with their physical textures as well as with their images in painting. The picture gallery of *Gilles* includes *la province* as well as Paris, making it perhaps the only sustained exercise in comparative museumgoing in French fiction. As a distant answer to Aragon's *paysan de Paris*, Drieu created Gilles, an aesthetic *paysan de France*.

As spectator and collector at once, the hero of Drieu's picture gallery novel wanders about in a world doubled by paintings. Gilles sees *multitextually*, in a shimmer of images perceived and images remembered such as operates in an informed perception of art—for example, in seeing Manet's *Olympia* as a naked courtesan/Venus that quotes Giorgione, Titian, Goya, and Ingres while at the same time declaring, by the textures of the painted surface and the boldly individualized specificity of her very French face (Venuses traditionally have missing or "neutral" heads), the emergence of the new modernist sensibility. The focus of such multitextual vision is at once on, behind, before, and all around what the eye takes in, producing something akin to the play of the brilliant, unreliable mirror in Manet's *Un Bar aux Folies-Bergère* (Fig. 11), where the posture of the attractive, neutral-faced girl behind the counter does not match the reflection behind her. Such plays of mirrors offer a fractionalized, ambiguous, newly created reality whose shifting surfaces suggest the elements of novels that might have been written and images that might have been painted *if things had been ever so little otherwise.*[32] Cervantes rendered both text written and text un-

32. My literary reading of "multitextuality" in *Gilles* has been stimulated by the densely informed art historical reading of Manet's *Un Bar aux Folies-Bergère* in Clark, *Painting of Modern Life*, esp. 239–55.

11. Edouard Manet, *Un Bar aux Folies-Bergère*. 1881–1882. Oil on canvas, 37¾ × 51¼ inches. Courtauld Institute Galleries (Courtauld Collection), London. Photo: Courtauld Institute of Art.

written operative in *Don Quixote* by bracketing his entire tale within the myth of an original text in Arabic accompanied by illustrations. Flaubert wrote a double text by placing side by side, with only rare spaces of intersection, his hero and the historical events of 1848–1851. Those small crosshatched areas where Frédéric and the revolution occupy the same spaces—in the Palais des Tuileries, in the streets of Paris—offer that form of illuminated darkness, of multiple textures, of fixity and motion at once opposed and fused that is one of the hallmarks of the picture gallery novel. Joyce in *Ulysses* and Céline in *Voyage au bout de la nuit* also create this *texture of specularity*, but they rely more heavily on language and sound, on aural/oral elements, than on pictures. In *La Comédie de Charleroi* Drieu renders the narrators' visions most completely through the sound of their voices and the apocalyptic shorthand of their words, but they are after all soldiers and not figures out of a painting.

Our present reading of *Gilles* will concentrate on scenes, on decorative details, on portraits and landscapes, on those iconic-thematic "knots" that Drieu saw as its most important formal elements, and on the broad bands of rhetoric (tirades, meditations, ideological dialogues) that have remained the greatest obstacle to readers. What plot there is falls quickly into place and rarely merits summary. There are numerous secondary characters, but their interest is largely visual or satirical rather than psychological. Gilles himself remains something of a puzzle, despite all the attention he manages to attract and despite the fact that the spotlight falls—as on Watteau's icon—directly on him. Gilles' opacity as a character is, of course, a direct function of his own status as an icon. A visual analogy can be useful here. A change of costume—imagine Watteau's *Gilles* in a French World War I infantry tunic, well fitted through the waist, flared out below. Replace Gilles' skullcap and broad-brimmed hat with a peaked army cap and his white satin shoes with well-shined boots. Replace the four half-length figures behind him with Galant and Caël and perhaps Mme Florimond; imagine Carentan riding on the donkey. Leave the vague platform in place, the feathery Paris park trees, the statue of a satyr. Leave the spotlight and the marvelous sky. Imagine the young aesthete with little money on leave in Paris in 1917. Look straight at him, and visualize his looking calmly back at you. Without the white suit, the riveting luminescence of the original picture is, of course, harshly dimmed. It's all different; but something essential remains. The underimage glows through, and one sees both Gilles at once.

WATTEAU'S PAINTINGS

Drieu had long lingered at the Louvre before Watteau's paintings, before *Le Pèlerinage à l'Isle de Cythère, Gilles*, and the museum's twelve smaller paintings of musicians, actors, and ladies and gentlemen in elegant dress inhabiting a tufted landscape. Antoine Watteau (1684–1721), the towering genius of French eighteenth-century painting, was born in the Flemish town of Valenciennes, which had become French only in 1677, and learned most of his craft in Paris. Because his subjects did not belong to the recognized academic categories—even as his work was being eagerly sought after by wealthy collectors—Watteau failed several times to be awarded the Prix de Rome, which would have allowed him to live and study in Italy. Initially formed by contact with northern painting, by the stunning revelation of Rubens' Marie de Médicis cycle at the Palais du Luxembourg, and by drawings and paintings by French, Flemish, and Venetian masters in the extraordinary private collection of banker and patron Pierre Crozat, Watteau developed his skills through a series of apprenticeships and through intensive copying. From early Flemish-inspired paintings showing country folk, craftsmen, vendors, and soldiers during their hours of leisure, Watteau moved on to theatrical illustrations and decorations under master engraver Claude Gillot. Soon after, Watteau's characteristic compositions began to emerge— delicate landscapes with vivid, seemingly quickly drawn figures engaged in talking, singing, dancing, flirting, staging or watching plays—pictures that seemed to express a new sensibility and a new mode of pictorial vision. He studied figure drawing from Rubens and other great draftsmen and from life, capturing many of his visions in extraordinary drawings done in three colors of chalk, then peopled his beautiful, deliberately vague landscapes with figures drawn from his own sketchbooks.

Official recognition and appreciation of Watteau's unique appeal was marked by his acceptance in 1712 as a candidate for membership in the Académie Royale de Peinture et de Sculpture, founded in 1648. Contrary to custom, Watteau was invited to choose his own subject for the required reception piece. After a five-year delay, during which his fame and popularity continued to grow, in 1717 Watteau at last submitted *Le Pèlerinage à l'Isle de Cythère*, which was recorded in the Académie's records as *une fête galante*, a new subject-matter designation. The painting became the property of the Académie, then entered the Louvre in 1795, where it remained the only work by Watteau until 1869. Briefly out of favor in the wake of the Revolution (the painting's title disappears from the Louvre catalogue for 1810), it is Watteau's best-known scenic allegory of love.

Interpretations of *Le Pèlerinage* (Fig. 12) trace the evolution of French attitudes toward Watteau's work. Throughout the eighteenth century and well into the nineteenth, it was regarded as a happy journey to a symbolic island of love. An expanding romantic sensibility fostered readings that stressed Watteau's "melancholy," canonized in 1856 by the Goncourt brothers' essay "La philosophie de Watteau." Seen within its original context, *Le Pèlerinage* is a new kind of mythological or history painting, an allegory of love, erotic poetry, and gallantry that seems to have filled a deep aesthetic need in the last years of Louis XIV's reign. The broad, rectangular canvas depicts eighteen women and men in

12. Antoine Watteau, *Le Pèlerinage à l'Isle de Cythère*. 1717. Oil on canvas, 129 ×
194 inches. Musée du Louvre, Paris.
Photo: Réunion des Musées Nationaux.

Louis XIII costumes, arranged in a fan-shaped curve over a hillock in the
shallow foreground, moving toward a body of water seen in the middle
distance and narrowing toward the upper left. The scene is enclosed on
the left by a thin segment of mountains behind which are visible some
distant hillside cabins and on the right by a broader segment of tall,
feathery trees against which is silhouetted an armless statue of Venus
decorated with roses. Cupids scattered through the middle distance
poke and pull at dresses and sails and arrange clouds. In the far middle
distance, toward the left, a gilded barge drawn up to the shore is visible,
much of it blocked from view by the large group of receding figures to
the left and by the gradual slope of the hillock. The sky glows with a
diffused, hazy light that illuminates the figures from several directions
at once—from a point behind the viewer's vantage point, reflecting off
the water, filtering through spaces in the trees. This is not natural light
from the setting sun but consciously controlled theatrical lighting that
heightens the sense of depth in the near and middle distances—where
the figures are—while giving the dreamlike rocks and the curves of green
shore in the far distance the look of a skillfully constructed, painted landscape. This is nature reconceived, a civilized, circumscribed wilderness.

Periodic art historical debates over whether the lovers are traveling to Cythera or returning from it underline the picture's deliberately ambiguous mood and message.[33] The delicate mottled bands of color, the varied poses and dancelike interactions of individual couples, the feathery foliage framing the scene and emphasizing the fantastic shapes of distant rocks shrouded in mists, a sky of no specific time or weather, all suggest a world that is neither reality nor fantasy but some place in between, just beyond the one we normally live in. In his brilliant essay accompanying a volume of Watteau's colored drawings, René Huyghe has described the Watteau *fête galante* as a processional gliding over a threshold as if through an opening door, into a distant landscape.[34] Huyghe interprets the visual suggestion of motion as being directed toward a goal, even if that goal is undefined. He also reads Watteau's sketchbooks as forms of narrative drawing, seeing in a page of slightly differing views of a single head, for example, the painter's record of the subject's movement. In this way, Huyghe relates Watteau's portfolio of motifs, which the painter reused and frequently replaced in new contexts, to the complexities of a literary reference system. In the absence of hard information on how Watteau himself conceived his sketches, it appears more sensible to interpret such multiple views on a single page just as what they appear to be, that is, as sketches, visual notes on plastic problems. Practically alone among Watteau scholars, Donald Posner has taken a refreshingly pragmatic, antiromanticizing stand on Watteau's subjects and on the mood of his pictures, emphasizing the robust, frankly erotic, and intensely fashionable character of many of his themes.[35]

All of Watteau's mature paintings are involved with some form of theater, or—more accurately—with *theatricality*, with the ambience of theater and theatrics, with settings, costumes, and the playing of roles, as well as with forms of portraiture. In its way the Académie Royale recognized this interplay of sets, characters, and scenes in designating Watteau a painter of *fêtes galantes*, costumed entertainments in outdoor

33. For a range of interpretations, see Donald Posner, *Antoine Watteau* (Ithaca, 1984), 184; Michael Levey, "The Real Theme of Watteau's *Embarkation for Cythera*," *Burlington Magazine*, CVI (1961), 180–85; and Pierre Rosenberg in the exhibition catalogue *Watteau, 1684–1721* (Washington, D.C., 1984), 396–406.

34. René Huyghe, *Watteau*, trans. Barbara Bray (New York, 1970), 60, 57, 70. Originally published as *L'Univers de Watteau* (Paris, 1968).

35. For a detailed analysis of Watteau's erotic themes and their relationship to eighteenth-century iconography, see Donald Posner, *A Lady at Her Toilet* (London, 1973).

settings. As Posner has pointed out, to the newly growing group of private collectors and the dealers who supplied them, Watteau's work was attractive and approachable, offering images of love, a refined form of landscape painting, and a light, informal approach to figure drawing and portraiture. Painters who followed him—Nicolas Lancret, Jean-Baptiste-Joseph Pater, François Boucher, Jean-Honoré Fragonard—borrowed from one or another of these features, but none combined them in the same way as Watteau. Watteau's beautiful, unofficial-looking paintings introduced the theater as subject matter into French painting, where its persistence has been notable in Daumier, Degas, Seurat, Toulouse-Lautrec, Rouault, and Picasso, to name a few.[36] Much of Watteau's appeal to the literary imagination relates directly to the theatricality of his work, to the look of painting that points to its own artificiality.

The spell of Watteau's painting has fueled debate over his works and speculation about his brief life, about which little is known except from scattered accounts by the few contemporaries who knew him. Dating most of his paintings has remained problematic. Twentieth-century interest in Watteau reached its first high point in 1921 with the bicentenary of his death and the publication of *Notes critiques sur les vies anciennes d'Antoine Watteau* by Pierre Champion in Paris. Drieu knew this collection of texts, the first significant step in disentangling the painter's work from the romantic legend that had culminated in the *Pierrot lunaire* of symbolist poetry, based on the reading of Watteau's *Gilles* as a deeply melancholy portrait of a suffering artist. The Watteau revival of the 1980s has seen the Champion volume republished, augmented by a few newly discovered *témoignages* by Watteau's contemporaries, as well as the mounting of a monumental retrospective in Washington, Paris, and Berlin in 1984–1985 and the appearance of detailed studies of Watteau's *oeuvre* by Posner and Mariane Roland-Michel.

For Drieu the "novel of Watteau" was less significant than the paintings. He was drawn to the same fusion of intimate portraiture, landscape, and theatricality that had made Watteau's work attractive to collectors and fellow artists in the early eighteenth century and that briefly made him indigestible to the immediate postrevolutionary sensibility that wanted its painted narratives dressed in Greek and Roman

36. For the suggestion of Watteau's founding role in the tradition, see Edward Lucie-Smith, *A Concise History of French Painting* (New York, 1978), 122.

clothes. In the modern era, Watteau's intense painterliness, his light "unlicked" touch, his ability to juxtapose previously drawn figures and idealized landscape in almost abstract, but highly emotive, compositions, have brought him back with a vengeance. In particular, Watteau's two late masterpieces, *Gilles* (1718–1719) and *L'Enseigne de Gersaint* (1720–1721), have commanded attention as predictions of the modernist sensibility.

Watteau's monumental, life-size portrait *Gilles* (Fig. 10) shows a riveting, still figure in a traditional clown suit, standing on a raised mound of earth, looking directly forward. He is silhouetted against a double scene. The upper two-thirds of the background includes a deliciously painted light blue sky heightened with pinks, yellows, and drifts of white. Feathery trees frame the slightly tipped, cup-shaped opening of light behind Gilles; its slant toward the upper left reinforces by opposition the strong vertical of Gilles' posture, rhythmically repeated by the sixteen closely spaced buttons on his jacket. Gilles' forceful verticality is softened a bit by the slight forward placement of his left shoulder, hand, and foot. He stands gracefully and firmly balanced in his white slippers decorated with scarlet satin bows. Gilles' impressive frontality is further emphasized by the eyeless gaze of a stone satyr figure in the middle distance on the right; this traditional symbol of comedy looks past and behind Gilles toward the man on the donkey. The scene in the lower third, its upper margins defined by a horizontal line suggested by the hemline of Gilles' jacket, shows four half-length figures engaged with a balky donkey. Two costumed men and a woman at the lower right pull on an unseen rope. The donkey's head emerges from mid-forehead to the left of Gilles' trouser leg, its round brown eye gazing softly forward. On the donkey rides a man in a black costume with a complicated, stiff white ruff, on his face a slightly mischievous smile.

The viewing point, just below the middle of the canvas, presents Gilles as one might see an actor onstage in a small open-air theater or in a life-size sign set up on a small platform. Posner's speculation that Watteau painted the picture for Belloni, a retiring actor friend noted for his portrayals of Pierrot or Gilles (the names were often used interchangeably), to be used as an advertisement for his café, *Au Caffé Comique*, seems reasonable.[37] It also seems to explain the painting's almost

37. Posner, *Antoine Watteau*, 267.

total disappearance from the art literature of the eighteenth century. In 1805 the huge portrait reappeared in the possession of a picture dealer, who sold it cheaply to Dominique Vivant-Denon, the director-general of museums under Napoleon, for his private collection. From that point, the painting's fame continued to grow. It entered the Louvre in 1869 as part of the La Caze bequest, where it has remained, in the early 1970s replacing Da Vinci's *Mona Lisa* as the keynote painting of the Grande Galerie, hanging at the center of French painting.

Gilles' elegant white clown suit—flannel for the jacket, satin for the pants—fills a huge portion of the canvas with a multiplaned, infinitely varied, luminous interaction of folds, creases, slopes and slides, accentuated by the red satin bows of the shoes and by the soft beige-brown of the hat, its brim repeating the white circle of the traditional skullcap beneath it and balanced by the intricate soft folds of the jacket's richly pleated collar. Gilles looks out, ignoring the scene below and behind him, involved only with his audience and the world out in front of the canvas. His silent, dignified gaze seems consonant neither with the early dunce Pierrot, who traditionally played the foil for the clever Harlequin, nor with the innocent *Pierrot lunaire* of symbolist poetry, a reading in large measure shaped, as Posner has pointed out, by the stage portrayals of master mime Jean-Gaspard Debureau. Posner comments snappily, "In Watteau's time Pierrots and Gilles were reprehensible in morals, obscene in language and gross in social behavior; they did not display the shy, lonely sensitivity . . . that since around 1850—but only since then—many critics have thought they see in the picture by Watteau." [38]

A theatrical painting or a portrait of a subject—like Gilles—obviously in costume tends to exert a mirror effect, emphasizing as it does the viewer's role as spectator. Watteau's viewers have varied widely in their visions. René Huyghe sees the clown as Watteau's perfect double, "the artist's reflection in the mirror," one of the two axes of the painter's final vision, in which the space of the "unreal theater" shown in all the earlier paintings is at last closed, with Gilles the only personage remaining behind, on this side of the threshold, near us. [39] Vivant-Denon, who bought *Gilles* in the 1820s against the advice of experts, including

38. *Ibid.*, 270–71.
39. Huyghe, *Watteau*, 69.

painter Jacques-Louis David, and loved the painting above all for its brilliant realism, wrote, "I own a painting of figures larger than life, in which [Watteau] made portraits of his friends and by which one can judge how much color and truth he retained in a size that was so foreign to him."[40] Posner appears to reconcile the two views when he writes, "Watteau has concentrated on appearances, on the broad features and hands, the heavy lidded eyes, and also on the shimmer of sunshine that strikes the white suit like a natural spotlight focusing on the lead actor. We perceive him simultaneously as the comic mask and as a man of serious, sober mien. But there is no tension or sense of contradiction between the two. Watteau's *Gilles*, monumental in scale and grand in conception, awes us by the power of its affirmation of a real, human presence in the world of theatrical fantasy."[41]

In 1941, as part of a fragmentary volume tracing the development of romanticism, realism, symbolism, and the beginnings of modernism in French literature and painting, Drieu put on paper his own reading of Watteau's *Gilles*. Armed with artistic intuition and a naturally intense sensitivity to painting, though lacking the significant historical information that has emerged in the intervening decades, Drieu evoked a vision of the painting in many ways remarkably similar to Posner's. The passage merits extended quotation:

> Until 1750, man is still substantial, solid, intimately related to himself, filled with a solid joy.
>
> I see him as painted by Watteau. *Gilles* is a crucial point of reference for those who love life and eagerly seek its incarnations. He is an important station between the graceful power, the velvety austerity of the figures in Reims and the shrinking bones, the tense nervous fatigue of men depicted at the end of the nineteenth century, the men of the impressionist and symbolist era, the last and most acute romantics. (The impressionists will no longer portray human beings: the end of the portrait is a sinister sign.)
>
> In *Gilles*, what vigor and health! What stability, certainty, tranquillity of equilibrium. . . . A hint of introspection is barely sketched. His faintly

40. Quoted in *Watteau, 1684–1721*, 433. For an interesting discussion of Vivant-Denon's career as a collector and of his role as an independent tastemaker, see Francis Haskell, *Rediscoveries in Art: Some Aspects of Taste, Fashion and Collecting in England and France* (Ithaca, N.Y., 1976), 42–45.
41. Posner, *Antoine Watteau*, 271.

mocking, imperceptibly disillusioned smile marks a turn toward the self that has not yet become wicked.

He still has an enigma in his eyes, a dimension of complexity. The contradictions still come together. Enough distance between the passions and the mind to allow freedom to the heart. But the passions have lost an element of their totality: he has no more heaven in his eyes, only the earth. . . . The movement of earthly passions is still impregnated with an ancient rhythm, ample, grave, total. From that rhythm comes the force of emotion communicated by the figures and the landscapes of Watteau. Christian humanism is not that far away: these men and women raised by an impoverished church put the residue of piety into matters of gallantry and honor.

The malady of the soul has not yet passed into the body. The body is softened but not attenuated: there is still geniune vigor in the shoulders and the relaxed hands of *Gilles*. Good eater, good drinker, good lover, good friend, good soldier. This is the man who will win the battle of Fontenoy and heroically defend India and Canada, the man who writes the comedies and the elegantly solid novels of Marivaux, the *Lettres persanes*.

This man is not yet the wounded and sneering Candide, not yet even Rameau's Nephew—a shade too frenetic in the display and scattering of his strength. This commoner still has modesty; he's not the extravagant dreamer who will declare war on the Europe of kings. . . . He's not the man of those convulsive generations that include . . . Laclos, Sade . . . Saint-Just, Bonaparte, Senancour, Chateaubriand. . . .

I compare the face of *Gilles* with one of those great portraits painted at the beginning of the nineteenth century by David or Ingres. I don't go as far as one of the emaciated faces in Géricault. . . . In David, in Ingres, beneath the still beautiful surface, not only the soul but the body have begun to change. The skeletal structure curves slightly, the hands become thinner, the eyes distracted.[42]

From the sketchy hero of *L'Homme couvert de femmes* with his Watteauesque name and the clownish lightness and awkwardness with which he periodically flits from one pose to another, to the slightly older Gille of *Drôle de voyage* playing out his role on a series of sets that suggest the aura of play, fantasy, and musicality of a painted *fête galante*, Drieu continued to use his vision of Watteau's landscapes with figures as a decorative and theatrical source for his fiction. With the inception of *Gilles* in 1937, the late Drieu turned to the late Watteau and to the

---

42. Pierre Drieu La Rochelle, "Rationalisme et romantisme," in *Notes pour comprendre le siècle*, rpr. in *Sur les ècrivains*, ed. Grover, 215–17.

painting that fused all the painter's apprenticeships—as genre painter of military life, as theatrical illustrator, as creator of decorative panels, as initiator of a new genre in French painting, as observer of his contemporaries in social settings, as landscape painter of Paris parks and *faubourgs*, as portraitist. In the odd stasis created by a life-size central figure who is so present, so real, who seems to wait patiently and eternally for recognition or applause or a handshake from the spectators, perhaps for silence from his fellow comedians in the middle plane of the picture, in the frontality of his stance and the confrontational effect of his outward gaze at the viewer, Watteau's *Gilles* presents a prototypical modernist vision. The richly suggestive irony of an actor in clown dress posing for his portrait, to be used as a sign for his new profession as owner of a theatrical café, is embedded in the picture. Drieu did not need all the historical information we now have to read with his eyes and imagination the complex semiotics on the canvas.

In Watteau's beautiful canvas combining portraiture, landscape painting, and theatricality in a monumental composition inviting infinite narration, Drieu found the form of his big novel. The portrait's size, its status as an icon of French art, its use of proportion, space, and relational portrayal all pointed toward Drieu's conception of his novel as a collection of pictures—portraits of Gilles in a series of roles, comic and dramatic scenes with figures, urban and rural landscapes, theatrical costume drawings, posters, caricatures. In such a novel, dominated and shaped by the presence of a single figure, Drieu could create the kind of novel he loved in Stendhal, the novel with an ironic hero set in "a universe that lives by itself, animated by its own music."[43] Drieu was forty-seven when *Gilles* appeared, the same age as Stendhal on the publication of *Le Rouge et le noir*—Stendhal, the only nineteenth-century novelist who, according to Drieu, still belonged by taste and temperament to Watteau's world and one of the few to succeed in combining in a single creation the infinitely particular and the infinitely symbolic, thus creating something intensely French that rivaled Dostoyevsky.[44] In Watteau Drieu found the iconographic and formal structures that would allow him to reconcile his gift for painterly detail and his bent

43. Pierre Drieu La Rochelle, unpublished journal, quoted in Andreu and Grover, *Drieu La Rochelle*, 425.
44. Pierre Drieu La Rochelle, "Naturalisme et symbolisme," in *Notes pour comprendre le siècle*, rpr. in *Sur les écrivains*, ed. Grover, 227.

for satire; he found the visual approach that would mark definitively his break with the linear, interconnected, synthesizing tradition of nineteenth-century realism. In this pictorial vision Drieu would at last be able to express the real meaning of the word that has elicited so much misguided critical commentary on his work. *La décadence*—the word that reappears, inconsistently used, throughout his essays of the twenties and thirties—is the artist's *complainte* for the loss of form in modern art, the expression of his longing for a world as ordered and spacious as the one in Poussin's scenes, for a landscape as beautiful and unspoiled as the controlled wilderness of Watteau's sophisticated pastorals. Drieu the decadent—the modernist—turned to Watteau. He had found his form, as valid and as unique as Malraux's swaying fictional constructs hung with memorable baroque scenes, as Céline's ruined medieval cathedrals filled with vituperating voices.

6

Gilles, II: On the Stones of Paris

PASSION, SPACE, A NOVEL OF PARIS

Gilles is an interartistic fiction about vision and society, a Paris novel in the grand tradition of the nineteenth century reshaped by the experience of World War I. Descendant of Julien Sorel and Rastignac, Gilles wanders among Paris scenes and provincial landscapes, past faces and figures out of Daumier and Balzac lit from within by demonic fires, and finds the terrain changed, the book of society waiting to be read, of *La Comédie humaine*, replaced by a strange, patchy, illegible jungle born of modern *machines*—practical, scientific, psychological, physiological, political—a newly created "lost world" whose only stable landmarks are icons from the past. The Paris of *Gilles*, of 1917, 1925, 1934, is a city that breathes drenching beauty and an overpowering odor of decay, a city suspended between the fires of its history and the ice of its dying soul, the city of novels and poetry and painting, the city of Watteau, Delacroix, Balzac, Daumier, Baudelaire, Flaubert, Manet, Zola, Seurat, Henri Rousseau, and Aragon—the city as landscape, as spectacle, as food for dreams, as political battlefield, the "beautiful theater of stone and sky" (*G* 432) resumed by the spaces and harmonies, the halftones and seasons, the dramas written and painted and soaked into the very pavement of the Place de la Concorde.

Drieu's novel *Gilles* suggests that in his relationship to the city of Paris—to its physical presence and its unique fusion of images and symbols of permanence inscribed with signatures of change, to its iconic interpenetration with the fabric of modernist art and literature— is to be found the most important source of his disastrous political engagements and also of some of his greatest strengths as an artist. Drieu's complex relationship to the major revolutions of his time—World War

115

I, surrealism, the moral and political crises of the thirties—represents a peculiar tangle of art and politics, a characteristically modernist network of antinomies stretched, like the novel itself, between chaos and form. To see into that tangle, to make some sense of its representations of the tensions between past and present, of its deliberate confusion of styles in art, of its clash of codes and its conception of fiction as an "inter-art," one must take account of the "light of the painters" that colors it, and one must include among the "painters" the novelists Drieu considered painters of another sort, the fictional realists whom he classified as romantics. For Drieu called the whole of the nineteenth century, the one from which he had been wrenched by the war but from which he derived much of his strength, *le grand siècle romantique* (the great romantic century). His dynamic opposition/attraction to the informing motifs of French nineteenth-century art and literature, juxtaposed with his growing ambivalence toward the arts of "disintegration"—cubism and surrealism—form the cement of his vast, difficult epic of the interwar years.

Drieu's conception of character in the novel leaps markedly backward, ignoring the new Freudian psychology and the scientific determinism that preceded it, to reach into the quintessentially romantic vision of character as destiny embodied in the novels of Benjamin Constant and Stendhal and in their relentlessly self-absorbed heroes. From Balzac and Daumier Drieu's secondary figures draw their look of being crouched on terra firma, of casting a big shadow. From Delacroix—by form and ironic contrast—Drieu's key confrontational scenes derive their powerful spirit of grandeur and loss. From Flaubert Drieu draws his passion for representing what he called "the decor of the disease of rationalism"—that hallucinating evocation of physical setting verging on the unreal that enchanted and nourished Marcel Proust and Joyce before him. And to this complex, multilayered fictional *gâteau* Drieu adds his oddest and most original decoration, his intense vision of the world of Watteau, which art historians of our own time have begun to view as the starting point of the modern era in France.[1]

Like the modernist painters whose work touched him most directly—Manet and Seurat—Drieu sought to model pictures of inter-

---

1. See, for example, Thomas E. Crow, *Painters and Public Life in Eighteenth-Century Paris* (New Haven, 1985); and Linda Nochlin, "Watteau: Some Questions of Interpretation," *Art in America*, LXXIII (March, 1986), 68–97.

penetrating perceptions of reality, to display ironically the strange and often contradictory imageries occasioned by social and historical events, to set down a highly personal reaction to a culture in the process of change and decay. Indeed, despite the overt political strands in *Gilles*— the hero's 1934 declaration of fascism and his somewhat "old-fashioned" anti-Semitism—the total effect of Drieu's novel, with its emphasis on portraits and landscapes and caricatures and its sense of heightened theatricality, is closer in spirit to painter Georges Seurat's *La Parade de cirque* (Fig. 2) than to novelist Louis Aragon's programmatic romance of class struggle *Les Beaux Quartiers*. As Richard Thomson's admirable study makes clear, Seurat's intense visual formalism comprehends an immense range of social observation and suggests incisive satirical readings of contemporary society; it also renders his local world of Paris as larger, and more artistically coherent and durable, than it was.[2] Like Daumier—another monumental satirist of modern society and Drieu's acknowledged model—Seurat elaborated a pictorial mythology of contemporary society that has permanently shaped our vision of his era. In the face of such intensely conceived images of reality—Daumier's Parisians, Seurat's leisure ritualists in *Un Dimanche à la Grande-Jatte*—it is almost impossible to separate the "myths," the artistic reconceptions, from their original sources.

Nineteen thirty-seven was a year for monumentalizing visions. Paris artists such as Raoul Dufy and Robert Delaunay and Fernand Léger, singly and in groups, elaborately and in suitably "modern" fashion, decorated huge surfaces—full walls of the Palais de l'Eléctricité, of the Palais des Chemins de Fer and the Pavillon de l'Air—in a huge rush of government-sponsored artistic employment spurred by the Exposition Universelle.[3] Commissioned in January, 1937, by the Spanish government to decorate a wall of the Spanish Pavilion, in June of that year— after the devastation bombing in April of the Basque town and a complex series of sketches and rethinkings—Picasso completed and hung *Guernica*, one of the most striking "manifesto paintings" (Thomson's phrase for *La Grande Jatte*) of all time.[4] Also in 1937, Malraux published his huge novel *L'Espoir*, and Drieu conceived *Gilles*, the vast iconic/

2. Thomson, *Seurat*, esp. 97–156, 185–223.
3. For detailed information on the 1937 show, see the catalogue of the 1987 retrospective, *Paris 1937*.
4. For a brief history of the 1937 Spanish Pavilion exhibition, see the opening sections of *Guernica-Legado Picasso*.

satiric narrative that illustrates the "peace" that Malraux called, with comprehending sympathy, the greatest disappointment of Drieu's inter-war years.[5]

"Nothing is accomplished in this world except by passion," Drieu wrote in July, 1937, in *Combat*, a militantly centrist journal of opinion. Denying that French culture was characterized by the rule of measure, Drieu summoned a roll call of "unreasonable" Frenchmen—historical figures such as Calvin, Robespierre, and Napoleon, writers such as Pascal, Corneille, Bossuet, Racine, Molière, Voltaire, Baudelaire, Rimbaud, Mallarmé, and blessedly passionate novelists such as Stendhal, Flaubert, and Balzac, and their totally "unreasonable" heroes. The France Drieu knew was created by the struggle between passion and form best exemplified by the work of its painters, by Watteau, Fragonard, Delacroix, Ingres, Manet, and Cézanne: "La religion de l'art a eu en France ses grands fanatiques."[6] 'In France, the religion of art has had its great fanatics.'

During the two-and-a-half-year struggle with his long, diverse, deliberately disjointed narrative, Drieu increasingly returned to themes first introduced in the 1923–1924 "Chronique des spectacles"—to the antagonisms between popular and high art, to the centrality of passion to creativity, to the rituals and theatricality of Paris life, to the linkages between spatial perception and form in art. As France went through a series of governmental changes and the war in Spain came and went, as Hitler became increasingly powerful and numerous European artists and intellectuals temporarily rallied in common causes, Drieu—as always dreaming of extreme solutions and pinning his hopes on images—continued to imagine that fascism might, in an apotheosis of heroism and strength, unite France and save Europe from the United States and Russia. But most of the time he lived emotionally and imaginatively isolated in the recent past, in the twenty years of *Gilles*, increasingly focusing his text on the visual and imaginative interrelationships between passion, space, and the representation of his fictional hero and his world.

Finding himself stumbling daily from his apartment on the Ile-

5. André Malraux, in an interview, quoted in Frédéric Grover, "Entretien entre André Malraux et Frédéric Grover sur Drieu La Rochelle (Paris, Octobre 1959)," in Walter G. Langlois (ed.), *André Malraux, I, du "farfelu" aux 'Antimémoires'* (Paris, 1972), 156.

6. Pierre Drieu La Rochelle, "Mesure et démesure dans l'esprit français," *Combat*, July, 1937, pp. 104–105.

St-Louis through a central Paris landscape altered and disarranged by temporary structures erected for the 1937 Exposition Universelle, Drieu protested in the pages of the March *Nouvelle Revue Française*. "They block her beautiful perspectives, fill up her open spaces, overburden the most sensitive lines of her composition. The Seine, the living axis of the beauty of Paris, is reduced to a corridor between two mountains of cement. . . . A nation that does not understand the power, the delights, the fecundity of space is no longer a nation of architects, no longer an intelligent nation. Intelligence operates in space."[7] This impassioned argument for the preservation of an aesthetic urban landscape coincided with the writing of the opening chapters of *Gilles*, where the fundamental patterns of the hero/comedian's experiences are figured in the rituals of his first incarnation as a poor and sensually greedy soldier on leave, adrift in the visual spaces of Paris. Drawn mothlike to the brightly lit *objets de luxe* of Parisian life, "with an eye honed on painting" (*G* 48), Gilles sees them as displays of planes intersecting, faceted, textured and colored, as forms harmoniously arranged in space, as elements of painted scenes he wants to enter. Surveying and judging, making selections, he reaches out to appropriate them.

The unusual conception and arrangement of *Gilles* vividly reflect Drieu's response to the 1937 Paris Exposition Universelle and its attempts to codify and display French culture for the eyes of visiting tourists, as well as his reactions to some permanent changes taking place in the world of Paris museums. The Palais de Tokio, the neoclassical double structure on the avenue du Président-Wilson that would later house the Musée d'Art Moderne (now designated "de la Ville de Paris" to distinguish it from the Musée National d'Art Moderne at the Centre Pompidou), opened with the only exhibit officially mounted for the exposition, "Chefs-d'oeuvre de l'art français," a collection of some four hundred paintings and three hundred drawings from collections in French provincial and foreign museums, grouped to illustrate the historical traditions of French painting up to Cézanne. The most notable work was a painting Drieu had already seen at the Schloss Charlottenburg in Berlin, Watteau's *L'Enseigne de Gersaint*, temporarily returned to France for the first time since its acquisition around 1744 by Frederick the Great of Prussia.[8] Timed to coincide with the exposition,

7. Pierre Drieu La Rochelle, "L'Intelligence et l'espace," *Nouvelle Revue Française*, XLVIII (March, 1937), 471–72.
    8. For a contemporary reaction to the Palais de Tokio show and in particular to Wat-

though not an official part of it, "Les Maîtres de l'art indépendant, 1895–1937," a collection of over fifteen hundred works by French artists conceived as the "modern" sequel to the show at the Palais de Tokio, was presented at the Petit Palais. From this exhibit of French nonsalon art after Cézanne would be drawn much of the basic collection of the first permanent museum—city or state—of modern art in Paris. Although limited by the inclusion of many now justifiably forgotten works and by the exclusion of most cubist, surrealist, and abstract art—beyond the range of taste of curator Raymond Escholier, a decorated veteran of World War I and author of books on Delacroix, Daumier, and Matisse—"Les Maîtres de l'art indépendant" was, along with *Guernica* and an ancillary exhibit at the Jeu de Paume of "foreign" modern painters such as Vincent Van Gogh, the major French cultural event of 1937.

Drieu's picture gallery conception explains his description, in the 1942 preface, of the novel's structure as a collection of parts "standing free, episodes detached from the background, in sharp focus," as a grouping of "intense highlights, knots that project forward, isolated from the long movement" (*G* 8), and makes specific the source of his deep discontent with the traditional novel of related sequence and expanded duration, which he often found boring and remote from his own perception of lived experience. The vocabulary of Drieu's retrospective account of the structure of *Gilles* underlines the intensely visual conception, the deliberate rethinking of narrative in spatial terms. Describing episodes as "bien dégagé," 'detached,' Drieu suggests the operation of detaching or ungluing a piece of a collage, then holding it closer to the eye, where it appears in sharper focus than the surfaces behind it. In speaking of the novel's parts as "des sursauts" (literally 'shudders'), "des péripéties saillantes," 'intense highlights,' knots that 'project forward,' he is comparing them to picture surfaces with the visible relief characteristic of paintings by Gustave Courbet, Edouard Manet, Claude Monet, and Vincent Van Gogh, paintings that stress the materiality of painting rather than its illusionism. Drieu's curatorial taste as novelist was fairly wide, ranging from Watteau, Ingres, Delacroix, Daumier, and Manet, to Van Gogh and Henri Rousseau, but much like Petit Palais curator

teau's monumental picture, not visible in France since the eighteenth century, see Louis Gillet, "A l'Exposition: Chefs-d'oeuvre de l'art français," *Revue des Deux Mondes*, September 15, 1937, pp. 274–303.

Escholier, born only a year earlier than Drieu in 1892, Drieu had a low opinion of most surrealist painting and excluded it from *Gilles*, after having given it center stage in *Le Feu follet*. His immersion in Paris art of the century's first three decades, however, had made the fundamental visual discoveries of cubism an integral part of his way of seeing the world, a necessity of expression, even if he did complain of "sardine cans stuck to canvases." But in his big novel, the art he loved most—the great French tradition encompassing Poussin, Watteau, Ingres, Delacroix, Daumier, Courbet, Manet, and Seurat—received the most prominent display. Within its contemporary Paris context *Gilles* assumes one of its most telling dimensions as one of the "monumental conceptions" of 1937, as Drieu's personal retrospective of French art.

Drieu's program in *Gilles* was immensely complex: to modernize the chronological picaresque structure, to achieve some of the imaginative density he found so attractive in Stendhal while avoiding the often tiresome, "patched together" effects of Balzac's sequential narrative method, to avoid Céline's medieval grossness and Malraux's olympian retreat from France, to be at once controlled and interesting, while remaining "French." The clearest exposition of what Drieu meant by this last goal—being French—appears in a December, 1939, review of Gide's *Journal* published in Buenos Aires. The essay turns on the relationship between lived experience and its rendering in art. In the *Journal*, which Drieu calls Gide's "finest novel" and the last literary "event" before the war (a fine edge of regret at the bad timing of *Gilles* comes through here), Drieu notes—with a sense of belonging to a younger generation—the sensibility and craft that permit Gide to tell all while revealing nothing. But above all, in his devotion to the minute rendering of lived sensation, Gide shows himself a worthy successor to Stendhal and to the Flaubert of the *Correspondance* and illustrates brilliantly what Drieu identifies as the essence of the French creative imagination—an intense preoccupation with the lived moment, an eternal love affair with the visible:

L'écrivain français s'apparente étroitement au peintre français. Qu'est-ce que le réalisme des peintres français, si ce n'est ce même besoin de noter la jouissance vécue, telle quelle? Ce matin-là, il y avait une fine brume sur la Seine, qui interprétait subtilement la lumière sur les feuillages: Corot en jouit, puis nota sa jouissance (non, certes, sans avoir amalgamé cette notation à la réflexion de tant d'années sur toute l'austère difficulté de la construction picturale). . . . Le Français s'en tient à l'immédiat de la vision, auquel il attache un prix infini.[9]

The French writer resembles the French painter. What after all is the realism of French painters, except that same need to take note of the experience of pleasure, just as it appears? That morning, there was a fine mist over the Seine, a mist that subtly interpreted the light falling on the leaves: Corot enjoyed the interplay, then noted his pleasure, incorporating into this notation a lifelong critical reflection on the austere complexities of pictural construction. . . . The Frenchman limits himself to the immediacy of vision, which he treasures above all else.

In the phrase "la jouissance vécue," 'the experience of pleasure,' Drieu identifies the most complex and sensitive element in his execution of his novel, most clearly visible in the careful separation and highlighting of scenes ("knots that stand out"), in the luminosity and relief of individual faces, in the shapes and colors of pieces of furniture and the highlights reflecting off their surfaces, in the detailed attention to textures and arrangements of fabrics, in the modeling and extraordinary coloring of faces, in the iconic use of landscape, the element of the felt and the visualized—the pictorialization of narrative—that has perplexed his critics both favorable and unfavorable. Dealing with the novel primarily in terms of plot or treatment of character or "contemptuous" point of view, concentrating heavily on social caricatures and political issues, they have ignored the fact that *Gilles is not a novel about events but about vision*.[10]

A broad survey of the distribution of figures, landscapes, theatrical compositions, portraits, portrait-landscapes, historical subjects, and cubist and futurist conceptions in the three major parts of *Gilles* reveals a similar emphasis on periods in painting, with a slow drift backward in time toward the high romantic climax scene on the Concorde. "La Permission," set in 1917 and the "between world" of Gilles' visit to Paris on leave from the war, favors painting of the 1860s, 1870s, and 1880s, with impressionist scenes and early modernist portraiture predominant and

9. Pierre Drieu La Rochelle, "*Le Journal* d'André Gide," *La Nación* (Buenos Aires) December 31, 1939, rpr. in *Sur les écrivains*, ed. Grover, 258.

10. Negative views of *Gilles* include Susan Rubin Suleiman, *Authoritarian Fictions: The Ideological Novel as a Literary Genre* (New York, 1983); Mary Jean Green, "Toward an Analysis of Fascist Fiction: The Contemptuous Narrator in the Works of Brasillach, Céline, and Drieu La Rochelle," *Studies in Twentieth Century Literature*, X (Fall, 1985), 81–97. The first detailed sympathetic study of Drieu, including a highly guarded assessment of *Gilles*, is Grover, *Drieu La Rochelle and the Fiction of Testimony*.

several key scenes relying on cubist and futurist effects. In the long and sometimes tiring section entitled *L'Elysée*, in which Gilles pursues a vague career in the political bureaucracy—and in which Drieu inter- weaves a satire on the surrealist movement, an extended account of Gilles' failed love affair with the American Dora, and a complicated po- litical intrigue culminating in the suicide of Paul Morel, son of the president of the republic—carefully rendered interior scenes, multiple caricatures, several notable landscape studies, and spectacle composi- tions predominate. "L'Apocalypse," the briefest and most intense of the major parts, with events concentrated in 1929 and 1934, "the end of Gilles' Parisian life," continues to emphasize realist painting but ex- pands to include large-scale depictions of rituals, revelations, and his- torical scenes emphasizing the influence of Watteau, Daumier, and De- lacroix. The brief Epilogue, set in a desolate region of Spain during the civil war in 1937, shifts gears radically, moving at first almost entirely away from pictorialism to pure dialogue, then returning to the visual with a vast, grim fresco executed entirely in gradations of brown and tan in the subdued tonal manner of *Guernica*.

Aware that no analysis of the kind possible here can offer even a par- tial account of Drieu's 501-page novel, I have organized the discussion of pictorialist elements in *Gilles* to focus on elements faithful to the pri- mary visual impact of the text rather than to its many complex details. The broad groupings of Paris scenes and landscapes, costume elements and their relation to fictional characterization, portraits and portrait- landscapes, spectacles, and historical subjects will permit us to wander, with the eye of a habitual museumgoer, lover of novels, and admirer of Drieu's most notable effects, observing, savoring, and making con- nections, with the intention of introducing readers and rereaders of Drieu's massive, flawed, and often marvelous novel to some of the pictures in his collection, pictures of a world he loved and condemned, a world caught—like the figure of his hero Gilles—between land- scapes, between cataclysms—the fast disappearing world of the inter- war years.

AMONG LANDSCAPES

The brilliantly conceived opening scene of "La Permission" (The leave), set at the Gare de l'Est in 1917 and modeled in broad oppositions be- tween light and darkness, Paris and the front, is a pictorialization of passion unfolding in space. The *mise en scène* of the traditional realistic novel is replaced by a modernist canvas, a broadly conceived scene in the manner of Manet's *Le Déjeuner sur l'herbe*, with a deliberately shallow background "sketched with a brush like a stage set behind the models" in thick patches that draw the eye forward to a few disturbingly vivid details.[11] A loosely defined, visually murky group is unloaded onto the platform. Soldiers and officers emerge slightly from the broader mass as dark, tanned faces barely distinguishable from the tired overcoats, then, as the cloud of "unreality" that had covered them all at the front begins to dissipate, the unnamed subofficer emerges from his darker surroundings as a series of facial changes, a few gestures. He comes to speaking life only when he walks outside and his eyes fill up with the "other world" of Paris.

> Par un soir de l'hiver de 1917, un train débarquait dans la gare de l'Est une troupe nombreuse de permissionaires. Il y avait là, mêlés à des gens de l'arrière, beaucoup d'hommes du front, soldats et officiers, reconnaissables à leur figure tannée, leur capote fatiguée.
>
> L'invraisemblance qui se prolongeait depuis si longtemps, à cent kilomètres de Paris, mourait là sur ce quai. Le visage de ce jeune sous-officier changeait de seconde en seconde, tandis qu'il passait le guichet, remettait sa permission dans sa poche et descendait les marches extérieures. Ses yeux furent brusquement remplis de lumière, de taxis, de femmes.
>
> "Le pays des femmes," murmura-t-il. (*G* 15)

> An evening in the winter of 1917, a train unloaded in the Gare de l'Est a large troop of soldiers on leave. There were, mixed in with noncombatant personnel, soldiers and officers, recognizable from their tanned faces and their tired greatcoats.
>
> The unreality that had been stretching on for so long a time, one hundred kilometers from Paris, was disintegrating right there on the platform. The young subofficer's face was changing from second to second, as he passed the gate, put his orders back in his pocket, and descended the exterior steps. His eyes were suddenly filled with light, with taxis, with women.
>
> "The land of women," he murmured.

The imperfect tense that dominates the beginning of the second paragraph—*mourait, changeait*—emphasizes ongoing motions, the vapor of unreality *thinning*, Gilles' expression *changing*, an effect of flickering like strokes of paint reflecting the light, like darkness on a stage lighten-

---

11. Françoise Cachin, on Manet's *Déjeuner sur l'herbe*, in the exhibition catalogue *Manet* (Paris, 1983), 167.

ing gradually to reveal an actor's eloquent facial gestures. The tense then shifts to the *passé composé*—*ses yeux furent brusquement remplis de lumière, de taxis, de femmes*—in a sensual rush of light, color, line, motion that depicts the scene as experienced, a picture Gilles enters, moving always toward its visual center. The pattern of desire and reaction established in the opening passages will hold throughout the novel: Gilles will *absorb* images, they will "fill up" his eyes. His thoughts and emotions will be born of responses to the visual; his actions will project forward like the mirror reflections in Manet's *Un Bar aux Folies-Bergère* (Fig. 11)—reversed, suspended, distorted, oddly lit—from his encounters with images.

Gilles emerging and coming into focus, then beginning to "compose" the world around him, his frequent, well-marked shifts from his private visual foreground to the middle distance inhabited by other characters, recall other, equally deliberate forms of modernist narrative "positioning"—the objectified, unintegrated perceptual psychology of Joyce's *Ulysses* and the indirect pictorial discourse of Hemingway's *Farewell to Arms*. In a sense, Stephen Dedalus, Frederic Henry, and Gilles Gambier are all "thinkers" in the modernist style, characters trying to organize their worlds by language and image, by arbitrarily imposed structures, Stephen with philosophical and religious conundrums, Lieutenant Henry with flatly observed, sharply dissociated, hard-edged, superimposed images. Gilles—less philosophical than Stephen and more visually literate and passionate (that is, French) than Lieutenant Henry—"sees himself before a mirror" (Drieu's phrase in "Le Héros de roman") in a constantly shifting play of possibilities. The keen impression of visual and psychological motion in "La Permission," built up, pasted together—*collaged*—from an interplay of plastic elements and from Gilles' constant air of playing a role and being in costume, resembles the visual effects of cubist painting that Winthrup Judkins has aptly characterized as "a deliberate oscillation of appearances . . . an iridescence of form." [12] Gilles' life is presented as a grouping and regrouping of patterns, as a collection of pictures, scenes, and performances, of miniature worlds desired and grasped and lost, of friendships disintegrated in a play of conflicting image systems.

Outside the Gare de l'Est, Gilles walks into another type of land-

12. Winthrup Judkins, "Toward a Reinterpretation of Cubism," *Art Bulletin*, XXX (December, 1948), 276.

scape, an urban scene in which figures of women move around him, "blind" women unaware of the world he has left behind. "Elles ignoraient absolument cet autre royaume aux portes de Paris, ce royaume de troglodytes sanguinaires, ce royaume d'hommes—forêt d'Argonne, désert de Champagne, marais de Picardie, montagne des Vosges" (*G* 18). 'They knew nothing of that other realm at the gates of Paris, that realm of sanguinary troglodytes, that realm of men—Argonne forest, desert of Champagne, marshlands of Picardie, mountains of the Vosges.' This roll call of battle sites—metaphoric, painterly, a list read aloud from a newspaper—appears as a thick, dark streak of color highlighted with touches of red (*sanguinaires*), with flat patches of beige-gray (*désert de Champagne*), with liquidy hollowed-out spaces (*marais*) and angular upward bulges (*montagne*), a streak pasted over the Paris evening scene, an incantation, a rhetorical surge of pain and poetry that will become submerged for a while as the front recedes from his vision and Paris fills up his soul as well as his eyes.

Gilles' visual adaptation to the city involves a series of optical corrections, of adjustments to shifts of angle and slippages of imagery, as objects and people that at one moment stand out clearly, at the next seem to have blurred edges and to pulsate and change as he moves between worlds, as he relearns how to see in the city, as he tries to become part of the picture, part of the landscape of women:

> S'il avait regardé le ciel, comme il faisait au front, mais oubliait aussitôt de faire dans la grande ville qui replie tous les sens de l'homme sur quelques fétiches, il aurait vu un ciel charmant. Ciel de Paris sans étoiles. C'était un soir doux, légèrement veiné de froid. Les femmes entrouvraient leurs fourrures. (*G* 17)

> If he had looked up at the sky, which he soon forgot to do in the city, which turns all man's senses toward a few fetishes, he would have seen a charming sky. A Paris sky with no stars. It was a mild evening, lightly veined with cold. The women were half-opening their furs.

The viewing angle here is close up, down-slanting, the light man-made, as Gilles' senses become magnetized by those *fétiches*, those secular icons that mark his passage through the assemblage of images that resumes the "leave." The perfumes of Paris, the textures of furs and fabrics, come together through the air "lightly veined with cold" and settle like a garment on the women he sees, the women of Kees Van Dongen, of Ernst Ludwig Kirchner's *Five Women in the Street* (Fig. 13), tantaliz-

13. Ernst Ludwig Kirchner, *Five Women in the Street*. 1913. Oil on canvas, 47½ × 35½ inches. Museum Ludwig, Cologne.
Photo: Rheinisches Bildarchiv.

ing, rapidly painted, densely colored forms that fill up the canvas and block from view the streets behind them.

   Appearing out of space as a luminously costumed figure poised in the interval between catastrophes, magnetized by heroism and by pleasure, actor and spectator, Drieu's Gilles is a wanderer between landscapes who sees the world as pictures.[13] On a winter day in 1917, his eyes dazzled by shards of light and cold, he contemplates the perspective of the avenue du Bois (later renamed the avenue Foch), the simple, rich landscape of a Watteau *fête galante* or a Pissarro Paris boulevard scene contrasted with another quickly sketched landscape, a few charcoal strokes evoking naked, stunted trees against an icy sky:

> La lumière et le froid avaient des pointes agaçantes. L'avenue du Bois, loin de la guerre, assez large pour que la masse de ses ramures noires restât basse sous un grand ciel calme, ouvrait sa perspective courte. . . . Il y avait les jeunes femmes et ces grands arbres de luxe, si bien soignés, qui arrondissaient leurs dômes dans la quiétude domestique. Quel contraste avec les arbres de Verdun. L'injustice s'étalait partout, souveraine, sereine.
>
> Gilles oublia un peu son angoisse, il était pris dans le rythme de va-et-vient des promeneurs et des promeneuses, dans le réseau de leurs regards, de leurs gestes, de leurs sourires. Il se tenait droit et il voulait croire qu'il ne manquait d'aucune élégance. (*G* 33)

> The light and the cold had sharp points. The avenue du Bois, far from the war, wide enough for the mass of its boughs to spread wide under a great calm sky, presented its short perspective. . . . There were young women and these great luxurious trees, so well cared for, their domes swelling in the domestic quiet. Injustice was spread over everything, sovereign, serene.
>
> Gilles let go of his anguish a bit, caught up in the back and forth rhythm of men and women promenading, in the web of their looks, their gestures, their smiles. He stood up straight and fancied himself elegant enough.

Gilles responds to the visual contrast between the *arbres de luxe* and the *arbres de Verdun* by reading the brightness and clarity that appear to cover the wide street before him as a glittering haze of "sovereign, serene" injustice, as a fabric of bedazzlement that billows and beckons, and into which—holding himself erect, like Watteau's *Gilles*—he plunges, ready to be carried along by the rocking, floating, turning rhythm, to bob up and down, back and forth, on the bright fabric of *regards*, *gestes*, *sourires* that covers the landscape of peace. This impression of brightness and of glinting light, of a colorful web of motion, recalls Mrs. Dalloway taking in the busy London scene on Bond Street in Virginia

13. For a splendid historical characterization of Drieu's generation and the discontents mirrored in this scene, see Robert Wohl, "Wanderers between Two Worlds," in *The Generation of 1914* (Cambridge, Mass., 1979), 203–37.

Woolf's equally syncopated and emotionally tense vision of the fragile enchantments of peace at the Great War's end. Aragon's restatement of this impressionist scene from *Gilles* as a panoramic genre scene—the Sunday morning promenade on the avenue du Bois in the early twenties, in *Aurélien*, written in 1941–1942—seems still another volley in the continuing Drieu-Aragon dialogue on art and life in the interwar years.[14]

At another moment in Gilles' life, in a striking mixed-genre landscape scene, the war appears to him in a different light, as a distant form of personal peace, as a space of revelation in a world grown too complex for ready comprehension, as "a high point, the treasure of a total absence of goal, being elastically suspended over an abyss of bottomless immobility . . . that state of grace he had known in the trenches" (*G* 386–87). This recollection operates through a rereading of a vision glimpsed on the battlefields of Champagne, when a small flower had appeared silhouetted against a ruined landscape:

> Il avait vu surgir entre les misérables trophées du parapet la primevère la plus naïve et la plus triomphale du monde. Parmi trois brins d'herbe, entre des détritus et des débris sardoniques, elle tintinnabulait faiblement comme une petite fille qui s'en va chantonnant se jeter dans les pattes du satyre, appelant par son ignorance provocante les plus atroces déchirements. . . . Tous les jours précédents, il s'était roulé . . . dans le tumulte énormément ivre et infatué d'un cosmos jouissant à pleins boyaux d'être . . . sans queue ni tête et de confondre ferraille, âmes, gaz, terre et ciel. Plus tard, les magasins d'uniprix . . . lui avait rappelé cette orgie, cette partouse insane où la démocratie des éléments semblait éclabousser dans son rut jusqu'aux étoiles. (*G* 387–88)

> He had seen spring up amid the wretched trophies of the parapet the most naive and triumphant primrose in the world. Among three blades of grass, amid the sardonic refuse and debris, she went tinkling quietly like a young girl who wanders singing into the satyr's paws, inviting by her provocative ignorance the most atrocious ravishments. . . . All the preceding days [Gilles] had rolled . . . in the vast, drunken, lascivious tumult of a cosmos taking its pleasure in huge bellyfuls of being . . . without head or tail and mixing together iron, souls, gas, earth, and sky. In later years, the Uniprix stores . . . had reminded him of this orgy, of this insane debauchery in which the democracy of elements seemed in its lust to explode to the stars.

His lyrical vision quickly forgotten on that field below Reims in the

14. Louis Aragon, *Aurélien* (Paris, 1944), 66–67.

business of loading shells, Gilles finds it returning at another suspended moment—his wife, Pauline, is pregnant, France is dying—a memory of renewal in the midst of destruction. But within the text, the recall undergoes still another, more painterly transformation: the word *primevère* (primrose) fuses with the Italian *primavera* (springtime) and the figure of Flora, the goddess of spring, crowned and garlanded with flowers and strewing them before her, from Botticelli's *Primavera* (Fig. 14) in the Uffizi appears. This brief flicker of the dazzling, joyous, rhythmic Florentine recreation of classical mythology against a richly tapestried sylvan background appears superimposed over the grim clutter beyond the parapet in a classic Joycean epiphany, an image of special personal truth, for Drieu framed by a tumultuous, futuristic evocation of the physical chaos of war. The central image, set off and framed between the suspended immobility of a long, rhythmic opening and the alternatingly slow and jolting motion of a closing orgy of destruction, fuses nature and art in one of the novel's most intense multilayered disclosure scenes, a fleeting but richly visualized integration of the ambiguous experience of war into the fabric of Gilles' peacetime existence. In Drieu's *Primavera*, glowing and evanescent, for a rare moment the picture gallery comes out to meet the trenches.

These landscape scenes, formed of visual contrasts, superpositions, and complex emotional responses, and unified by an intense personal vision, illustrate the strange, strong, complex angles of vision that enclose each of the novel's sequences. Visual elements are presented as consciously selected, savored, considered and reconsidered, touched up or worked over or repositioned, their coloring adjusted to a shifting context. In the *Primavera* scene *pentimenti*—alterations that become visible through the completed surface of an oil painting as the paint becomes more transparent with age—show through, a series of iconic references, with Botticelli, Magritte, and Drieu the most readily identifiable but far from the only ones. In the avenue du Bois scene, in the "landscape of women," in the Forêt de Lyons (*G* 212–13), on the Cotentin seacoast of Normandy (*G* 100), in a still unspoiled fishing village in the Midi of 1917 (*G* 1917), elements of nature become part of a transfixed spectacle, framed, hung, on view, each touch of color, each line the effect of a consciously applied stroke. Drieu is laying on his effects, modeling his scenes, emphasizing the *visual availability* of places, pointing to them as images and not as mirrors of reality. The deliberate self-referentiality of such an arrangement—rich, ironic, never wholly

14. Sandro Botticelli, *La Primavera*. 1477–1478. Oil on canvas, 80 × 123¾ inches. Galleria degli Uffizi, Florence.
Photo: Marburg/Art Resource, N.Y.

stable, almost belligerently unprogrammatic—defines the "pleasure" of Drieu's text and also helps to locate its capacity to arouse and irritate, to leave questions unanswered and arguments unsettled. There is, after all, no way to argue effectively with the conventions of a picture gallery, except perhaps by constructing another, countervailing one.

COSTUMES, PORTRAITS, PORTRAIT-LANDSCAPES

Between Paris and the war, between poverty and *luxe*, Gilles appears as a passion in flux, a core of emotion enclosed in a changing envelope of costume, a portrait of the hero as a series of slippages and restructurings, of mirror effects, as a consciousness poking through the interstices between rising and falling spells of inattention. "Myriam admirait la brusquerie des entrées en matière de Gilles où elle voyait la rapidité de son esprit, mais qui provenait du fait que Gilles fort enfoncé en lui-même et rêvant tout haut ne distinguait point toujours entièrement ses interlocuteurs les uns des autres, et continuait avec celui-ci la conversation commencée avec celui-là" (*G* 98), 'Myriam admired the suddenness of his materializations, which seemed to her reflections of the quickness of his mind, but which were in fact the effect of his self-absorption and his habit of dreaming out loud, so that he failed to recognize whom he was speaking to, and sometimes continued with one person the conversation begun with another.' Gilles the *comédien* often has difficulties with his masks, with "this separate personage who had sprung up exterior to him, an effect of half-sincerity, half-hypocrisy, of distraction, of whims, whom Gilles saw reflected in Myriam's eyes" (*G* 98).

His sense of performance, his curiosity about audience reaction, at intervals impel Gilles onstage. In an early scene, after squeaking under the lowering blind at Charvet's on the rue de la Paix at closing time, buying some unclaimed custom-made shirts (the sleeves turn out to be too long) and a striped silk ascot that sets off his fitted army tunic, after having his secondhand boots shined and rolling himself in "a delicious shroud" of fragrant linen at the barber's, Gilles penetrates the bar (narrower and less impressive than he had expected) at Maxim's and, in a room filled with elegant men of rank and aviators, sees his image in others' eyes—an odd figure who stands out, noticed by all, "a well turned-out infantryman who's not an officer" (*G* 18). This performance, like all of Gilles' "materializations"—as military hero, reluctant husband, lover, victim, political journalist, aesthete, provincial romantic, urban dandy—produces an ambiguous image, a representation that hovers between classes, falls between codes, that calls attention to its own artificiality. His costume always fits handsomely but is just a hair too loose or too long or too short (like the trousers of Watteau's *Gilles*), somehow not quite "correct," so that he looks not dressed but *en costume*, moving with a faint incongruity of gesture that suggests an unfilled space between body and fabric, a figure out of place, out of time, out of synchronization with his surroundings.

The "other Gilles" reflected in Myriam's eyes, the double who "refuses to come unglued," reappears elsewhere with slight alterations of shading, with a few elements rearranged. On his trip to Cannes with the married *Américaine* Dora, Gilles is two distinct characters within twenty-four hours: in the cool, crystalline light of Provence, clever, healthy, and attractive; when the sun goes down, stripped of his "fine and sober eloquence," looking "infinitely sad" (*G* 275). At their wedding in a country church in Normandy on a windy, rainy February day, Pauline *l'Algérienne*, Gilles' second wife, sees standing beside her the man "of those crushing melancholies that whirled him into dark twilight meditations . . . with that lost, nostalgic, wild look he sometimes had in Paris" (*G* 396). Gilles is the "perverse Parisian" identified by his former schoolmaster, a multiple creature shadowed by tempestuous provincial melancholies, a celebrant of spectacles and texts of the city, a connoisseur of luxuries (gilt-tooled volumes in the quiet, spacious Falkenberg library; the fine cheviot twill of politician Clérence's black suit; the beautiful, superbly styled blue chair Myriam buys by accident) and of the luxuries of deprivation (his mentor Carentan's grim, smelly provincial study and toothless, ugly peasant housekeeper; the dying, cancer-ridden Pauline's terrible beauty; the austere light of Normandy in winter)—the fictional hero as dandy, as *flâneur*, as the ultimate *stranger*, as exile and star, like Watteau's *Gilles* on his platform, his marvelous white suit glowing in the diffused outdoor light, calm and composed and *almost* oblivious of the ruckus going on behind him, the Frenchman as comedian and artist.

The novel's strongly illuminated, "forward-projecting" scenes, its deliberate display of roles and costumes, of decors and stagings, emphasize the fact that Gilles is not a "character" in the traditional sense, that a curious recombination of the representational elements in realist fiction and the mimetic modalities of theater is operating to subvert traditional parameters of characterization and setting, that each of Gilles' materializations is something more than a charade, yet something less than an event-in-narrative. Stepping back, one notices that each of his *appearances* posits a momentary Gilles who stands next to or behind or in front of the figure identified by that name, someone who is not his double or one of his *personae*, but rather more like a *version* of the same figure. One is reminded of photographic images imperfectly superimposed, of iconological strata in a painting, of double vision, of a play of incomplete definitions in a tale by Borges (whom Drieu knew and who made Drieu a character in one of his most famous tales, "Tlön, Uqbar, Orbis Tertium"). Each materializing Gilles is *une esquisse*, a sketch or study occupying common space with the original, like Watteau's multiple views of a single face drawn in three colors of chalk on a single sheet, his recurring refigurations of one mask in many paintings. This metaphor, with all it implies of lightness of touch, glow of light, play of the visual, comes close to describing the subtle flickers of color and light that play around Drieu's Gilles as he slips into and out of his costumes. In a very real way, failing to be defined by what he says and how he comports himself, Gilles *is* his costumes, he is an effect of his decors, in disguise all the way through, pure surface to the core, and yet wholly tactile—a three-dimensional appearance painted in two dimensions.

The central motifs of this "life" presented as spectacle, of these portraits of the hero as surface, as the sum of multiple, finely worked strokes interlayered over rough, built-up, thick surfaces, as a character not quite finished, still to be rendered,[15] appear most clearly in those visually framed moments when the intensity of Gilles' desire for textures and colors transcends acquisitiveness and becomes the affair of art rather than of social distinctions, when, for example, he enters a tailor's shop:

> Il entra chez le tailleur avec le même frémissement intime et lent que chez les filles. Il aimait cette caverne d'Ali-Baba où, de tous côtés, les étoffes anglaises s'empilaient et retombaient à longs plis. Il se retenait de se rouler dans cette matière solide et souple, n'en jouissant pas assez du nez, des yeux, du bout des doigts. (*G* 47)

> He entered the tailor's shop with the same intimate, slow, quivering sensation as a brothel. He loved this Ali Baba's cave where, from all sides, English fabrics were piled and hung down in long folds. He wanted to roll himself in this solid and supple matter, not getting enough of it with his nose, his eyes, the tips of his fingers.

This controlled orgy of sheer sensual pleasure in textures and arrangements of forms evokes the desire rather than the character, presenting in a framed scene the kind of transcendent, immaterial visual pleasure Drieu experienced in the fabrics and folds, the colors and slippages of surfaces in Watteau, Ingres, and Delacroix, the almost untranslatable sensation he suggested in a letter: "Yes, looking at a Watteau, I knew . . . that it is everything . . . and nothing."[16] Compared with Gilles' vision in the tailor's shop, the sartorial strategies of a Rastignac or a Julien Sorel seem almost pragmatic.

Gilles' thirst for *luxe*, echoed in the high relief given to the depiction of costumes, decors, pleasures and deprivations, places him squarely in the line of Watteau and Manet and Baudelaire, in the French aesthetic

---

15. For the basis of this comparison, see the analysis of Monet's intricate painting techniques and complex layering of colors in Robert L. Herbert, "Method and Meaning in Monet," *Art in America*, LXVII (September, 1979), 90–108.

16. Pierre Drieu La Rochelle, unpublished journal entry of October 16, 1939, quoted in Lansard, *Drieu La Rochelle*, I, 23.

tradition. The word *luxe*, inadequately translated as *luxury*, has vast resonances in French literature and art of the nineteenth and early twentieth centuries; it connotes lavishness, richness of texture, detail, color—and pleasure. There is *luxe* in the infinitely detailed, deeply colored jumble of fabrics and objects that fills the foreground of Delacroix's *La Mort de Sardanapale*, in the metaphysical sensuality of Baudelaire's phrase *luxe, calme, et volupté* in "L'Invitation au voyage," in the cushions, fabrics, and skin textures of Ingres' paintings of odalisques, in the thick circular strokes that shape a wrist or a face in a Manet painting.[17] The tables, walls, windows, and floors of Matisse's Mediterranean interiors vibrating with deep colors and contrasting patterns and Flaubert's costume and food descriptions in *L'Education sentimentale* are modes of *luxe*. So, too, are the beautiful flowing fabrics worn by the women turning from view in Watteau's paintings and the thick, rich abundance of the trees that surround them. There are also sparer forms of *luxe*, such as that dense materiality, that color seeming to glow out of representation in black on white that Baudelaire identified in Daumier and that the French call *le gras* (fatness), substantiality of form expressed through line. *Luxe* is a confluence of beauty, quantity, and texture, governed by an exercise of artistic selection that creates quality, a level of distinction. Simply assembling a lot of something—fine fabrics or money or paint on canvas—does not ensure the presence of *luxe*. The costumes, decors, and portraits in Drieu's novel are signs of *luxe* or of its absence. The hero's vision—formed by an aesthete's taste, a critic's bent for judgment, a painter's feel for the details that sum up a scene or a face in measured strokes—in its sparest form, motivated by anger or discontent, resembles that of a caricaturist like Daumier; in its most expansive, swelled by a thirst for more reality than life has to offer, his vision for a few moments discerns in the scene before it the potential elements for "a Delacroix."

Watteau and the early modernist painters—and the literary modernists who followed them—shared an intense perception of the interpenetration of theatricality into broad areas of Paris life. Watteau's painted *fêtes galantes* and theatrical scenes reflect a changing world of French society, a world in which fashion was growing more important, where a new public was seeking lighthearted theatrical entertainment,

17. For a detailed examination of Manet's structural brushstrokes, see Anne Coffin Hanson, "Manet's Pictorial Language," in *Manet*, 20–28.

where a lively café society was springing up near the principal Paris theaters, where pleasure was taking on new "spectacular" forms.[18] Like
Daumier, Manet, and Seurat—and Drieu and the early Aragon after
them—Watteau drew his essential subject matter from real events.
Masked balls at the Opéra and *fêtes galantes* held at wealthy private resi-
dences in Paris and the nearby countryside provided models for the delicious, far from innocent pleasures evoked in his paintings, scenes that
prefigure some of the most notable nineteenth-century portrayals of
theatricalized, licentious Paris life—scenes such as the costume party in
L'Education sentimentale and Manet's *Bal masqué à l'Opéra*. The links
between Watteau and modernist painters—including Henri Rousseau,
whose *Moi-même, portrait-paysage* (Fig. 15) is a clear quotation of *Gilles*—
are most readily apparent in their common use of costume as a central
figure of representation. Manet was a startling and controversial painter
as much for his insistence on using costume in nonhistorical compositions as for his often confrontational subjects. His toreadors, gypsies,
Spanish dancers, and figures in glaringly modern dress all underline, in
good Baudelairean fashion, the centrality of costume to the representation of modern life. Manet and Watteau were both deeply formed by
the experience of "museum art." Both kept a stock of costumes in their
studios for professional models or friends to don when sitting for them.
Manet openly acknowledged his admiration for Watteau in the original
name of his notorious *Le Déjeuner sur l'herbe—La Partie quarrée*, after a
painting by Watteau. Seen within the broad artistic context that shaped
his sensibility, viewed as a re-vision of the *modernité* of Baudelaire and
Manet, Drieu's version in his *Gilles* of the modernist vision appears less
strange, less culturally isolated; his passionate attachment to Watteau—
totally puzzling to some of his friends—comes into clearer focus.[19]
Without ignoring their justly admired pleasures of ambiguity, their
notes of melancholy, or their often dreamlike quality, Drieu also perceived in Watteau's paintings their intense plastic materiality, their elements of satire, their network of self-referentiality, their complex social
and artistic roots, and their fund of potentially translatable imagery.

18. For some of the extensive background to these remarks, see in particular François
Moureau, "Watteau in His Time," in the exhibition catalogue *Watteau, 1684–1721*,
469–507.
19. See the mystified comments by Jean Bernier on Drieu's attachment to Watteau's
paintings, quoted in Lansard, *Drieu La Rochelle*, I, 271.

15. Henri Rousseau, *Moi-même, portrait-paysage*. 1890. Oil on canvas, 56¼ ×
43¼ inches. National Gallery of Prague.
Photo: Giraudon/Art Resource, N.Y.

In viewing the extensive range of portraiture levels in *Gilles*—from partial portraits that analyze the techniques of figurative representation, to quotations of notable painted portraits, to full-blown *portraits-paysages* and theatrical compositions—the example of Watteau is immensely useful. Clearly, for Drieu and the special requirements of his modernist picaresque epic, the theatricality of portraiture, its use of an image that calls attention to itself *as image*, as well as its increasingly precarious status in modernist art, were particularly appealing. Although Watteau was not known primarily as a portrait painter, his practice of portraiture—a form that by the time of the high Renaissance had moved well beyond a simple record or true likeness of the sitter[20]— was extensive, evolving, over the brief years of his career, through many degrees of likeness and varied uses of context toward the major late portraits that include *Gilles* and the Louvre's *Portrait d'un gentilhomme*. There are, to draw on Posner's useful distinction, significant differences between "people in pictures" and "pictures of people."[21] Watteau's practice of portraiture frequently falls on the line between the two categories, especially in his theater subjects, some of which show actors performing a specific stage action—*L'Amour au Théâtre Français*—and others that organize forms of portraiture into a portrayal of a company—*Le Théâtre Italien*, in which the actors appear in *une vaudeville*, an onstage assembly at the end of the performance. From their reappearance in other pictures, often in radically different poses and subjects, it appears that many of the actors and musicians Watteau portrayed were friends or models dressed in actors' costumes. Watteau also developed another, more generalized form of portraiture in which carefully individualized figures were used to represent types. Most strikingly, in the monumental late painting *Les Comédiens Italiens* (Fig. 16), a scene composed of a vast network of contrasting and complementary gestures and poses, the theater itself appears as a massive mythology of presentation. This striking composition, which invites the viewer to behold critically the visual components of role-playing and to speculate on the relationship between staging and painting, reappears signifi-

20. See Rémy Saisselin, in the exhibition catalogue *Style, Truth, and the Portrait* (Cleveland, 1963); and John Pope-Hennessy, *The Portrait in the Renaissance* (Princeton, 1966).

21. Posner, *Antoine Watteau*, 263.

16. Antoine Watteau, *Les Comédiens Italiens.* 1719–1720. Oil on canvas, 25¼ ×
30 inches. National Gallery of Art, Washington, D.C., Samuel H. Kress
Collection.
Photo: National Gallery of Art.

cantly in Daumier's watercolor *La Parade de foire* (Fig. 1), Seurat's *La
Parade de cirque* (Fig. 2), and once again in the "last banquet" and Radical Congress scenes in *Gilles.*[22]

The portraits in *Gilles*—from those that refer directly to specific
paintings and others that fuse elements from several portrait types and
periods to some that function primarily as ironic illustrations of the decline of portraiture to which Drieu referred in his text on Watteau's
Gilles—all emphasize Drieu's quintessentially modernist vision, his

22. There is some disagreement about the authorship of the painting, now in the National Gallery of Art in Washington, D.C. Posner judges it "a very fine old copy," while
Pierre Rosenberg accepts it as being from Watteau's hand. See Posner, *Antoine Watteau,*
263; and Pierre Rosenberg, in *Watteau, 1684–1721,* pp. 439–43.

preference for human images that seem to belong in the picture gallery. Unlike Henry James, who frequently used widely known portraits to suggest psychological and moral traits and who, in Adeline Tintner's view, came in late career to prefer the "natural" masterpiece to the museum version, Drieu relished literary portraits that not only *looked* like painted portraits but that shared their iconic fixity, their "framed" presence.[23] His insistence on the picture gallery quality of his fictional characters recalls Gertrude Stein's strikingly articulated preference for scenes glimpsed through the windows of museums.[24]

The "partial" or secondary portraits in *Gilles* offer a scattered survey of painterly preparations for formal portraits. Monsieur Falkenberg's corpse a few hours after his suicide is an oil sketch of decomposition: "M. Falkenberg was already far advanced in the metamorphoses of death. Greens, grays were beginning to explore the white. On his vest no blood" (*G* 124). In Gilles' eyes, Mabel, the nurse who has shed her saintly image along with her uniform, appears "in the soft afternoon light [that] came in through the curtains" as a study of a sleeping nude, "a charming body that no longer spoke to him. All those lines, which had briefly been so eloquent, were now silent" (*G* 74). The *demi-portrait* of Mme Florimond, mother of two illegitimate sons, the surrealist poet Galant and the young Third Republic politician Clérences, draws on several visual traditions. From Watteau's *demi-caractères*— costumed figures representing social or national classifications, peasants, pilgrims, *Espagnolettes, Orientales*[25]—comes "the dress of a provincial intellectual"; from the vividly painted faces of Van Gogh's portraits and the boldly simplified figure poses in Lautrec come the face and figure glowing with the demonic individualism of nineteenth-century French realism. The whole is then resumed in three carefully balanced sentences that capture the essence of *l'accent Drieutique* (the Drieu

23. For a discussion of James's use of portraits, see Tintner, *Museum World of Henry James*, esp. 81–100.

24. For critical viewpoints on the technique of literary framing in Woolf, see Mary Ann Caws, *Reading Frames in Modern Fiction* (Princeton, 1985), 237–62; in Proust, see Meyers, *Painting and the Novel*, 96–123; in Stein, see Wendy Steiner, *Exact Resemblance to Exact Resemblance: The Literary Portraiture of Gertrude Stein* (New Haven, 1978).

25. François Moureau, "Theater Costumes in the Work of Watteau," in *Watteau, 1684–1721*, pp. 507–31.

touch) that fuses complex visual and verbal traditions into an instantly, viciously memorable minor figure:

> Mme Florimond était une petite boulotte de quarante ans. Dans son visage couperosé et fripé, surmonté d'une batailleuse chevelure rousse, il y avait des yeux d'un cynisme et d'une curiosité si ostensibles, qu'ils en paraissaient naïfs. Elle avait une étrange robe démodée et provocante d'intellectuelle de province où une paire de seins très blancs et fort bien conservés étaient mis en évidences. (*G* 127)

> Mme Florimond was a round little loaf of forty. In her red-veined, worn face, topped by a quarrelsome head of red hair, were eyes of such palpable cynicism and curiosity that they looked naive. She had on the strange, outmoded, provocative dress of a provincial intellectual that showed off a pair of very white, very well-preserved breasts.

Stripped of its costumes, Gilles' own body is a black and white partial portrait, the strange growth of the "two landscapes" between which he lives, "totally unsettling, divided in half like an anatomical drawing: on one side, the body of a full-grown, almost athletic man, with a firmly seated neck, a full right shoulder, an ample chest, narrow hip, well-formed knee; on the other, a carcass struck by lightning, tormented, twisted, dried out, stunted . . . the side of war, massacre, torture, death. The stealthy arm wound had hooked its iron fingernail into the flesh right to the nerve and had there surprised and suspended the life current, and by a vast countershock had corrupted its muscular architectonics" (*G* 364). Morel, president of the republic, appears dressed as a fake warrior, "in evening dress, wearing the pale mask with the little, carefully twisted beard he had fashioned for himself as a shield from the humiliation of his duties" (*G* 313). Many of the secondary characters appear as colored *caricatures*, figures defined by the visual language of physiognomy, pose, and gesture and heightened by strong, heavily outlined patches of color—Daumier plus Rouault—their physical density compressed and accentuated by vivid *décors*: the elegantly, soberly attired Clérences in his ostentatiously bare-walled dining room and *atelier* (artist's studio, his pretentious name for the living room), marked by "two or three revoltingly austere cubist paintings" (*G* 175, 177); Morel in mask silhouetted against his *salon*, "une salle de musée," 'a room in a museum,' filled with the spoils of the *ancien régime* (*G* 309).

17. Jean-Auguste-Dominique Ingres, *Portrait de Mademoiselle Rivière*. 1806. Oil on canvas, 39¼ × 27½ inches. Musée du Louvre, Paris.
Photo: Réunion des Musées Nationaux.

The novel's first major portrait, a bust of Myriam Falkenberg, the young Jewish intellectual who becomes Gilles' first wife, comes into view as a painting moving through the somber, luxurious apartment on the avenue de Messine:

> Un visage s'avançait vers lui. Un visage lumineux. Tout y semblait vaste, parce que la lumière y régnait. Gros yeux, front découvert, prolongé par une chevelure d'un noir éclatant. Avec tout cela faisait contraste une bouche épaisse, sombre, qui était comme une allusion enfantine à la volupté. Ce ne fut qu'au bout d'un moment que Gilles perçut que sous ce visage il y avait un corps, un corps frêle. Le buste était délicat, les jambes fines. (*G* 30)
>
> A face was moving toward him. A luminous face. Everything in it seemed vast, because it was glowing with light. Big eyes, bared forehead, accentuated by brilliantly black hair. In contrast with all this, a thick, dark mouth, a childlike allusion to sensuality. Only after a few minutes did Gilles notice that below this face there was a body, a frail body. The bust was delicate, the legs thin.

Myriam's striking coloring, full lips, childlike body, the luminosity of her face clearly recall Ingres' *Portrait de Mademoiselle Rivière*, hanging in the Louvre (Fig. 17), and the Raphael faces that stand behind it. The undercurrent of darkness and potential disaster (Mlle Rivière died at fourteen, a year after the portrait was completed, Gilles abandons Myriam, unable to relate to her physically) also leads the mind's eye back to Bronzino's *Portrait of a Lady in a Black Dress* (Fig. 18), underlining the emphasis on strong light, high finish, and stylized form that link two of Drieu's most cherished portraitists.[26] Gilles will continue to prefer Myriam as a portrait, as a face without a body; her full-length image will be an artistic failure: "One day . . . he saw her coming toward him. She was walking from the end of a long garden path. We rarely see the people we live with in long perspective. . . . She walked badly. . . . Something essential in Myriam displeased him" (*G* 45).

Pauline, Gilles' second wife, is a full-length seated figure out of Delacroix's *Les Femmes d'Alger dans leur appartement* (Fig. 19): "There was movement in her body, fire in her face. . . . A brunette with amber skin, with deep eyes with dark shadows under them, the head and upper body very erect. . . . Badly dressed like a Bovary or a *poule* [prostitute]

26. See Hélène Toussaint, *Les Portraits d'Ingres* (Paris, 1985); and Robert Rosenblum, *Ingres* (New York, 1967).

18. Agnolo Bronzino, *Portrait of a Lady in a Black Dress*. 1559. Oil on panel, 47¾ × 38 inches. Galleria degli Uffizi, Florence.
Photo: Alinari/Art Resource, N.Y.

19. Eugène Delacroix, *Les Femmes d'Alger dans leur appartement.* 1834. Oil on canvas, 70 × 89¾ inches. Musée du Louvre, Paris.
Photo: Réunion des Musées Nationaux.

who wants to transcend her station. . . . A woman of the native soil" (*G* 366). At their wedding in Normandy, Pauline's exotic coloring at first appears heightened and made more glowing by the wind and the rain, framed by her dark, wild hair; then, a "mortal pallor" seems to show through the amber skin in the filtered light of a small Romanesque church (*G* 396–97). Undermined by illness and the legacy of her promiscuous past, the girl from the south withers in "the winter of society" of France in the late twenties and early thirties, and as her body decays and her beautiful, ravaged face takes on the luminosity of Myriam's (*G* 426), the voluptuous *Algérienne* becomes another still and glowing bust-length portrait in Gilles' collection.

Berthe Santon, Gilles' last romance, is from the beginning "nothing but an image" (*G* 242), a modernist icon whose context is defined by color and style and nourished by money, whose exterior is a display of

20. Edouard Manet, *Nana*. 1877. Oil on canvas, 60¾ × 45¼ inches. Hamburger Kunsthalle, Hamburg.
Photo: Elke Walford, Hamburg.

class and sex, a striking rereading of Manet's *Nana* (Fig. 20) with black hair instead of reddish-blonde, of Seurat's *Jeune femme se poudrant*: "Gilles was obsessed by Berthe's hollow and deceptive form. She was beautiful, a milky pool with black hair floating on it. Her eyes were mineral blue. . . . With Santon's money she had constructed a perfect cage with platinum bars. . . . She dressed with a marvelously mortifying simplicity. Exquisite poverty of colors and lines" (*G* 425). As Gilles prepares to leave Paris in 1934, he sees the sobbing Berthe, mumbling romantic clichés out of novels, as another framed portrait in the picture gallery of beautiful "dead women."

Drieu's most complex, vivid, and visually ironic portraits are three studies of Carentan, the politically and racially biased country philosopher, political propagandist, and ethnographer of religions who was Gilles' guardian and mentor before the war. Elements of costume, decor, landscape, and literary and painterly quotation all come to bear in a densely detailed, satirical portrait of a late nineteenth-century sage who has raised a strange "modern" child—the tall, elegant veteran and dandy who comes in 1917 to visit his "natural father" in the novel's "third landscape," neither Paris nor the war but a small Norman town near the wild, rocky coast evoked by Michelet's *La Mer* in 1860 and painted by Monet and Seurat in the 1880s. Enchanted by the glaucous sea and the steep, irregular coastline of his fondest childhood memories, Gilles glimpses through a "flaw" in the cliffs the postromantic, decaying Norman town of symbolist literature (epitomized in the now-lost painting by J.-C. Cazin, *La Ville morte*, of a town in the Pas-de-Calais).[27] Turning his back to the sea, Gilles gazes down at Carentan's house in the valley, "a long, low cottage, totally isolated . . . a thatched hut cluttered with gods" (*G* 101). Stopping at a distance, he "composes" the first portrait of Carentan, the "old prodigal son," who appears at his doorway, standing next to his servant-mistress. Both are tall, "of the Norman race," seen in vivid patches of color against the browns, grayed greens, and muddy yellows of their background. At closer range

---

27. For an excellent brief study of the impressionists' reactions to the northern coasts, see Sylvie Gache-Potin and Scott Schaefer, "Impressionism and the Sea," in the exhibition catalogue *A Day in the Country: Impressionism and the French Landscape* (Los Angeles, 1984), 273–98. For an examination of the relationship between impressionist and symbolist views of Normandy, see Thomson, *Seurat*, 176–87. The Cazin painting is illustrated on page 181.

Gilles feels himself gripped by Carentan's strong arms and assaulted by his "powerful, stinking breath, the healthy stink of tobacco, alcohol, solitude, meditation" (G 102). He hugs the servant, with her "bald spots, terrible little blue eyes, huge mouth with few teeth . . . magnificent, dressed in her work clothes and her native coiffe" (G 103)—a peasant figure out of a postimpressionist painting—and is revolted by the smell.

Carentan in his study becomes the subject of a second, seated portrait. First, his costume and features are painted in quickly, with firm, crusty strokes—rugged painting student's costume, heavy white mustache, regular features, large, slightly dilated and blurry blue eyes, strong, straight nose. Then the details of the room complete the picture. As in Manet's *Portrait d'Emile Zola* (Fig. 21), the essence of the portrait is in the network of emblems, the objects disposed on tables, the images affixed to the wall—some of them invented, some belonging or referring to the painter and not to the subject.[28] The relative quantities and disposition of emblematic objects in the two portraits stand in interesting contrast. In the Zola portrait a large Oriental screen appears to the left, cut off by the picture's edge. To the right, open in Zola's hand is Charles Blanc's *Histoire des peintres*, one of Manet's most frequently consulted books. Arranged in meaningful disorder on the table are a blue Zola pamphlet (Manet's name on the cover serves as the painter's signature), a porcelain inkstand, a pipe, several other pamphlets, a row of books, and a few reed pens in a jar. Above the table to the right on the dark wall behind the subject is a frame with three carefully disposed images slipped into it—a photograph or lost print of an early version of Manet's *Olympia*, a portrait of a sumo wrestler, and an engraving after *Los Borrachos* by Velasquez. Manet's portrait of the young Zola shows an almost neutral-faced figure—"the writer" set into a "text" of literary and artistic references. Drieu's portrait of Carentan begins with a satiric icon of the smelly, saintly philosopher, then proceeds—by highlighting crudeness and disorder—to overwhelm his subject with a ludicrous surfeit of texts and images. On the study table next to him are "many piles of paper, flasks, a thick lamp, pipes, the

28. See Theodore Reff, "Manet's Portrait of Zola," *Burlington Magazine*, CXVII (July, 1975), 34–44.

21. Edouard Manet, *Portrait d'Emile Zola*. 1868. Oil on canvas, 57¼ × 45 inches.
Musée d'Orsay, Paris.
Photo: Réunion des Musées Nationaux.

whole romantic prejudice for the picturesque, for dirt and disorder."
To Carentan's left we see "a monstrous heap of books," to his right
"on the bare wall roughly painted with beige . . . 'the whole divine
bazaar' . . . as many images of gods from all eras and places as he had
been able to find. . . . Statues and statuettes, engravings, photos (many
photos taken, with great care, on his travels), pages torn out of books,
drawings from his own hand so awkward they verged fantastically and
humorously on caricature. There were primitive gods, evolved gods,
skeletal figures, grimacing figures, others highly finished, too perfect,
almost cold. All of this was arranged on the wall according to a complicated genealogy, tangled with arrows and brackets painted directly on
the wall." Looking at "the wall of gods," Gilles thinks, "Enough to sat-
isfy Flaubert and Pécuchet" (G 104–105).

When Gilles revisits Carentan in the winter of 1923, the landscape
of *contre-Paris* dominates once again, with its solitude, silence, and
space for meditation. But the land is visibly dying, the remaining peasants trailing through the landscape like a ragged army in retreat. In this
"winter of society," Gilles sees a different Carentan on the icy road
beside him, a figure "whitened and losing color, aged, beginning to
bend," a partially transparent image viewed against the whitened and
grayed landscape, "a tall silhouette whose slow caving-in still filled the
scene. With the majestic remains of his vast shoulders the old man still
filled up space; there were still powerful tendons in his scrawny neck, an
inextinguishable vitality still ran beneath his red cheeks, through the
white hair of his mustache and his brows and the very pale water of his
eyes. . . . In his big stinking mouth he held a pipe" (G 353–55). In this
portrait-landscape, the central figure, if not yet totally hollow, begins to
take on the look of a cheap illustration, a faded *image d'Epinal* barely
distinguishable from the grim winter landscape behind him except for
the dark outlines, the strokes of black showing up tendons, the spots of
red on his cheeks. Only a huge beech tree in a thicket beyond the
road—outside the frame of the portrait-landscape—has density, deep
color, the majesty of a persistent image out of art, of the trees in Poussin
and the Barbizon landscapes. When Carentan with his stinking pipe
points to the beech tree and pompously asserts its immortality, Drieu
puts a dark, heavy, satirical frame around his almost effaced icon of a
dirty, aging provincial saint.

LA COMÉDIE FRANÇAISE AND THE PORTRAIT-SPECTACLE

The most vigorous and controlled male icon in the novel is the brilliant formal portrait of Chanteau, the political leader who takes center stage in a massive spectacle composition depicting a Radical Party Congress in the late twenties. In this sequence, carefully framed, elaborated, and orchestrated, Drieu brings together the multiple strands of romantic, realist, and modernist painting and literature, of visual and verbal caricature and rhetorical collage developed earlier in the novel, deliberately working and rearranging them, braiding and twisting them to the point where the extravagance of images and language becomes a virtuoso exercise in sheer *luxe*. From crisply sketched dialogue to interior and spoken monologue to diatribe, from caricature to portraiture to a parody of grand historical painting, the Radical Congress episode shows Drieu at his most powerful, infuriating best. Far more artistically concentrated than the expanded satire on the surrealists in "L'Elysée," this finely nuanced, temporally fractionalized staging of a three-day political convention achieves the unlikely fusion of painterly with literary effects Drieu had attempted with uneven results in episodes of *L'Homme couvert de femmes*, *Le Feu follet*, and scenes of his unfinished play *Gille*.

The narrative situation is close to ideal for working out a "big picture" set within another even bigger one: a ritual within a ritual, observed from a densely informed focus, inviting a dazzling display of visual distance and depth. Because Gilles attends the congress primarily as a professional spectator, because he has at his fingertips the literary and art history that illustrate and explain what he sees, because he is comfortable and less conspicuous than usual in his current costume as a free-lance political journalist, and probably most of all because he really expects little of his friend Clérences, whom he is encouraging to challenge Chanteau for leadership of the party, he can both observe and react, see and comment, with more art than passion.

Thus at the Radical Congress the novel's recurrent dialectic between visual representation and social and political polemics is literally dissolved into the fabric of the text: painting and politics become part of the same visual and verbal structure. The fiction stops, stands still, as the crowd breathes in the cadences of the speeches, as Gilles watches and his mind moves backward and forward in time, as multiple images appear and cover one another, then are rocked and shuffled until they fall separated again like a deck of cards thrown down. The closest parallel to the peculiar time sense of this episode is the Nighttown sequence in *Ulysses*, with Joyce's stagy, comic, recollective-allusive perspective reduced to the optic of a single character, Gilles, whose center stage is toward the back of *le cirque* (the arena).

Chanteau on his platform, adjusting his bulk and mouthing clichés, is viewed at a grand, brilliant distance. He is seen larger than life-size, so that even from the back of the meeting hall he takes up a huge amount of space. The fine details of his portrait appear magnified as if under a gigantic enlarging glass, so that the high "finish" of the canvas can be examined scrupulously. Miraculously, it holds together. Chanteau's portrait is so compactly painted, so brilliantly colored, so hallucinatingly conceived, that even from a distance it has the illusionistic finish and the rhythm of line of its major model, Ingres' *Portrait de Monsieur Bertin* (Fig. 22), mirror-smooth, luminous, unchangeable, overpowering—and to some viewers menacing—the image of a powerful man wholly at ease in his skin. Baudelaire, in his *Salon of 1845*, called it "the most beautiful portrait Ingres has painted. . . . It seems the proud stance and majesty of the model have further advanced the audacity of Monsieur Ingres, the man of audacity par excellence." [29]

The most striking reaction to the Bertin portrait, and the most significant for understanding the use Drieu makes of it, came from Edouard Manet, who said, "Ingres chose *père* Bertin to stylize an era; he made him the Buddha of the bourgeoisie, satiated, rich, triumphant." [30] As Hélène Toussaint points out, "Manet spoke knowingly, as a craftsman in precious metals, as someone who belonged to the same class." [31] In Ingres' portrait Manet caught hold of precisely the element Drieu exploits, its hallucinating tension between surface and suggestion, its vibrating "thirstiness," its air of being about to swallow up the viewer, what I have earlier characterized as *hollowness*. In the Radical Congress scene, Chanteau orating literally absorbs his audience, swallows them up into his vast bulk, where they create not even a shimmer.

The episode opens with a dense paragraph that sketches in with

29. Baudelaire's comment is quoted in Toussaint, *Les Portraits d'Ingres*, 75.

30. Manet's comment is quoted in Henri Mondor, *Mallarmé*, (2 vols.; Paris, 1941), II, 393.

31. Toussaint, *Les Portraits d'Ingres*, 75.

22. Jean-Auguste-Dominique Ingres, *Portrait de Monsieur Bertin*. 1832. Oil on canvas, 45¾ × 37½ inches. Musée du Louvre, Paris.
Photo: Réunion des Musées Nationaux.

quick, firm strokes the company of delegates, a vast group of figures gesturing and responding to one another, with hands greeting and shaking and slipping into other hands, with presidents kissing militants and militants kissing presidents, with a long series of actions, "a lively preliminary prostitution" composed of forms of recognition, familiar address, congratulation, pardon, suspicion, filling up the hotels, cafés, street corners, arena. "The thick cloud created by this swarm of petit bourgeois flies circling around power buzzed with extravagant indulgence, with luxuriant complicity" (*G* 397).

Gilles watches the assembly watch the speakers, meditating, commenting to himself and occasionally aloud, riffling through his mind a vast collection of images, layer upon layer—medieval churches, robed monks, old monuments and pieces of public statuary, rooms filled with paintings and drawings—centuries of French history as embodied in French art, images lapping and overlapping, interrupted occasionally by a few words drifting into his sphere of attention from the speakers' platform. Then he watches Chanteau advance "with the same tragi-comedian's gait . . . every year since the war, onto the national stage, the accustomed scene of his triumph," proudly carrying before him the paunch that identifies him as a successful bourgeois (*G* 406–407). Gilles sneeringly mumbles a remark about placing another wreath on the bust of Molière. Chanteau then "slowly rotates his shoulders" in preparation for the opening line of his speech. At that point the Bertin image glows demonically from the stage, corpulent, topped with a "wiry salad of hair," looking out at the audience, preparing to pacify the flock, to swallow them. Drieu's careful emphasis in this scene on pose and gesture, on complementary and contrasting stances, on extensive classifications of *métiers* and types vividly echoes the densely populated visual world, the richly inflected caricatural language of Daumier.[32] "Chanteau went on speaking. The crowd of spectators, militants, petits bourgeois from the city and the provinces, lawyers, veterinarians, doctors, pharmacists, small industrialists, farmers, journalists, magistrates, free-masons . . . listened to him and were profoundly reassured. . . . Chanteau filtered them and let them settle, purified them" (*G* 409). As Gilles the spectator-artist himself "filters" and "lets settle" the colors, lines, and shapes of the scene, an odd, dramatic disjunction takes place. The entire arena becomes a picture, a vast composition filled with faces and bodies, all lines of motion turning toward the platform, illuminated from above and to one side by a dim, dirty light, a vast confrontation

32. For a detailed and superbly informed analysis of the visual language of pantomime and caricature as practiced by Daumier, see Wechsler, *A Human Comedy*, esp. 132–72. The broad lines of inquiry I follow here are based in large part on Wechsler's clarifications.

23. Eugène Delacroix, *Boissy d'Anglas à la Convention, esquisse*. 1831. Oil on canvas, 31¼ × 41 inches. Musée des Beaux-Arts, Bordeaux.
Photo: Musée des Beaux-Arts, Bordeaux.

composition like Delacroix's *Boissy d'Anglas à la Convention* (Fig. 23), translated into the postrevolutionary world of the "last revolution," the Great War. The precipitating crisis now is not lack of bread, as in the scene Delacroix painted, but a dim, unrecognized menace whose outlines Gilles can make out—a war still unsettled, ready to begin anew. In place of a symbolic head on a pike presented to Boissy by the crowd, the weak, conceding smile of Clérences, who fails to make his little political revolution, hovers before Chanteau, the gleaming "Buddha of the bourgeoisie." Into the dark spaces filled by crowd masses in Delacroix's historical scene Drieu has stuffed the vast repertoire of French types smiling and fawning and grimacing and posing recorded in the lithographs of Daumier, creating out of the Radical Congress a singular, startling modernist hybrid: a romantic historical canvas filled with realist caricatures and organized around a startling neoclassical portrait icon, the whole striped and crisscrossed with rhetorical commentary and art historical comparisons—a massive collage, a *portrait-spectacle* conceived in the late thirties, vivid and self-contradictory, a work—to borrow Daumier's phrase—very much "of its time."

PAINTED REVOLUTIONS

The "painted revolution" of February 6, 1934, on the Place de la Concorde is the epicenter of the novel, the scene where Paris as museum and Paris as fortification merge, where the art of the barricades confronts the modernist gallery. Gilles' preceding involvements with painting have followed a similar pattern of beholding, adjusting, fixing, acquiring. From his walks "among landscapes" in "La Permission," through his multiple interactions with portraits and portrait-landscapes, to his virtuoso creation for the novel's private *salon carré* of the portrait-spectacle at the Radical Congress, the given and the visible have responded by yielding up pictures for his collection. On the Concorde, for a few hours, Gilles walks inside the frame for an art of revolution; there he attempts to compose a canvas that will hold. Instead, he participates in a stunning visualization of narrative checkmate that marks the novel's central closure, "the end of Gilles' Parisian life." The textual and conceptual difficulties of the Epilogue, set in Spain in 1937 and divided into two ill-connected sequences, reinforce vividly the ultimate revelation on the Concorde—that there can be no more grand compositions, only fragments and vortices and "terrible" frescoes in the manner of *Guernica*.

In fractional increments, with oblique deformations and multiple iconological layerings, to this point *Gilles* radiates out into a series of "long perspectives," each leading to a picture dominated by the costumed figure of Gilles, seconded or opposed or "presented" by secondary figures inhabiting a separate visual plane. A life-size icon who reads himself in the eyes of others, the clown as artist as Parisian, soldier, diplomat, journalist, he floats through segmented narrative time, collector and critic, observer and participant, watching everything he sees— including himself interacting with others—in a complex play of forms that gather, separate, and re-form, creating an odd scrapbook filled with stills of Paris life, with reproductions of paintings, with snapshots, caricatures and *grotesques*, snippets of speeches and harangues and *faits divers*. The text becomes a vast "realist collage," resembling a cubist composition in which we distinguish many of the elements but perceive them in unexpected spatial relationships to one another. The novel's dialogues, meditations, polemics, journalism, fragments of dramas constitute a rich plastic *résidu* of images and roles and social groupings, a residue sorted, "filtered and settled," arranged and layered and superimposed like the sliding and overlapping planes in a cubist painting, a densely textured visual setting for a familiarly modern, unsteady hero, as ill at ease in the cafés of Paris as in the *boîtes* of Barcelona, at his best as an *amateur* of the visual arts, seeing everyone he meets as a picture. His vision crowded with images demanding to be arranged, but lacking the confidence in heroic portraiture and eternal icons of Malraux's heroes or the sheer verbal energy of Céline's Bardamu, Gilles fluctuates between outraged eloquence and angry silence. Most naturally Gilles is an impatient satirist, an inveterate citizen of Paris and of its small quarrels and grand squares and homey river running quietly through its middle, most at home somewhere in the literary neighborhood of Zola and Céline and Malraux and Aragon, taking walks and rereading his Flaubert and dreaming of Rastignac and Julien Sorel—a bookish veteran who would have wanted to be a painter.

Taking his daily walk from the Ile-St-Louis along the Seine toward the Concorde on February 6, 1934, Gilles composes the prescene: "the angle the Louvre makes in the curve of the river. . . . the angle [that] inscribes the empire of beauty over the city that remains, in spite of the smears and scribbles of the era, one of the most beautiful in human history" (*G* 430). At the Place de la Concorde he enters the vast open space, oddly empty, with just a few blurred, dark silhouettes at the edges. "At the end of a deserted street, at the edge of a square, a dark mass of police crouched. . . . An emptiness, a silence stretched along the quais and across the Tuileries. . . . Nothing was going to happen here today." With its monuments, its sense of scale, the square is a huge empty canvas, prepared for a historical painting in the grand manner, for a Delacroix. Gilles' gaze seeks out the missing elements in all directions. The Pont de la Concorde leading to the Palais Bourbon is blocked by armed men, men on horseback, "men and horses facing something absent. In the background, the normal swarm from the rue Royale is cut off sharply by a thin line of police" (*G* 430–31). Crossing over to the Left Bank on the Pont de Solférino, Gilles comes around behind the Chamber of Deputies; here he finds the narrow streets empty, each closed off at the end by a line of police. A gravitational pull from the direction of the boulevard Raspail draws him along the Esplanade des Invalides back toward the Seine.[33]

A spreading patch of demonstrators is gathering near the Chamber. Crossing the Pont Alexandre III, he sees another group around the Grand Palais. Forms hover at the edges of the empty Concorde, "a theater of stone and sky" aspiring dim shapes toward its center. The scene begins to take on shape, another crowd moving onto the square, a sacked taxi with a wounded man lying on it, blood, motion, shooting. The big painting is coming together. An overturned bus flames, men warm themselves near the fire. A large, moving group brightened with flags appears from the direction of the Rond-Point, les Anciens Combattants, a right-wing veterans group. Gilles moves through groupings of forms, patches coming together, then disintegrating almost immediately. Daubs of color appear, then are smudged as crowds coagulate and disperse. The historical painting is struggling to come into existence, pulsating and running and smearing. Other images are called up—Frédéric Moreau stumbling through the revolution of 1848, Fabrice del Dongo looking for the battle of Waterloo—but there is nothing to make them cohere, nothing to supply the missing painter's hand, the strokes to make a picture that holds, a Delacroix, *La Liberté guidant le peuple* (Fig. 24), formed of bodies and light and color and icons and an overpowering vision of chaos dominted by an ideal. Gilles' picture needs stronger lines of force, a central icon, a focus of compositional beauty, an illusion of purpose in the perception, to be able to fill this curve of the Seine with something that can hold next to the framed canvas hanging in the Louvre—a massive vision of flow and cohesion and transforming perception. Gilles' picture is slipping out of control before it is fully sketched in. The smudged canvas is put aside for a moment as he runs off to enlist other spectators and other participants, but in the tight little offices he visits literary-political figures huddle—tiny caricatures—afraid to come outdoors and engage in a real battle, on

33. Gilles' path retraces most of the trajectory of Delacroix's nostalgic walk through Paris in 1859, with the Rond-Point the western axis, the Louvre the eastern, moving from Right Bank to Left Bank to Right again. For a map of Delacroix's path, see Tom Prideaux, *The World of Delacroix, 1798–1863* (Amsterdam, 1984), 132–33. For a full discussion of Delacroix's "only major painting on a contemporary subject," see Lee Johnson, *The Paintings of Eugène Delacroix, A Critical Catalogue, 1816–1836* (2 vols.; Oxford, 1981), I, 144–51.

24. Eugène Delacroix, *La Liberté guidant le peuple*. 1830. Oil on canvas, 102½ ×
138 inches. Musée du Louvre, Paris.
Photo: Réunion des Musées Nationaux.

any side. Alone, Gilles returns to the Concorde and plunges into a preliminary oil sketch for a painted revolution. Intense color and drama fill
up a single paragraph:

> A partir de ce moment-là, il fut dans le tourbillon tour à tour cinglant et
> flasque des foules jaillissantes et refluantes, amoncelées et perdues. Sur
> le beau théâtre de pierre et de ciel, un peuple et une police, demi-choeurs
> séparés, essayaient vainement de nouer leurs furieuses faiblesses. Gilles
> courait partout aux points de plénitude qui lui apparaissaient dans la nuit et
> dans les lueurs et, quand il arrivait essoufflé, il trouvait un carré de bitume
> déserté qu'un corps couché ne comblait pas. (*G* 434)

> From that moment, he was caught up in the pulsating whirlpool of crowds
> spurting up and flowing backward, coming together and disintegrating. On
> this beautiful theater of stone and of sky, a people and a police, divided half-
> choruses, were trying vainly to unite their furious weaknesses. Gilles kept
> running to the patches of plenitude that were appearing in the darkness and

the patches of light and each time, arriving breathless, he found a bare patch of asphalt unfilled by a prone body.

But there is no grand painter, there is no orchestrating vision, and the picture falls apart as the darkness of the asphalt drinks up the puddles of color and night swallows up the picture. The scene ends, and the novel returns to spare modernist forms and subdued colors, to the satirical lithographer's crabbed strokes. There will be no grand composition, no Delacroix in the thirties. Gilles will leave Paris.

The final painted revolution, set in a small town in Estremadura during the Spanish civil war, closes the Epilogue of *Gilles*. The Epilogue's first part, composed largely of dialogues and cinematic effects—violence, dramatically underlit interiors, pans on streets and landscapes slipping into the distance—with Gilles appearing under the pseudonym Walter, seems a parody of scenes from Malraux's *L'Espoir* and is strangely out of character with the rest of the novel. Jean Lansard plausibly suggests that Drieu, tired by his massive work on the body of the novel, hastened its completion by inserting the Walter section, published earlier as a story, then adding to it the brief final episode.[34] The last scene, set in an abandoned bullring, carefully structured, deliberately and drenchingly plastic, forms a dramatic counterpoint to the Concorde scene, a *Götterdämerung* of surrender to war and annihilation painted into the Spanish landscape, a visual challenge to Picasso—once again as in 1925 in *L'Homme couvert de femmes* the painter with whom Drieu argues violently—and his *Guernica* (Fig. 25), which Robert Hughes has aptly called "the last great history-painting."[35] Drieu composes his scene in horizontals, as opposed to the vertical frontal assault of *Guernica;* muted tans and ochres and browns oppose the dazzling grisaille; a vortex that sucks everything to its center counters the angles and juttings and figures exploding outward in Picasso's "manifesto" for the Republican cause.

The tiny town Gilles visits as itinerant reporter appears, from the top of an old monument, almost totally flat on the flat landscape, dominated by two stone structures, to one side the ruins of an old Roman

---

34. For details on the earlier version of the Epilogue's first part, see Lansard, *Drieu La Rochelle*, I, 452.

35. Robert Hughes, *The Shock of the New* (New York, 1980), 110–11.

25. Pablo Picasso, *Guernica*. 1937. Oil on canvas, 137½ × 306 inches. Museo del Prado, Madrid. Copyright 1990 ARS N.Y./SPADEM.
Photo: Giraudon/Art Resource, N.Y..

aqueduct, one of its remaining arches silhouetted starkly against the blue sky, to the other an ugly modern bullring, "stupidly round, as much like a gas reservoir as anything else" (*G* 494). The Plaza de Toros, with its posters for events that never took place—a bullfight scheduled for the first week of July, 1936—forms a natural fortification, its open arcades now enclosed by concrete pierced by small apertures through which machine guns point out in all directions. From the top gallery of the Plaza, Gilles has a bird's-eye view of Spain, a "land of exile and grandeur," of that "horizontal vertigo" so remote from the rush of imagery with which Paris assaults the senses:[36]

> De là, on voyait toute l'Espagne: une immense étendue de plateaux et de chaines de montagnes qui alternaient et enchevêtraient leurs plans dans un chaos qui était un ordre complexe et tourmenté. Le froid était assez mordant et le pâle soleil d'hiver soutenait mal cette harmonie des bruns, des bistres, des fauves, des ocres, des terres de Sienne, que le soleil d'été pousse les uns par-dessus les autres vers un paroxysme unique. (*G* 495)

> From there, one could see all of Spain: an immense extent of plateaus and mountain chains that alternated and tangled their networks in a chaos that formed a complex and tormented kind of order. The cold was biting and the pale winter sun weakly supported this harmony of browns, bistres,

36. For Drieu's conception of "horizontal vertigo" and his planned but never written book, see "L'Espagne et Argentine," in *Drieu La Rochelle*, ed. Hanrez, 73.

fawns, ochres, Siennese earth tones that the summer sun pushes one on top of the other toward a single intensity.

Gilles walks inside this picture of Spain, this "new Orient," with its patches of subdued color remaining separated under the winter light, visible daubs, as in a Manet "prospect" or a cubist view of the Midi. As gunfire breaks out, he looks toward the Plaza, from whose steps flashes of scenes from Goya float up into his consciousness—"women, with their small feet laced and gay, climbing up the Plaza steps on Sundays" (*G* 497). In this remote corner of Europe the sputtering passions of Paris are flaring up, men are fighting and dying in scenes "that would be so exciting from the seat of a movie house on the Champs-Elysées" (*G* 497). Taking refuge in the interior of the bullring, looking up through the semidarkness of the *vomitoire*—the wide main exit of an amphitheater or a theater—at the sky, Gilles carefully plots the position of the door opposite the shooting, then turns in the other direction and climbs the interior stairs to a post at one of the loopholes. There he finishes his picture, firing, "applying himself to his composition," concentrating intently. There the novel ends.

Gilles dies on the barricades, not on the stones of Paris, but in a remote place, inside a dark, ugly stone structure from which he can see a ruined aqueduct, "a gigantic piece of old debris weighing on the landscape, like a meteor fallen from another planet" (*G* 495). The painted revolution in Spain comes together, a darkness within a paler darkness, a vortex on an alien landscape, a terrifying picture closer to Max Ernst's *Europe after the Rain* or *The Spanish Physician* than to Delacroix, a return to what Marjorie Perloff has called "the language of rupture." [37] In his essay "Le Héros de roman," Drieu explained his conviction that there could be no old "heroes," no middle-aged Julien Sorels, that the only option the novelist has is to kill his hero at the appropriate moment. [38] Gilles the *flâneur*, the dandy, ends his *vie de spectateur* by dying in the Orient, inside the bullring, in an anti-urban landscape, his bird's-eye view of the Spanish plains reduced to a gun sight through a small aperture in concrete, vision at once projected out and closed down, his painting gone in a few pages from "doing" Manet doing Goya back to

37. Marjorie Perloff, *The Futurist Moment: Avant-Garde, Avant Guerre, and the Language of Rupture* (Chicago, 1986).
38. Drieu La Rochelle, "Le Héros de roman," p. 1.

that apocalypse of futurism, of surrealism he had lashed out against in the twenties and satirized in the thirties.

Drieu's epic of the interwar years ends where it must, at the moment when the only answers seem to be big ones—manifesto paintings, huge novels, little wars paving the way for bigger ones. Gilles in Spain, inside the bullring, firing at an unseen enemy and expecting to die, is the logical culmination of Drieu's ongoing rereadings of World War I. Throughout the novel, Gilles' memories of battle fluctuate between romantic idealizations of heroism and the glories of conflict and another, infinitely darker view of war as a total revolution of matter, the elements unleashed, the reign of an unnatural "Nature" set in motion by the miscalculations of political bureaucrats and cheered on by all the "old men," a world exploding and destroying an entire generation. In the "Chronique des spectacles" Drieu tried to make sense of the war by reading the rituals that succeeded it. In *La Comédie de Charleroi* he reexamined the experience of the war from multiple retrospective distances and found himself unable from any angle to shape it into a stabile plastic whole.[39] In *Gilles*, the fruit of Drieu's maturity as a writer, the war is most of all *an absence*, a counterimage, *les arbres de Verdun* as opposed to the avenue du Bois. In the *Primavera* sequence Drieu calls the physical forms of war "la démocratie des éléments," 'the free rule of the elements,' by which he means chaos. The vision on the battlefields of Champagne that inserts an image out of Renaissance art over the debris beyond the parapet is a "miracle" and never happens again. Gilles' battlefield lyricism quickly "loses its color." The whole of *Gilles*, then, is *une permission*, the interlude between one war and another, a brilliant and devastating picture gallery of Paris and the provinces in the interwar years.

39. For an analysis of the multiple and unstable distances constructed in Drieu's 1934 novella and of his striking use of the phrase "the three old men" (Wilson, Clemenceau, and Lloyd George, who created an impossible peace), see Reck, "Drieu La Rochelle's *La Comédie de Charleroi*."

7

Mémoires de Dirk Raspe: Margins, Visions, Departures

Drieu's last, unresolved vision of the painted novel moves beyond the walls of the fictional picture gallery toward the unchronicled space where paintings begin to take on shape, in the artist's vision and on the canvas. *Mémoires de Dirk Raspe*—a fictionalized memoir conceived as "a reply to Van Gogh's painting" and loosely based on the painter's life— was written between late September, 1944, and mid-January, 1945, while Drieu lived in hiding in the countryside outside Paris.[1] Discovered at his death in Paris in March, 1945, and published in 1966, this sedimentation of a passage from vision into darkness has had an unquiet afterlife, stirred by sporadic gusts of interpretation, then once again allowed to settle into the obscurity and confusion surrounding Drieu's work.[2]

Fitful critical discussion of the novel has become mired in the dual hagiographies of Drieu and Van Gogh, both artists who committed suicide and whose work has been slow in finding rational assessment. One has only to read Frédéric Grover's account of *Dirk Raspe* as the pinnacle of Drieu's career as a novelist and the real reason for his suicide (because he found out he was a great writer!) to get some sense of the problems on the literary side of the fence.[3] Judging an unfinished novel by the same standards as work the author revised, rewrote, and worked over intensely is probably no more foolish than rereading an entire fictional career primarily as a prelude to its end. Not a culmination, not a

---

1. Drieu's characterization of his novel appears in Pierre Drieu La Rochelle, unpublished letter to Suzanne Tézenas, November, 1944, quoted in Pierre Andreu, Preface to Pierre Drieu La Rochelle, *Les Mémoires de Dirk Raspe* (Paris, 1966), 7. Hereafter cited in the text as *DR*.
2. The earliest and still one of the most perceptive analyses of Drieu's unfinished novel is Hanrez, "Le Dernier Drieu."
3. See Andreu and Grover, *Drieu La Rochelle*, 565–70.

touchstone work, *Dirk Raspe* is nonetheless an artistically logical and frequently compelling closure to Drieu's twenty year-long exploration of visual fiction. In the unforeseen "truce" between his first two suicide attempts and his last, Drieu was drawn to a *roman du peintre* in the tradition of Zola's *L'Oeuvre*.[4] Moving from his earlier heroes, who like the "center of consciousness" characters of Henry James have the vision of painters without possessing their plastic skills,[5] Drieu embarked on a new creative task as potentially complex as *Gilles:* to trace and penetrate a unique mode of vision, to relate that vision to a concrete historical and cultural world, and to mirror in verbal structures some of the most intensely seen and emotionally rendered images in modern art.

The two brief, deeply flawed novels Drieu published after *Gilles* mark phases of his discouragement with the timing and reception of what he considered his major work. *L'Homme à cheval* (1943), a dreamy mythological-poetic parable of the relationship between the man of action and the man of art and meditation set in Bolivia in the 1880s, collapses under the weight of cinematic and psychological mannerisms. *Les Chiens de paille* (1944), a disjointed fable of petty politics and dark personal meditations set in the occupied France of late 1942, is partially illumined by a flash of Rabelaisian-Célinean humor—occupied France seen as a huge food-trading fair decorated with political banners—and a visual sequence foreshadowing the directions of Drieu's last novel. Seen against their background, the habitués of a Parisian bistro painted a saturated Prussian blue by an unknown painter drunk on color (for the "blue-out" imposed by the war) look like Van Gogh portraits. In *Dirk Raspe* Drieu abandons the fables and mannerisms and cinematic games of *L'Homme à cheval* and *Les Chiens de paille* and turns to a first-person narrative, a modernist *roman du peintre* that traces the glimpses and dimmings, the affirmations and retrenchments, the fissures and strains and flashes of vision that mark a painter's discovery of vocation.

Drieu's growing interest in Van Gogh vividly reflects the French art historical context of the thirties. The first de La Faille catalogue raisonné in four volumes of Van Gogh's complete work appeared in Brussels and Paris in 1928. Quarrels over the attribution of some of the paintings began to surface, with de La Faille writing in *Formes* (an art

4. For a detailed account of Drieu's last years, see Reck, "Pierre Drieu La Rochelle."
5. For a brilliant and detailed exposition of this Jamesian theme and its techniques, see Viola Hopkins Winner, *Henry James and the Visual Arts* (Charlottesville, 1970).

journal to which Drieu contributed in the thirties), Elie Faure (whose work would be a major influence on Malraux's art histories) replying in 1930 in *L'Art Vivant*, and de La Faille counterreplying.[6] While Drieu and Malraux argued privately about Van Gogh, the museological world of Paris began to assess the immense impact of his painting on the non-salon painters of the century's first two decades. Detailed studies of Van Gogh's life began to appear in the Netherlands and to filter to Paris. Picture dealer Wilhelm Uhde's melodramatic essay "La Vie et l'oeuvre de Vincent Van Gogh" prefaced Ludwig Goldscheider's selection of paintings, drawings, and letters in the Phaidon volume of 1936. John Rewald's more scholarly articles in *L'Amour de l'Art* related Van Gogh's work to the development of Cézanne. Julius Meier-Graefe's deeply emotional biography, first published in Munich in 1921 and based almost entirely on Van Gogh's letters, appeared in London in 1922 in an equally passionate English translation by J. Holroyd-Reece and was widely circulated in Paris in a 1936 reissue. A one-volume French translation of Van Gogh's letters to his brother Theo, culled from the three-volume collection published in Amsterdam in 1914, appeared in Paris in 1937, as did art dealer Ambroise Vollard's *Souvenirs d'un marchand de tableaux*, with a chapter on Cézanne and Van Gogh. Painter Maurice Vlaminck confessed in *Le Ventre ouvert*, published in 1937, his stunned reaction at seeing Van Gogh's work for the first time in 1902.[7] With preparations under way for the 1937 Exposition Universelle, partisans of Van Gogh's work pressed for a major retrospective to be held in Paris.

In 1937 Drieu attended the important Van Gogh exhibit (226 works) held from June through October at the newly opened Palais de Tokio, where for the first time he immersed himself in the full sweep of a vision until then viewed piecemeal in small groupings and in printed reproductions. The early paintings and drawings on loan from Dutch collections and the impressive assemblage of portraits would be particularly important to Drieu's later fictional rendering of the genesis of Van Gogh's vision. The 1937 Van Gogh exhibit, mounted by art histo-

6. J. B. de La Faille, "Les Faux de Van Gogh," *Formes*, December, 1929; Elie Faure, "A propos des faux Van Gogh," *L'Art Vivant*, April 1, 1930; J. B. de La Faille, "Réponse à l'article de M. Elie Faure," *L'Art Vivant*, June 15, 1930.

7. For an account of other painters' reactions to Van Gogh's work, see Pierre Cabanne, "La Leçon de Van Gogh," in Camille Bourniquel et al., *Van Gogh* (Paris, 1968), 259–73.

rian René Huyghe and in part inspired by Alfred H. Barr, Jr.'s, 1935 Van Gogh show at New York's Museum of Modern Art, aroused considerable controversy in Paris art circles. The exhibit's odd, didactic arrangement, with biographical materials, paintings, drawings, and iconographical items displayed in separate rooms, with green background walls, and with a heavy emphasis on the painter's life and letters, set off a series of critiques that led Huyghe to defend his project eloquently in the pages of *Micromégas* and the *Revue des Deux Mondes*, arguing both for the importance of Van Gogh and for the significant role of museums in modern life.[8] The Parisian furor over Van Gogh's paintings, fueled by the growing legend of his difficult life, dramatic suicide, and slowly discovered influence on modern painting, appears never to have totally died down. To this day writing on Van Gogh, stirred by the fatal appeal of "artistic madness," or genetically inherited epilepsy, or painterly martyrdom through lead poisoning, tends to swell with hyperbole and bend under the weight of unverifiable speculation.[9] In the troubled years of the late thirties, to Drieu as to others, the ferment over the war in Spain, the political and cultural battles of Paris, and the rising specter of another European war all seemed connected somehow through the brilliant, violent, beautiful paintings that Van Gogh had been unable to sell in his lifetime.[10]

Drieu's choice of hero in 1944 is the logical culmination of his growing interest in Van Gogh's paintings and of his deepening sense of the war's futility. Pierre Andreu's contention in his preface to *Dirk Raspe* that until 1944 Drieu did not consider Van Gogh a significant modern painter or even mention him in his writings is incorrect. I have already noted references in letters composed during the writing of *Gilles* to

8. For defenses of the Paris show, see René Huyghe, "Querelles muséographiques—pour ou contre l'exposition Van Gogh," *Micromégas*, October 10, 1937; and Huyghe, "Le Rôle des musées dans la vie moderne," *Revue des Deux Mondes*, October 14, 1937. For a reprint of the New York show's catalogue, followed by an annotated bibliography of literature by and on Van Gogh through 1940, see *Vincent Van Gogh*, followed by *A Bibliography* (New York, 1966).

9. For a psychological reading of Van Gogh's illness, see Marthe Robert, "Le Génie et son double," in Bourniquel *et al.*, *Van Gogh*, 171–97. For a fascinating new theory, based on recent medical evidence, suggesting that Van Gogh's madness was caused by lead poisoning absorbed through the skin from cinnabar contaminated with red lead, see Berton Roueché, "Cinnabar," *New Yorker*, December 8, 1986, pp. 94–102.

10. For the history of the paintings' economic fortunes, see François Duret-Robert, "Destin de ses tableaux," in Bourniquel *et al.*, *Van Gogh*, 217–43.

"the apparently excessive but in reality so brilliantly observed" land-scapes of Van Gogh. In the late thirties, Drieu increasingly began to connect Van Gogh's emotionally expressive style with an imminent European apocalypse. In "Artistes et prophètes," a December, 1939, article intended for *La Nación* in Buenos Aires, Drieu mused on the Nazi exclusion of Van Gogh's paintings from German museums a few years earlier because he was considered a "dangerous" painter. He concluded that the Germans were—like most men of radical action—no more than ignorant *bourgeois* frightened of what they did not understand, brothers to those enemies of art guarded against by French museum regulations requiring visitors to check their umbrellas. "Hitler was simply sharpening the metal point at the end of a weapon dear to Joseph Prudhomme [the *bon bourgeois* of nineteenth-century caricature] and to Mister Chamberlain."[11] Seeing everywhere banality triumphing over artistic vision, convinced by July, 1944, that Europe would soon die over-whelmed by Russia and the United States, Drieu regarded Van Gogh's late paintings, "with their enormous suns rolling over ravaged fields," as prophecies of the apocalypse and thought of the painter himself as the artist "who would flood with light the last vision of unreality" (*DR* 7).

Van Gogh's letters vividly display the passions in art Drieu found im-mediately sympathetic: Delacroix, Daumier, the landscape painters, Watteau, Seurat.[12] At still another level, Van Gogh's letters—containing some of the most extraordinary passages on the plastic arts ever written by any painter—exerted what might be called a painterly refraction effect, leading Drieu to look in new ways at Ernest Meissonnier and Félix Ziem, whom Van Gogh called "master colorists," and at Adolphe Monticelli, Marseille-born disciple of Watteau and friend of Cézanne,

11. Pierre Drieu La Rochelle, "Artistes et prophètes," in *Drieu La Rochelle*, ed. Hanrez, 88–89.

12. My analysis of Van Gogh's tastes in painting and literature is based on a close reading of his letters. A particularly valuable collection of extended excerpts from the letters appears in A. M. Hammacher and Renilde Hammacher, *Van Gogh, A Documentary Biography* (London, 1982). The first important biography, also based on the letters, was Julius Meier-Graefe, *Vincent Van Gogh, A Biography*, originally published in Germany in 1921 and widely circulated both in France and the United States in J. Holroyd-Reece's translation (London, 1922, 1933, 1936). A more recent and up-to-date biography, incor-porating material suppressed by Joanna Van Gogh-Bonger, Theo Van Gogh's widow, ap-pears in Pierre Leprohon, *Vincent Van Gogh* (Paris, 1986).

whose late canvases Van Gogh considered precursors of his own use of heavy impasto and of paint applied directly from the tube.[13] In Van Gogh's rare ability to describe the specific qualities of work he admired, in his talent for evoking in words the sensations aroused in him by painting, Drieu found a painter himself offering a basis for fiction. Following the methodology of Van Gogh's extraordinary letter describing the gray-clad figure standing to the left of Franz Hals's and Friedrich Codde's *The Company of Captain Real* in Amsterdam as a modulated visual symphony in "orange, white, blue"—a letter that is itself a model for verbal description of plastic art—Drieu began to glimpse the possibility of a new type of picture gallery novel, a metatext tracing the crystallization of a creative vision by means of a series of pictures intensely seen, plastically described, leading the reader's gaze gradually forward toward an effect of pure light—a kind of inverse *Paradiso* ending in total destruction. As Drieu became increasingly saturated in the fall of 1944 in Van Gogh's letters, as he revisited in his mind Rembrandt and the world of the Dutch landscape painters, as he looked again at reproductions of Van Gogh's drawings and of his early, earth-colored paintings, he began at moments to see as Van Gogh might have seen.

Attracted by Van Gogh's attachment to literature and by his literary taste—as a passionate realist and a sporadic mystic—for Michelet, Baudelaire, Flaubert, Zola, and the English romantic poets, Drieu also became aware of the literary references in many of Van Gogh's paintings. Zola's *La Joie de vivre* sits on the table to the left of the still life *Oleanders* (1888). Van Gogh's letters specifically identify Pierre Loti's *Mme Chrysanthème* as the primary inspiration for *La Mousmé* (1888), a portrait of a young Provençal girl seen as *une Japonaise*.[14] The copies after Delacroix (Fig. 26), Millet, Daumier, and Rembrandt executed during Van Gogh's confinement at Saint-Rémy are at once gestures of homage and something close to a visionary form of literary illustration: drawings based on memory or on black and white reproductions, then

13. The most complete study of Monticelli's work is the exhibition catalogue prepared by Aaron Sheon, *Monticelli, His Contemporaries, His Influence* (Pittsburgh, 1978). For a useful discussion of the nostalgia wave of which Watteau and, later, Monticelli were a part and of the varying political implications of nineteenth-century defenses of eighteenth-century painting, see Haskell, *Rediscoveries in Art*, 59–64.

14. These connections are reviewed in Meyer Schapiro, *Van Gogh* (New York, n.d.).

26. Vincent Van Gogh, *Le Bon Samaritain, d'après Delacroix.* 1890. Oil on canvas, 28¾ × 23¾ inches. Rijksmuseum Kröller-Muller, Otterlo.
Photo: Rijksmuseum Kröller-Muller.

colored in "in a personal way." Almost alone among the painters of his time, Van Gogh delighted in novels that attempted to portray painters and admired what Zola had done in *L'Oeuvre*—creating a fiction sympathetic to the aims of painting without understanding its material conception from within—although he remarked that Zola's *Salon* reviews of 1866 were superficial and full of errors because the novelist did not know enough about art.[15] Van Gogh's encyclopedic memory for paintings, down to their placement on the walls of specific rooms in a museum, and his absolute recall of color and detail all contribute to the vivid literary appeal of his letters, some of which achieve in monumental detail effects Drieu had suggested in his own picture gallery novel, *Gilles*.

The novel *Dirk Raspe* owes as much to oppositions, however, as it does to sympathies. From the telling divergences between Drieu and Van Gogh, from those points of strain and conflict, of impossible "fit," that underline the desperate character of Drieu's last venture into fiction, come both the novel's unique character and its massive instability. Van Gogh was specifically *not* French, *not* a Parisian dandy (he disliked Paris and fled from it twice), *not* a devotee of elegance, and *not* fundamentally a satirist. Van Gogh was not involved in the wars and revolutions that informed Drieu's vision of modern French life. He died in 1890, on the threshold of modernism but to the far side of it. In choosing to write *for Van Gogh*—a foreigner of another time, a self-mortifying, self-styled peasant-prophet who rejected Paris and moved to the sun, a warrior of intensely personal battles, a "madman"—Drieu was literally *translating* himself into another century, another skin, other eyes, onto a different turf.

From this massive exercise in novelistic expatriation come the artistic counterrhythms and deepening fault lines of a text destined from its inception to remain unfinished, to form an imaginative plank out into the void. Drieu's novel—like Van Gogh's painting—points in the direction of ultimate abstraction, moving toward its own extinction. Becoming intensely immersed in the writing, Drieu lent himself fully to the joyous and ironic pretense of making a new—and impossible—beginning, noting in a journal entry of October, 1944, the splendid gratuitousness of his final fiction: "So I've learned nothing from experience, nothing has changed? I take it all up again: the journal, a novel. If all this continues, I'll end up writing on politics again" (*DR* 9). "If all this continues"—this ironic qualifying phrase underlines Drieu's complete awareness of his situation, in hiding, watching the *épuration* (the

15. For a useful exposition of reactions by a number of his contemporaries, who were themselves painters, to Zola's novel, see John Rewald, *Cézanne, A Biography* (New York, 1986), 161–86.

"settling of accounts" with collaborators in Paris) begin to gain momentum. As the novel became "a big, important machine," Drieu watched himself work: "I am writing *Mémoires de Dirk Raspe* facing the debris of a park mutilated by a hasty woodsman. I write eight pages effortlessly, without rereading what came before. I'm writing the whole novel without concerning myself with what I've already done; perhaps this way I can capture the groping about of life itself. Besides, in this type of thing, my memory is sure. I'll revise too much, later on, as I always do" (*DR* 10).

The four parts of *Dirk Raspe* share a common structure: an intensely visualized opening scene—the interior of an English country parsonage, London streets seen through fog under a low-hanging sky, the dark plain of the Belgian mining country, the interior of a cheap café in The Hague—followed by a slowly emerging nucleus of realization that scatters before it a series of portraits and smaller scenes, then a trailing off into silence as Dirk finds himself on the outer margins of a vision, facing undefined, imageless space.

This series of incomplete epiphanies, reminiscent of the shape of Joyce's *Portrait*, is—like the implied fictional structure of Drieu's 1923–1924 "Chronique des spectacles"—strangely negative. Dirk's realizations appear inverted, leading inward, moving away from understanding. The three major parts—the second, third, and fourth—of *Dirk Raspe* show vision narrowing and becoming constricted; a physical sense of possibilities becoming closed off haunts Dirk's awakening sense of artistic vocation. He describes, in cyclical waves, a feeling of pressure building up, concentrating, his eye beginning to exclude what it cannot use, his fingers sketching, his hand and arm painting like the outermost gestures of a spirit turning in around itself. With the novel stopped short of Van Gogh's stays in Paris, Arles, and Saint-Rémy—the center of what would have been Dirk's most joyous creative years as a painter—Drieu's "memoir" of a painter's road toward his most lasting work reads like a condemnation, a stumbling descent into a hell at whose center shines the hallucinating sun of Provence.

Dirk Raspe suggests many of the issues raised by the existence and the form of Van Gogh's letters. Beyond the significant literary questions of the relationship between the memoir and the painted self-portrait, between the forms of language and of pictures, between emotion and vision, Drieu's novel probes some even knottier—and still unexplored—questions about the total configuration of Van Gogh's painting and its literal inseparability from his "written" self.[16] Theo Van Gogh's widow, aware of the potential appeal of the huge cache of Vincent's letters her husband had scrupulously preserved, tried following his death in 1891 to assure that the fame of the paintings would precede that of the letters. With the publication of the letters in Amsterdam between 1914 and 1925, the already emerging legend of Van Gogh's life and personality became inseparable from his painting. Drieu, at once sensitive to the problems of Van Gogh's posthumous fame and attracted by its "fictionality," in 1944 set out—perhaps not consciously at first—to beat the odds by portraying the painter from an unguarded and almost inchoate perspective, not in letters written to be read by someone else but in a journal. To simplify and concentrate the many brief false starts of Van Gogh's life, Drieu combined all the early years— the least well-documented until recently—into a crudely symbolic period as a boarder with an English clergyman and his family. Drieu collapsed several periods of employment with foreign branches—in Paris, London, and The Hague—of the Goupil Galleries, owned by Van Gogh's relatives in Amsterdam, into Dirk's period of employment for London picture dealer Philip Mack. Three stabs at an evangelical vocation became a single stay with Belgian miners at Hoeuvre. The brief period of studying painting became Dirk's unhappy stay in The Hague. With the pieces sorted into relatively manageable heaps, Drieu proceeded to try to capture the vision and the voice and to follow, from the plastic and written evidence—"groping about" as he went—the difficult terrain that led to the *oeuvre* he was trying to understand from the inside.

When Dirk asks *while writing* how one can write more than a single page "sans s'empêtrer dans soi-même, se répéter, s'exploiter, s'ennuyer avec soi-même ou s'habituer à soi-même" (*DR* 32), 'without getting entangled in oneself, repeating oneself, getting bored or used to oneself,' Drieu is making explicit an important question raised by an attentive reading of Van Gogh's letters. Was Van Gogh, who wrote so much and so eloquently, aware of the intrinsically *literary* appeal of his writing?

16. A brief commentary on the relationship between Van Gogh's letters and his fame as a painter appears in John Rewald, "The Posthumous Fate of Vincent Van Gogh, 1890–1970," *Studies in Post-Impressionism* (New York, 1986), 244–54.

Did he glimpse what would over time come to seem the almost illustrative appeal of his painting, its look of translating almost literally fear and terror and religious fervor into corkscrew lines and whirling stars and fields that flee vertiginously into the uptilted, high horizon? The patterns of Van Gogh's life suggest that he often experienced himself as suspended between words and pictures. His serious hesitations between the life of a preacher and the life of a painter stemmed from a deep-seated conviction that both vocations were forms of the same enterprise, two different approaches to making the transcendent accessible. He deeply valued being understood; he sought to communicate with ordinary people, to find images that would have the appeal and the currency of colored illustrations. In capturing the dazzling and at times naive literariness of Van Gogh—his strange, sometimes quaint diction, his frequent reference to the Scriptures, his insistent and complex critique of art criticism, his highly personal theories of art history—by conceiving Dirk's memoirs as a collection of notes to the self, as an album of images and counterimages located beyond the margins of the novel, Drieu was attempting to write the novel that Van Gogh approached writing in his letters.

Van Gogh's unusual skill at communicating his insights verbally combines with Drieu's extensive knowledge about the physical dimensions of a painter's craft to make Dirk Raspe an immensely complex fictional character. Unlike Zola's Claude Lantier, whom John Rewald has characterized as the son of a novelist rather than of a painter, Dirk is, like the man he is modeled after, that most curious of artists—a painter who is also close to being a major writer.[17] Striking a largely successful balance between the tone of Van Gogh's own writing—intense, often ponderous, wearing its literariness heavily at times, insistently looking for the right words to communicate both the seen and the felt—and the traditional fragmentation of fictional journal entries—Alissa's journal in Gide's *La Porte étroite*—Drieu skillfully maneuvers the focus of Dirk's text to create strong visual and physical rhythms. Obvious lapses juxtaposed with passages of intense expansion recalling a Proustian visual sequence—the writer Bergotte in *La Prisonnière* looking at the little patch of yellow wall in Vermeer's *View of Delft*—point to the presence of a vast network of intertexts, some based on Van Gogh's detailed

17. Rewald, *Cézanne*, 166.

accounts of paintings (including an account of the *View of Delft*, concentrating most of all on the application of color, "citron yellow, pale blue and pearl-grey"), others based on Drieu's interest in fictional treatments of the experience of looking at painting.[18]

Mémoires de Dirk Raspe becomes the occasion for an impressive critique of the literary epiphany. By comparing what is seen in novels with what he himself sees, Drieu's character Dirk the painter suggests directions for a fuller and more accurate form of the literary epiphany, a form better suited to the internal necessities of plastic vision. Dirk would like to see more attention to modeling and relief. He wants novelists to visually "scan" their scenes several times, the way his own eyes take in views and paintings. He regrets the almost total absence of attention to the tactile impact of color. He notices that most novelists miss the intense identification of color with smell he often experiences. He looks for a radical expansion of the Baudelairean theory of *correspondances*—of synesthetic imagery—to include the intersense perceptions and reactions that arouse a painter to the physical application of paint to canvas. With the assistance of remarks scattered through Van Gogh's letters, in *Dirk Raspe* Drieu maps out some exciting avenues of exploration for bridging far more successfully than Zola ever did the distances between verbal art and painting. Whether Drieu would have succeeded in writing the painted novel he was groping toward early in 1945 we cannot know. Perhaps not. Perhaps it is the very nature of the painted novel—and the essence of its appeal—forever to reach toward an impossible fusion without achieving it.

Ironically conscious of the visual difficulties implicit in realist fiction, Dirk frequently stresses that he is not a novelist and therefore not obliged to make linguistic compromises or to pretend to "locate" and methodically spell out what he sees. After an unusually detailed verbal-visual portrait of the woman he comes to call Tristesse, Dirk notes:

> Je conçois que toutes ces descriptions n'auraient rien à faire dans un roman et n'ont rien à faire dans la littérature d'aucun genre, car qui peut se situer comme l'auteur par rapport à un visage, un paysage, des aîtres, prendre son angle? J'ai souvent constaté dans mes lectures qu'il est impossible de reporter sur un plan les indications données par un romancier sur une maison

18. Vincent Van Gogh, *The Complete Letters of Vincent Van Gogh* (3 vols.; London, 1958), II, 433–34. For an analysis of Proust's treatment of Vermeer, see Meyers, *Painting and the Novel*, 112–23.

ou un jardin. Mais ce qui est intéressant dans une description, ce sont les soins et les soucis qu'elle implique. Et puis ce livre n'est pas un roman, mais les mémoires d'un peintre, ou d'un homme qui. . . . (*DR* 179–80, ellipsis Drieu's)

I understand that all these descriptions would have no place in a novel and have nothing to do with literature of any genre, for who can situate himself in the author's place in relation to a face, a landscape, doorways and squares, who can assume his angle? In my readings I have often noticed that it is impossible to trace on a map the information a novelist provides about a house or a garden. But what is interesting in a description is the care, the effort it implies. Besides, this book is not a novel, but the memoirs of a painter, or a man who. . . .

Mirroring Van Gogh's passionate concern for portraiture, and his own, Drieu uses Dirk's scrutiny of faces—including his own in the mirror—to study the way the painter's eye passes from color to character and from character to color, the way his use of rough pigment textures and striking applications of reds and greens and blues—emanations of what Meyer Schapiro has called "a spectrally colored world"—in place of the strong light and shade of traditional portraiture gives the human face the quality of extraordinary landscape objects.[19] The portraits in *Dirk Raspe* trace a broad spectrum of representations of the human image. From the rough sketches of Mrs. Heywood and the ugly servant girl Sybil, to the early modernist full-length figure of the epicene Mr. Wristhelay surrounded by his expensive candelabras and looking like a figure out of Robert Delaunay—candlewax yellow circles upon circles from head to toe—to the magisterial harmonies and tensions of one of the greatest of Van Gogh's self-portraits, *Self-Portrait with Easel* (Fig. 27), Drieu attempts to follow the painter's gaze searching appearances and attempting to penetrate substance.

The novel opens with the interior of the Reverend Heywood's country parsonage, its floors and walls splashed with rectangles of green light reflecting off the lawn into the house, playing on the old sofas, then settling like slow and stagnant water in the corners of the rooms (*DR* 17), suggesting Matisse's mildly cubist *Piano Lesson* (1916), with a pale green triangle receding from the room where the boy sits playing out

19. Schapiro, *Van Gogh*, 18.

27. Vincent Van Gogh, *Self-Portrait with Easel.* 1887–1888. Oil on canvas, 25¾ × 20 inches. Rijksmuseum Vincent Van Gogh/Vincent Van Gogh Foundation, Amsterdam.
Photo: Stedelijk Museum.

past the balcony grillwork into the garden. Still uncertain of his direction and lacking compelling visual sources for this period in Van Gogh's paintings or letters, Drieu draws the visual structure of this period of Dirk's life from his own youthful memories of England. Several references in Drieu's letters to the novel's "three" parts suggest that he might ultimately have recast or eliminated entirely this first section, which converts Van Gogh's Dutch childhood into an idealized Rousseauist "natural upbringing." A background of light, quiet, and pale colors—even the Reverend Heywood's eyes are pale blue water, reflecting back everything they look at—leave the narrator free to grope with the process of learning to see and of finding ways to communicate his vision. As Dirk begins feebly to sketch, Drieu mixes images suggested by Van Gogh's earliest work—books on tables, worn pieces of furniture, glimpses of houses inhabited by the poor, church buildings—with others that suggest the background against which Dirk defines himself. Tiresome pre-Raphaelite reproductions connote the dismal artistic taste of the Heywood family, while the two older Heywood brothers—Robert the pastor to the poor and Cyril the would-be poet—represent the evangelical and artistic vocations.

The London cityscape opening part two traces one of Dirk's habitual walks through London after work at art dealer Philip Mack's picture gallery and introduces visually the recurrent themes of the section: Dirk's unfolding perception of the visual equivalences between things and people, his ongoing examination of line versus color as the central element in painting, his sensitivity to costumes and decorative detail, his vision of the city as an album of signs and sites, and, a bit later, his vivid reactions to the museum experience, his discovery of great painting, and his first dim awareness of the aesthetic battles concealed behind the facades of the London art world.

> Tout m'était bon, les lignes et les couleurs. Les figures des passants et les figures des maisons recevaient la même lumière, diffuse, humanisée, tout à fait assimilée à l'enfer humain dont elle semblait, dans le plafond du ciel, dans le gris opaque, la réverbération exténuée. Dans cet air humide, liquide, les couleurs étaient rares et choyées. Souvent effacées, brouillées par la suie, elles ressortaient soudain délavées, avec une force douce, soumise mais insistante. . . . C'était soudain un mur de briques d'un rose malade mais obstiné qui s'efforçait vers l'orange et dans un secret triomphe parvenait à le suggérer; ou bien un beige qui cherchait à me rendre la jouissance de ce

"tabac d'Espagne" que j'avais savouré déjà à Aterbury. . . . Ces beiges qui
s'ensoleillaient dans la bruine, ces roses qui rougeoyaient et découvraient
parfois dans leur coeur un pistil de carmin, cela était soutenu par la belle
baie des grands et forts chevaux pattus et par le cuivre de leurs superbes
harnais. Les vêtements des hommes et des femmes étalaient leurs touches
successives sur le fond terne soudain avivé des maisons. . . . Devant chaque
façade de briques tendant son suaire humide, trois marches de pierre blanche,
bien passées au blanc d'Espagne, traçait une barre rassurante et exaltante.
(*DR* 49–50)

Everything nourished me, lines, colors. The figures of passersby and the
figures of houses were bathed in the same diffused, humanized light, a light
totally assimilated to the human inferno whose exhausted reverberation it
appeared to be, in the ceiling of the sky, in the thick grayness. In this humid,
liquid air, colors were rare and carefully cultivated. Often erased, dimmed
by the soot, they would suddenly emerge washed clean, with a soft, subdued, but insistent force. . . . Suddenly there would be a brick wall of a
sickly but obstinate rose color that was trying to become orange and in a
kind of secret triumph succeeding in suggesting it; or a beige that was trying
to bring back to me the pleasure of that "Spanish tobacco" I had already
savored in Aterbury. . . . Those beiges that became sunny through the mist,
those rose colors that were going red and occasionally revealing at their
center a pistil of carmine, all of this was sustained by the handsome reddish-
brown vertical of the big, strong, thick-footed horses and by the copper of
their superb harnesses. The clothes of the men and women spread their successive touches on the dull background of the houses, lighting them up. . . .
In front of each brick facade spreading out its humid shroud, three white
stone steps, thickly painted with Spanish white, traced a reassuring and ex-
ultant horizontal stroke.

This is a London street scene as the early Van Gogh might have
painted it, the luminous overarching sky of seventeenth-century Dutch
painting reread through the imagery of Van Gogh's stays in Amsterdam
and Scheveningen—Drieu's memory of a Van Gogh painting superimposed over Van Gogh's memory of a Dutch landscape painting.
Dirk's text follows the painter's eye across and back again over the
scene, noting the intensity and interaction of colors, the diffused,
liquidy, varyingly intense light, the costumes of the small figures of pe-
destrians making bright notes of color against the dark walls of houses,
the architectural bay of the line of cab-horses and their copper harness
trim domesticizing and making a "story" of the view. The scenic pre-

sentation of the low sky, the enclosed sense of space, the restrained use of color seen as emerging from shadow and declaring itself in a few strong "notes," the deliberate compositional blending of light with sound and smell, the whole defined and "reassuringly" put in place by the repetition with each pair of steps of three heavy strokes of Spanish white, achieve the verbal rhythms and progressively built-up visual detail of a Van Gogh scene or letter on painting.

Visiting the museums of London, looking at the commercially successful paintings in Mack's gallery, Dirk begins to perceive a hierarchy of aesthetic levels. Comparing the quality of light in French painting with the skies of the Dutch, he finds it weak; the delicacy and originality of the French painters appear sickly to him: "Leur lumière n'était pas cette héroïne traquée qui vainquait dans les tourments et les supplices. Je regardais Watteau, Corot d'un oeil lointain. Les Flamands, c'était trop pour moi; Delacroix, c'était trop pour moi" (DR 58–59). 'Theirs was not that hunted heroine who wins out through torments and tortures. I looked at Watteau, at Corot with a distant eye. The Flemish painters were too much for me; Delacroix was too much for me.' Aroused by the physical stimulus of the smell of oil paints and varnish at a painter's studio, Dirk tries to paint. But the color he puts on canvas is formless; discouraged at never "possessing things" (DR 63), he returns to drawing in black and white.

The central revelation of Dirk's London stay is his confrontation in Philip Mack's locked back room—entered with a key deliberately left in the open—with Delacroix's La Femme au perroquet (Fig. 28), a small, exquisite painting of a nude that resumes "with an ease having nothing to do with facility the infinite battle between darkness and light" (DR 76).[20] Seeing in this canvas the physical representation of Genesis, "the assault of light on shadow," Dirk finds his vision temporarily transformed by Delacroix's use of color as line. But soon the London winter settles in, the light stops scintillating, the fog thickens. "Dans les musées, les toiles se mouraient, couvertes de croûtes mornes" (DR 102). 'In the museums, the canvases were dying, covered with dark crusts.' Depressed, Dirk thinks he was mistaken about the centrality of painting to his existence. In his rush to absorb colors, he has forgotten human beings; he has been misled "by appearances" (DR 104–105).

20. For a philosophical reading of Dirk's encounter with Delacroix, see Guy-Félix Duportail, "La Femme au perroquet," in Drieu La Rochelle, ed. Hanrez, 201–17.

28. Eugène Delacroix, *La Femme au perroquet*. 1827. Oil on canvas, 9¾ × 12¾ inches. Musée des Beaux-Arts, Lyon.
Photo: Studio Basset, Caluire (Lyon).

On the plain of Hoeuvre in the Belgian mining country Dirk seeks his religious vocation as evangelist to the poor. The third part opens with a scene resembling an early Van Gogh landscape. A desolate sea of fleeing fields and furrows, knobby trees, and crows, sparely dotted with squat, sturdy farmhouse buildings, executed in gradations of black, brown, and gray heightened with barely perceptible touches of blue, green, lighter gray, strokes of pale orange, presents a vision of light concealed inside shadow (*DR* 111–12). The scene's low, light-filtering sky, its compositional organization around several points of focus, the domestic scale of the vision of nature and its minute clarity of specific detail all mirror Van Gogh's conscious use, at this point in his development, of his Dutch roots. In Hoeuvre Dirk has deliberately separated himself from painting; he looks at no pictures and does not draw or paint. He does not need to flee to exotic places, as did Rimbaud and Gauguin, he boasts; he has "la tropique des mines" (*DR* 112), 'the tropic of the mines,' and the exotic mountains of the slag heaps. He is determined to see exclusively with "the other eye," *not* to become immersed in things. "Surely," he speculates, "Saint Francis carried all the painting of Fra Angelico within himself, but turned it aside" (*DR* 133).

But Dirk's physical struggle against the visual arts only increases the pressure; everything he looks at becomes a picture. The Belgian plain stretching away from the mine is a painting, a vision of dark brown "rich with a Siennese brown that gave it unexpected opulence." Light is concealed in even the most humble color: the "oily black," the twisted trees, a faint stroke of green, a thin patch of sun turns this dark country into "a distant Mediterranean place" (*DR* 162). Confused and wounded by his inability to renounce the world of appearances, Dirk goes out onto the plain at night at the height of an electrical storm. In a flash of lightning that turns the night into day, he sees revealed the light concealed in darkness: "Le jour terrible et créateur qui sculpte la nuit, fait jaillir la forme, le jour qui arrache à la nuit une vision, le jour des peintres, le jour de Rembrandt, de Delacroix!" (*DR* 167). 'The terrible, creating light that sculpts the night, from which form springs, the light that tears a vision from the night, the light of the painters, of Rembrandt, of Delacroix!' The vision of light being born out of darkness, of forms whitened and glowing against an undefined background, recalls a less apocalyptic but no less dramatic vision—Daumier's *L'Artiste à son chevalet* (Fig. 29), showing the artist himself as a form born out of darkness. Significantly, at the conclusion of the third part, the light of *Dirk Raspe* reaches from Delacroix to Daumier to Van Gogh.

The difficult and truncated fourth part opens on the interior of a café in The Hague, filled with a sticky, glaireous yellow light falling on small figures of men and women, a sea of slowly turning and oozing light punctuated with accents of red and green strikingly echoing the enclosed, menacing colored space of Van Gogh's *Café de nuit* (Fig. 30). Dirk the painter-spectator sits in the café watching and sketching the "comedy of forms" (*DR* 175) that he has begun to seek in his work, the substance and design of those metaphysical skeletons hidden beneath the clothes and the flesh. In the vertigo of colored light and strong human smells Dirk begins to experience himself as an *object* threatened by what he sees.[21] The joy of knowing himself a painter is also beginning to become tainted by an expanding awareness of the world of con-

---

21. For an excellent discussion of the odd effect of perspective in Van Gogh's paintings recalled by this sequence in Drieu's novel, see Schapiro, *Van Gogh*, 29–32.

29. Honoré Daumier, *L'Artiste à son chevalet. ca.* 1870. Oil on panel, 13¼ × 10¼
inches. Phillips Collection, Washington, D.C.
Photo: Phillips Collection.

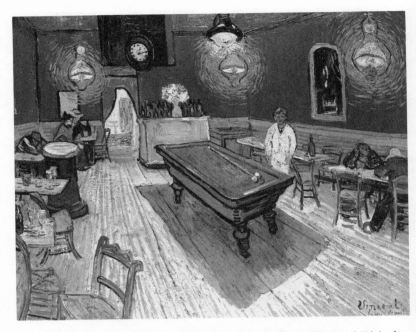

30. Vincent Van Gogh, *Café de nuit*. 1888. Oil on canvas, 28½ × 36¼ inches. Yale University Art Gallery, New Haven, Bequest of Stephen Carlton Clark, B.A. 1903.
Photo: Yale University Art Gallery.

temporary art. Dirk is taking note of the dangerous role of art critics; he is learning of the public's hostility to originality; he is made uneasy by the current triumph of impressionism, which he reads as a triumph of surface and facility, as realism gone disastrously astray. "In the faces of Renoir I read the perverted ascesis of a materialist era" (*DR* 215). Depressed by the lack of sunshine and lonely for the company of real painters, disappointed in his courtship of a young widow, Dirk quickly approaches the artistic despair that will drive him to leave Holland and go to Paris.

As Drieu neared the end of the fourth part of *Dirk Raspe*, he grew tired and discouraged; his writing became choppy and terse, the voice of Dirk increasingly dim and inarticulate. Andreu and Grover have speculated that it might have been interesting to read, had Drieu written it, the part of *Dirk Raspe* based on Van Gogh's two years in Paris. But Drieu's deepening sense of physical decrepitude, his belief that suicide was the only possible resolution to his collaborationist activities, and— most important of all—his conviction that the world being born in the final months of the war was not one he wanted to live in were all brought inevitably to a head by the organic form of his new literary venture. At the end of the Hague section, Drieu reached the unforeseen dead end built into the text—Van Gogh's fundamental dislike of and sense of alienation in Paris, mirrored in his concentration in the paintings of that period on what T. J. Clark has aptly characterized as the unfilled spaces and empty margins on the edges of the city and on self-portraits—some twenty-five in less than two years.[22]

With the end of the Dutch portion of the novel, Drieu's fictionalized memoir came up against a period of Van Gogh's life for which there are practically no letters, when what biographer Pierre Leprohon calls the "conducting thread" of the painter's life breaks.[23] For the years 1886–1887, Van Gogh's written voice is suddenly silent. Thinking the flaw was in the biographies he had at hand, in December, 1944, Drieu asked a friend to send him a volume of Van Gogh's collected letters. When they arrived, he wrote, "Alas! These are just extracts" (*DR* 9). At that point Drieu moved toward the end of his own expatriation and the beginning of Van Gogh's. In mid-January, 1945, Drieu stopped writing. A few weeks later, he went back to Paris, where he died by his own hand on March 15, 1945, a few months before the official end of the other war that framed his life.

22. Clark, *The Painting of Modern Life*, esp. 25–30, 191–92. For a rich exploration of Van Gogh's Paris stay, based on recent research, see also the catalogue of the Musée d'Orsay's first major special exhibit, *Van Gogh à Paris* (Paris, 1988).
23. Leprohon, *Vincent Van Gogh*, 189.

Bibliography

WORKS BY PIERRE DRIEU LA ROCHELLE

Books

Reprinted editions are indicated by date only, except when the publisher differs from the original.

Avec Doriot. Paris: Gallimard, 1937.

Beloukia. Paris: Gallimard, 1936.

Blèche. Paris: Gallimard, 1928; rpr. Lausanne: Editions Rencontre, 1964.

Charlotte Corday; Le Chef. Paris: Gallimard, 1944.

Les Chiens de paille. Paris: Gallimard, 1944; rpr. 1964.

Chronique politique 1934–1942. Paris: Gallimard, 1943.

La Comédie de Charleroi. Paris: Gallimard, 1934; rpr. 1960.

Les Derniers Jours. With Emmanuel Berl. 7 vols. Paris, 1927; facsimile rpr. 1 vol. Paris: Jean-Michel Place, 1979.

Doriot ou la vie d'un ouvrier français. Saint-Denis: Editions Populaires Françaises, 1936.

Drôle de voyage. Paris: Gallimard, 1933; rpr. 1977.

L'Eau fraîche. Cahiers de Bravo, XVIII, Supplement for August, 1931.

Ecrits de jeunesse. Paris: Gallimard, 1941.

Etat civil. Paris: Gallimard, 1921; rpr. 1977; Paris: Collection L'Imaginaire, 1980.

L'Europe contre les patries. Paris: Gallimard, 1931.

Une Femme à sa fenêtre. Paris: Gallimard, 1929; rpr. 1976.

Le Feu follet. Paris: Gallimard, 1931.

Le Feu follet, suivi de Adieu à Gonzague. Paris: Gallimard, 1963.

Fond de cantine. Paris: Gallimard, 1920.

Fragment de mémoires, 1940–1941. Paris: Gallimard, 1982.

Le Français d'Europe. Paris: Editions Balzac, 1944.

Genève ou Moscou. Paris: Gallimard, 1928; rpr. following *Le Jeune Européen,* 1978.

Gilles. Censored edition, Paris: Gallimard, 1939.

Gilles. Complete edition, with new Preface. Paris: Gallimard, 1942; rpr. 1962; Paris: Livre de Poche, 1969.

Histoires déplaisantes. Paris: Gallimard, 1963.

L'Homme à cheval. Paris: Gallimard, 1943; rpr. Paris: Club des Librairies de France, 1962; Paris: Livre de Poche, 1965.

L'Homme couvert de femmes. Paris: Gallimard, 1925; rpr. 1977.

Interrogation. Paris: Nouvelle Revue Française, 1917.

Le Jeune Européen. Paris: Gallimard, 1927.

Le Jeune Européen, suivi de Genève ou Moscou. Paris: Gallimard, 1978.

Journal d'un homme trompé. Paris: Gallimard, 1934.

Journal d'un homme trompé. Definitive edition, including "Le Mannequin." Paris: Gallimard, 1978.

Mémoires de Dirk Raspe. Paris: Gallimard, 1966.

Mesure de la France. Paris: Grasset, 1922.

Mesure de la France, suivi de Ecrits, 1939–1940. Paris: Grasset, 1964.

Ne plus attendre (Notes à leur date). Paris: Grasset, 1941; rpr. in *Chronique Politique 1934–1942.*

Notes pour comprendre le siècle. Paris: Gallimard, 1941.

Plainte contre inconnu. Paris: Gallimard, 1924.

Plaintes contre inconnue. Paris: Frédéric Chambriand, 1951.

Récit secret. Limited edition of 500 copies. N.p.: A.M.G., 1951.

Récit secret, suivi du Journal, 1944–1945 et d'Exorde. Paris: Gallimard, 1961.

Rêveuse bourgeoisie. Paris: Gallimard, 1937; rpr. 1960.

Socialisme fasciste. Paris: Gallimard, 1934.

La Suite dans les idées. Paris: Au Sans Pareil, 1927.

Sur les écrivains. Edited by Frédéric Grover. Paris: Gallimard, 1966.

La Voix. Paris: Edouard Champion, 1928; rpr. in *Journal d'un homme trompé.* Paris: Gallimard, 1978.

Prefaces, Translation

Czapska, Maria. *La Vie de Mickiewicz.* Paris: Plon, 1931.

Hemingway, Ernest. *L'Adieu aux armes.* Paris: Gallimard, 1931.

Lawrence, D. H. *L'Homme qui était mort.* Translated by Pierre Drieu La Rochelle and Jacqueline Dalsace. Paris: Gallimard, 1934.

Le Marois, J.-L. *L'Ode aux voiles du Nord.* Paris: Henri Jonquières, 1928.

Articles and Reviews

This comprehensive listing of 244 items includes a number of articles and reviews that do not appear in other bibliographies of Drieu's occasional writings.

Some of these items replace the "phantom articles," repeated over the years, created by excerpts reprinted with vague citations and with titles different from those Drieu gave them. A number of other items dating from the early 1920s, the late 1930s, and from the *Nouvelle Revue Française* between December, 1940, and June, 1943, many of considerable literary and artistic import, are included here for the first time.

"A certains." *Nouvelle Revue Française*, LV (August, 1941), 200–205.

"A propos d'*A l'ouest rien de nouveau.*" *Nouvelle Revue Française*, XXXIII (November, 1929), 725–30. [On Remarque's *All Quiet on the Western Front*]

"A propos d'un certain A.V." *Nouvelle Revue Française*, L (January, 1938), 117–23.

"A propos d'un roman anglais." *Nouvelle Revue Française*, XXXV (November, 1930), 721–31. [On Huxley's *Point Counter Point*]

"A propos des cent cinquante ans de la Révolution Française." *Revue de Paris*, June 1, 1939, pp. 577–89.

"A vomir." *Emancipation Nationale*, November 18, 1938, p. 5.

"Abus de confiance." *Ecrits Nouveaux*, No. 5 (1922), 3–10.

"L'Actualité du XXe siècle." *Nouvelle Revue Française*, LIII (November, 1939), 782–89.

"L'Affaire Hanau." *Nouvelles Littéraires*, November 8, 1930, p. 1.

"L'Agent double." *Nouvelle Revue Française*, XLV (July, 1935), 26–37.

"Air de février 34." *Nouvelle Revue Française*, XLII (March, 1934), 568–69.

"Allemagne européenne." *Nouvelle Revue Française*, LVI (January, 1942), 104–12.

"Alliances spirituelles et politiques." *L'Europe Nouvelle*, XVIII (June 1, 1935), 524.

"L'Ami du front." In *Drieu La Rochelle, Cahiers de l'Herne*, edited by Marc Hanrez. Paris: Editions de l'Herne, 1982, pp. 107–109.

"*Anicet ou le panorama*, par Louis Aragon." *Nouvelle Revue Française*, XVII (July, 1921), 97–99.

"Anniversaire." *Nouvelle Revue Française*, XLIV (February, 1935), 319–20.

"Appel aux communistes." *La République*, November 30, 1935, p. 1.

"Après la métropole, c'est l'Empire." *Emancipation Nationale*, February 18, 1938.

"Aragon." *Nouvelle Revue Française*, LV (October, 1941), 483–88.

"Artistes et prophètes." In *Drieu La Rochelle, Cahiers de l'Herne*, edited by Marc Hanrez. Paris: Editions de l'Herne, 1982, pp. 88–91.

"*Athènes et l'Attique*, par Emmanuel Boudot-Lamotte; *Les Arts primitifs français*, par Léon Gischia et Lucien Mazenod." *Nouvelle Revue Française*, LVI (February, 1942), 247–49.

"Au temps des surréalistes," *Je Suis Partout*, March 11, 1938; rpr. in *Sur les écrivains*, edited by Frédéric Grover. Paris: Gallimard, 1966, pp. 314–17.

"Audiberti." *Nouvelle Revue Française*, LVII (September, 1942), 358–63.

"L'Automate." *La Revue Européenne*, XXXV (January, 1926), 11–15.

"*Aux Fontaines du désir*, par Henry de Montherlant." *Nouvelle Revue Française*, XXIX (November, 1927), 676–81.

"Avant le *Retour de l'U. R. S. S.*" *Emancipation Nationale*, September 26, 1936; rpr. in *Sur les écrivains*, edited by Frédéric Grover. Paris: Gallimard, 1966, pp. 158–59. [On Gide, Malraux, communism]

"Avant-Propos." *Nouvelle Revue Française*, LIV (December, 1940), 1–6.

"Avènement d'un prince décapité." *L'Oeuf Dur*, November, 1922, pp. 2–3.

"Après le *Retour de l'U. R. S. S.*" *Emancipation Nationale*, November 21, 1936; rpr. in *Sur les écrivains*, edited by Frédéric Grover. Paris: Gallimard, 1966, pp. 160–61. [On Gide, Aragon, Malraux, communism]

"Bilan." *Nouvelle Revue Française*, LVIII (January, 1943), 103–11.

"Bilan 'fasciste,' 15 juillet 1944." *84 (i.e. Quatre-Vingt-Quatre)*, December, 1950, pp. 47–55.

"Les Bords de la Seine." *La Revue Européenne*, 1927, pp. 1237–44.

"*Les Bourgeois et l'amour*, par Emmanuel Berl." *Nouvelle Revue Française*, XXXVII (December, 1931), 944–47.

"La Brouille des poètes et du public." *Le Figaro*, September 24, 1934.

"Camping." *Le Figaro*, September 11, 1935, p. 1.

"Le Cas de Violette Nozières." *Marianne*, September, 1933, p. 10.

"Ce qui meurt en Espagne." *Nouvelle Revue Française*, XLVII (November, 1936), 920–22.

"Ceux qui tremblotent." *Emancipation Nationale*, June 12, 1937, p. 2.

"*Chacun pour soi*, par Constance Colline." *Nouvelle Revue Française*, XL (January, 1933), 186–87.

"Chardonne." *Nouvelle Revue Française*, LV (December, 1941), 737–41.

"Cherbourg, port Américain." *Rivarol*, March 22, 1951.

"Chesterton, orthodoxe paradoxale." *La Flèche*, June 27, 1936; rpr. in *Sur les ecrivains*, edited by Frédéric Grover. Paris: Gallimard, 1966, pp. 120–26.

"*Choléra*, par Jean Delteil." *Nouvelle Revue Française*, XXII (February, 1924), 227–28.

"Christianisme et paganisme." *Nouvelle Revue Française*, LV (November, 1941), 610–15. [On Montherlant, addressed to him]

"Chronique des spectacles." *Nouvelle Revue Française*, XXI (November, 1923), 588–96.

"Chronique des spectacles." *Nouvelle Revue Française*, XXI (December, 1923), 729–35.

"Chronique des spectacles." *Nouvelle Revue Française*, XXII (January, 1924), 96–99.

"Chronique des spectacles." *Nouvelle Revue Française*, XXII (February, 1924), 209–13.

"Chronique des spectacles." *Nouvelle Revue Française*, XXII (March, 1924), 342–46.

"Cinq lettres inédites." *Magazine Littéraire*, No. 143 (December, 1978), pp. 35–36.

"La Coalition rebelle." *Emancipation Nationale*, September 19, 1936.

"Colonialisme." *Nouvelles Littéraires*, November 30, 1935, p. 1.

"Commentaire sur 'L'U. R. S. S. et les Anglo-Américains,' par Demarée Bess du *Saturday Evening Post*." *Révolution Nationale*, March 4, 1944, pp. 1, 2.

"Commentaire sur 'La Trahison en Afrique du Nord, vue par un Américain.'" *Révolution Nationale*, April 22, 1944, p. 4.

"Commentaire sur 'La Trahison en Afrique du Nord, vue par un Américain, II.'" *Révolution Nationale*, April 29, 1944, p. 4.

"Commentaire sur 'Le Testament de Pierre le Grand.'" *Révolution Nationale*, June 10, 1944, p. 1.

"La Concision, vertu française: Racine ou Hugo?" *Nouvelles Littéraires*, May 4, 1940, pp. 1–2.

"*La Condition humaine* en 1933." *La Nación* (Buenos Aires), 1933, rpr. in *Sur les écrivains*, edited by Frédéric Grover. Paris: Gallimard, 1966, pp. 284–91. [On Malraux]

"Confidences." *Révolution Nationale*, January 29, 1944, p. 1.

"Le Corps." *Nouvelle Revue Française*, LIV (February, 1941), 352–55.

"Le Corps des Français." *Le Figaro*, April 7, 1936, p. 1.

"La Crise décisive du capitalisme et le communisme de demain." *La Revue Européenne*, August, 1928, pp. 787–94.

"Cuadro de la literatura francesa actual." *La Nación* (Buenos Aires), September 19, 1937, p. 1.

"Dans l'atroce et vivante réalité." In *Drieu La Rochelle, Cahiers de l'Herne*, edited by Marc Hanrez. Paris: Editions de l'Herne, 1982, pp. 114–20.

"*Demain la France*, par Robert Francis, Thierry Maulnier, Jean-Pierre Maxence." *Nouvelle Revue Française*, XLIII (August, 1934), 287–91.

"Dérivation de la violence." *Nouvelles Littéraires*, April 11, 1936, p. 1.

"Les Deux jeunesses." *Le Figaro Littéraire*, May 9, 1936, p. 5.

"Deux opinions sur le Front commun (en collaboration avec Bertrand de Jouvenel)." *Lutte des Jeunes*, June 3, 1934, pp. 1, 4, 5.

"Deuxième lettre aux surréalistes." *Les Derniers Jours*, February 15, 1927, pp. 3–5.

"Dialogue avec un pauvre de droite." *Lutte des Jeunes*, March 25, 1934, p. 2.

"La Dictature dans l'histoire." *Nouvelles Littéraires*, August 18, 1934, p. 1.

"Diderot." In *Tableau de la littérature française de Corneille à Chenier*. 2 vols. Paris: Gallimard, 1939, II, 303–13.

"Discours aux Français sur les etrangers." *Revue Hebdomadaire*, October 9, 1926, pp. 141–61.

"Le Don." In *Drieu La Rochelle, Cahiers de l'Herne*, edited by Marc Hanrez. Paris: Editions de l'Herne, 1982, pp. 75–83.

"L'Echec de Doriot et la défaite de Blum." *Emancipation Nationale*, June 26, 1937.

"Une Ecole des chefs." *Marianne*, June 24, 1936, p. 9.

"L'Economie de Barrès." *Nouvelles Littéraires*, December 8, 1923, p. 3.

"L'Ecrasement des Latins par les Anglo-Saxons." *Révolution Nationale*, February 12, 1944, p. 1.

"Edouard Bénès et son peuple." *Marianne*, January 23, 1935.

"En Afrique." *Révolution Nationale*, April 8, 1944, p. 1.

"En marge, I." *Révolution Nationale*, March 25, 1944, p. 1.

"En marge, II." *Révolution Nationale*, July 15, 1944, p. 1.

"Encore et toujours Nietzsche." *Je Suis Partout*, March 3, 1939, rpr. in *Sur les écrivains*, edited by Frédéric Grover. Paris: Gallimard, 1966, pp. 91–94.

"Encore les toits de Paris." In *Mesure de la France, suivi de Ecrits, 1939–1940*. Paris: Grasset, 1964, pp. 210–20.

"Enquête sur l'opinion publique." *Marianne*, April 25, 1934, p. 10.

"Enquête sur le rajeunissement de la France. Réponse de M. Drieu La Rochelle." *Grande Revue*, March, 1934, pp. 13–17.

"Entre Bude et Pest." *Marianne*, November 28, 1934.

"Entre l'hiver et le printemps." *Nouvelle Revue Française*, LVI (April, 1942), 468–79.

"Ephémères." *Révolution Nationale*, February 19, 1944, pp. 1, 4.

"L'Espagne et Argentine." In *Drieu La Rochelle, Cahiers de l'Herne*, edited by Marc Hanrez. Paris: Editions de l'Herne, 1982, pp. 71–74.

"Esquisse." *Nouvelle Revue Française*, LVI (May, 1942), 567–71.

"*Essai sur la misère humaine*, par Brice Parain." *Nouvelle Revue Française*, XLII (June, 1934), 1019–21.

"Est-ce l'automne de l'humanité?" *Chronique filmée du mois*, March, 1937.

"L'Etat inspiré." *Le Figaro*, May 23, 1935.

"Eternelle Germanie." *Je Suis Partout*, January 12, 1940, p. 7.

"L'Europe aux 'extra-Européens.'" *Révolution Nationale*, January 15, 1944, p. 1.

"L'Europe socialiste." In *Drieu La Rochelle, Cahiers de l'Herne*, edited by Marc Hanrez. Paris: Editions de l'Herne, 1982, pp. 121–24.

"L'Exemple." *Nouvelle Revue Française*, XXIV (April, 1925), 649–51. [On Jacques Rivière]

"L'Exemple canadien." *Petit Dauphinois*, February 1, 1940, p. 1.

"L'Exemple de l'Algérie." *Emancipation Nationale*, October 22, 1937.

"Expériences." *Nouvelle Revue Française*, XXIV (April, 1925), 649–51.

"Une femme et une déesse." *La Revue Européenne*, 1928, pp. 1026–32.

"Le Fait." *Nouvelle Revue Française*, LIV (June, 1941), 855–59.

"La Fin des doctrines." *Nouvelles Littéraires*, February 22, 1936, p. 1.

"La Fin des haricots." *Nouvelle Revue Française*, LVII (December, 1942), 744–51.

"La Fin du Parti Radical et de l'esprit petit-bourgeois." *Revue Hebdomadaire*, July 3, 1926, pp. 5–16.

"Les Français et le voyage." *France-Japon*, VII (January, 1940), 21–23.

"France, Angleterre, Allemagne." *Deutschland-Frankreich*, Vierteljahresschrift des Deutschen Instituts, Paris, 1943, fascicule 3, pp. 28–42.

"La France découvre l'Italie." *Marianne*, December 26, 1934.

"La Gaîeté française." *L'Europe Nouvelle*, XVIII (February 23, 1935), 180–81.

"Goya." *L'Europe Nouvelle*, XVIII (May 11, 1935), 455–56.

"Le Grand Bonheur ancestral." *Emancipation Nationale*, November 5, 1937.

"Grosses échéances." *L'Homme Nouveau*, March, 1935.

"Guerre et révolution." *Nouvelle Revue Française*, XLII (May, 1934), 887–88.

"La Guerre mondiale de 1936." *Nouvelle Revue Française*, LVIII (April, 1943), 503–12.

"Guerres de religion." *La République*, October 19, 1935, p. 1.

"Le Héros de roman: De Fabrice à Gilles." *Nouvelles Littéraires*, December 16, 1939, p. 1.

"Hitler et Staline." *L'Europe Nouvelle*, XVIII (November 9, 1935), 1094–95.

"Hommage à L.-P. Fargue: Rôdeur, gourmand." *Feuilles Libres*, June 1927, pp. 51–53.

"L'Homme mûr et le jeune homme." *Nouvelle Revue Française*, XLIV (February, 1935), 190–210.

"Un Homme, une femme." *Nouvelle Revue Française*, LIV (May, 1941), 720–26. [On Céline]

"La Hongrie et ses voisins." *Marianne*, December 12, 1934.

"L'Idée de décadence." *La Revue Européenne*, 1928, pp. 557–76.

"Ils n'ont rien oublié ni rien appris." *Je Suis Partout*, June 23, 1941, p. 8.

"L'Instinct de la guerre." *Nouvelles Littéraires*, November 25, 1933, p. 1.

"L'Intelligence et l'espace." *Nouvelle Revue Française*, XLVIII (March, 1937), 471–72.

"L'Italie remise à neuf." *Marianne*, January 2, 1935, p. 2.

"L'Italie Sociale." *Marianne*, January 9, 1935, p. 3.

"*Le Journal* d'André Gide." *La Nación* (Buenos Aires), December 31, 1939; rpr. in *Sur les écrivains*, edited by Frédéric Grover. Paris: Gallimard, 1966, pp. 254–58.

"Jugement de l'auteur sur lui-même; Une Ville d'Europe." In *Anthologie de la nouvelle prose française*. Paris: Le Sagittaire, 1926, pp. 343–53.

"Une Leçon vieille de vingt ans." *Emancipation Nationale*, November 11, 1938, p. 2.

"Lettre à un ami gaulliste." *Révolution Nationale*, August 12, 1944, p. 1.

"Lettre d'un agent secret." *Feuilles Libres*, May–June, 1926, pp. 3–7.

"Libéraux." *Nouvelle Revue Française*, LVII (November, 1942), 601–607.

"Lindbergh et ma vie." *Nouvelle Revue Française*, XXX (May, 1928), 608–13.

"Littérature communisante." *L'Europe Nouvelle*, XVIII (June 22, 1935), 602.

"Littérature du Front Commun." *L'Europe Nouvelle*, XVIII (July 20, 1935); rpr. in *Sur les écrivains*, edited by Frédéric Grover. Paris: Gallimard, 1966, pp. 155–57.

"Malraux, l'homme nouveau." *Nouvelle Revue Française*, XXXV (December, 1930), 879–85. [On *Les Conquérants, La Voie royale*]

"Mauriac." *Nouvelle Revue Française*, LV (September, 1941), 243–50. [On *La Pharisienne*]

"Maurras ou Genève." *Nouvelle Revue Française*, LIV (February, 1940), 243–46.

"*Ma vie sans moi*, par Armand Robin." *Nouvelle Revue Française*, LIV (December, 1940), 111–12.

"La Mauvaise conscience des bourgeois." *L'Europe Nouvelle*, XVIII (August 17, 1935), 798–99.

"Méditation entre les deux tours." *Gazette de Lausanne*, May 1, 1936, p. 5.

"*Méditation sur un amour défunt*, par Emmanuel Berl." *Nouvelle Revue Française*, XXV (December, 1925), 750–51.

"Mémoires inédits." *Nouvelles Littéraires*, January 16 and 23, 1964, pp. 1, 7, and 7.

"*Le Messager* de Bernstein." *Nouvelle Revue Française*, XLII (January, 1934), 148.

"Mesure de l'Allemagne." *Nouvelle Revue Française*, XLII (March, 1934), 450–61.

"Mesure et démesure dans l'espirit français." *Combat*, July, 1937, pp. 104–105.

"Mitos e imperios." *La Nación* (Buenos Aires), June 2, 1940, Sec. 2, p. 1.

"Le Monde pharisien." *Nouvelle Revue Française*, XLIII (August, 1934), 309–10.

"Montesquieu ou le pire et le meilleur." *Je Suis Partout*, April 21, 1939, p. 10.

"Le Mouvement dramatique." *Revue de Paris*, I (1930), 926–36.

"Ne nous la faîtes pas à l'oseille." In *Drieu La Rochelle, Cahiers de l'Herne*, edited by Marc Hanrez. Paris: Editions de l'Herne, 1982, pp. 27–29.

"Le Norvège en France." *Petit Dauphinois*, May 5, 1940, p. 1.

"Notes sur l'Allemagne." *Défense de l'Occident*, February, 1958, pp. 136–43. [Written December, 1944]

"Notes sur la Suisse." *Nouvelle Revue Française*, LVIII (March, 1943), 376–84.

"Notes vraiment peu politiques." *Nouvelle Revue Française*, LVII (August, 1942), 229–37. [On Daudet, Robin, Guillevic, Follain]

"Notre allure." *Le Figaro*, June 16, 1934, pp. 1–2.

"Notre force et la faiblesse des autres." *Emancipation Nationale*, March 26, 1938, p. 2.

"*Nouvel empire*, par Fritz von Unruh." *Nouvelle Revue Française*, XXV (November, 1925), 627–30.

"Nouvelle époque." *L'Homme Nouveau*, January, 1935.

"La Nouvelle fidelité." *L'Homme Nouveau*, September 1, 1935.

"La Nuit du 4 août." *Révolution Nationale*, May 21, 1944, p. 1.

"Paris part pour la guerre." *Annales*, August 3, 1934.

"Paris, ville d'exilés." *Nouvelles Littéraires*, January 28, 1933, p. 1.

"Le Parti de la bonne humeur." *Emancipation Nationale*, July 10, 1937, p. 5.

"Le Parti vivant." *Emancipation Nationale*, July 3, 1937, p. 5.

"Pas de concentration." *Emancipation Nationale*, September 2, 1938.

"Paul Adam." *Nouvelle Revue Française*, XIV (April, 1920), 577–79.

"Pauvre Europe." *Révolution Nationale*, April 15, 1944, p. 1.

"La Pensée du P.P.F." *Emancipation Nationale*, June 10, 1938.

"*La Percée*, par Jean Bernier." *Littérature*, II (September–October, 1920), 37.

"Perspectives socialistes." *Révolution Nationale*, March 11, 1944, pp. 1, 2.

"*Pétrus*, de Marcel Achard." *Nouvelle Revue Française*, XLII (January, 1934), 149.

"Pierre Emmanuel." *Nouvelle Revue Française*, LVII (October, 1942), 466–83.

"La Plaine Hongroise." *Marianne*, December 5, 1934.

"*Plutarch a menti*, par Jean de Pierrefeu." *Nouvelle Revue Française*, XXII (August, 1923), 220–23.

"Le Poème en prose." *Nouvelles Littéraires*, May 5, 1934, pp. 1, 2.

"La Poésie au-dessus de tout." *Je Suis Partout*, September 3, 1937; rpr. in *Sur les écrivains*, edited by Frédéric Grover. Paris: Gallimard, 1966, pp. 310–14.

"*La Politique et les partis*, par Emmanuel Berl." *Europe*, May, 1932, pp. 135–39.

"La Position de l'Eglise." *La République*, November 2, 1935, p. 1.

"Pour ceux qui veulent s'instruire." In *Drieu La Rochelle, Cahiers de l'Herne*, edited by Marc Hanrez. Paris: Editions de l'Herne, 1982, pp. 104–106.

"Pour sauver la peau des Français." *Le Flambeau*, June 27, 1936.

"Premier appel aux communistes." *La République*, November 9, 1935, p. 1.

"Premier Article de Critique, ou La Poutre." *Littérature*, II (June 1920), 13–15.

"Près d'une mitrailleuse." *Le Figaro*, September 11, 1936, p. 1.

"*Présentation de Swift*, par A. Petitjean; *Le Journal à Stella*, traduit par Renée Volloteau." *Nouvelle Revue Française*, LIII (November, 1939), 800–802.

"Prestige de la femme." *Le Figaro*, February 21, 1936, p. 1.

"Le Printemps dans la ville." *Le Figaro*, May 15, 1935, pp. 1, 3.

"Procès-verbal." With Louis Aragon *et al. Littérature*, II (December, 1920), 2–4.

"Professeurs marxistes." *L'Europe Nouvelle*, XVIII (August 24, 1935), 821.

"Propos parmi les ruines." *Révolution Nationale*, June 25, 1944, p. 1.

"Propos sans illusions." *Je Suis Partout*, June 12, 1937; rpr. in *Sur les écrivains*, edited by Frédéric Grover. Paris: Gallimard, 1966, pp. 163–67.

"*Le Puits de Jacob*, par Pierre Benoît." *Nouvelle Revue Française*, XIV (June, 1925), 1069–70.

"Quand les femmes votent." *Le Figaro*, January 11, 1935, p. 1.

"Quelques écrits 'farfelus.'" In *Drieu La Rochelle, Cahiers de l'Herne*, edited by Marc Hanrez. Paris: Editions de l'Herne, 1982, pp. 23–24.

"Questions d'avenir." *Nouvelle Revue Française*, LVI (February, 1942), 229–33. [On Daniel-Rops]

"El Racionalismo francès y su critica francesa." *La Nación* (Buenos Aires), November 3, 1939.

"Radio-dialogue avec Frédéric Lefèvre." Cited in Frédéric Grover, *Drieu La Rochelle*. Paris: Gallimard, 1962, pp. 217–19. [Recorded in 1939, never broadcast]

"Récidive à propos de Bourget." *Je Suis Partout*, January 6, 1939, p. 8.

"Réflexions sur le 6 février." *Lutte des Jeunes*, February 25, 1934.

"*La Reine morte*, par Henry de Montherlant." *Nouvelle Revue Française*, LVIII (February, 1943), 249–56.

"La Relève de Barrès." *Emancipation Nationale*, December 3, 1937; rpr. in *Sur les écrivains*, edited by Frédéric Grover. Paris: Gallimard, 1966, pp. 162–64.

"Repères." *Nouvelle Revue Française*, LIV (January, 1941), 200–207.

"Réponse à Claudine Chomez: 'En vous relisant . . . Drieu La Rochelle.'" Cited in Frédéric Grover, *Drieu La Rochelle*. Paris: Gallimard, 1962, pp. 215–16.

"Réponse à Pierre Varillon." In "Enquête sur les maîtres de la jeune littérature." *Revue Hebdomadaire*, IV (November 4, 1922), 93–94.

"Retour au front pendant la Guerre d'Espagne." In *Drieu La Rochelle, Cahiers de l'Herne*, edited by Marc Hanrez. Paris: Editions de l'Herne, 1982, pp. 84–87.

"*Le Réveil des morts*, par Roland Dorgelès." *Nouvelle Revue Française*, XXI (September, 1923), 358–61.

"Robinson." In *Drieu La Rochelle, Cahiers de l'Herne*, edited by Marc Hanrez. Paris: Editions de l'Herne, 1982, pp. 35–49.

"Romanciers du XIXe siècle." *Je Suis Partout*, December 16, 1938, p. 8.

"*Russie 1927*, par Alfred Fabre-Luce." *Nouvelle Revue Française*, XXX (February, 1928), 252–55.

"Saint-Denis," *Nouvelle Revue Française*, XLV (October, 1935), 627–28.

"Saint-Denis contre les vieilles routines." *La Liberté*, June 18, 1937, p. 5.

"Le Salut de la jeunesse." *La Liberté*, May 25, 1937, p. 2.

"Le Sang dans les veines d'un mot." *Feuilles Libres*, May–June, 1928, pp. 79–89.

"Une Semaine à Berlin." *Nouvelle Revue Française*, XLII (February, 1934), 393–94.

"Si j'étais La Roque." *Lutte des Jeunes*, Mau 20, 1934.

"Le Siècle des maréchaux." *Révolution Nationale*, December 18, 1943, p. 1.

"*Signes des temps*, par Maurice Martin du Gard." *L'Oeuf Dur*, June, 1922, p. 10.

"Signification sociale." *Revue du Siècle*, July–August, 1933, 89–93. [On Mauriac]

"Socialisme à l'épreuve." *Révolution Nationale*, June 3, 1944, p. 1.

"Solitude de Buenos Aires." *L'Intransigeant*, January 6, 1934; rpr. in *Sur les écrivains*, edited by Frédéric Grover. Paris: Gallimard, 1966, pp. 119–20. [On J. L. Borges]

"*Le Songe*, par Henry de Montherlant." *Nouvelle Revue Française*, XX (February, 1923), 455–56.

"Sous le dôme." *Nouvelle Revue Française*, LIV (March, 1941), 492–96.

"Sur les lettres d'un propriétaire noble." *L'Europe Nouvelle*, XVIII (January 19, 1935), 61–62.

"Un Tableau militaire." *La Liberté*, June 11, 1937, p. 2.

"Los Techos de Paris." *La Nación* (Buenos Aires), March 17, 1940, p. 2.

"Témoignage dans 'L'Affaire Barrès.'" With André Breton *et al. Littérature*, III (August, 1921), 20–24.

"Thèses." *Révolution Nationale*, May 6, 1944, p. 1.

"Le Toboggan du pouvoir." *Le Figaro*, June 19, 1935; p. 1.

"Une Tradition française." *L'Assaut*, December, 1936.

"Les Trois tares du Front Populaire." *Emancipation Nationale*, January 21, 1938.

"Troisième lettre aux surréalistes." *Les Derniers Jours*, July 8, 1927, pp. 1–17.

"Valéry contre Pétain?" *L'Europe Nouvelle*, XVIII (January 26, 1935), 80–81.

"*Vauban*, par Daniel Halévy." *Nouvelle Revue Française*, XXI (October, 1923), 484–86.

"La Vénus de Milo vivante et cruelle." *Le Figaro*, November 10, 1936, p. 1.

"*La Vénus internationale*, par Pierre Mac Orlan." *Nouvelle Revue Française*, XXI (October, 1923), 496–98.

"La Véritable erreur des surréalistes." *Nouvelle Revue Française*, XXV (August, 1925), 166–71.

"Verra-t-on un parti national et socialiste?" *Lutte des Jeunes*, March 25, 1934, p. 2.

"Vers une conception réaliste de l'homme." *Emancipation Nationale*, July 22, 1938.

"Les Vertus d'un grand parti." *Emancipation Nationale*, March 11, 1938, p. 2.

"La Vieille force radicale." *Emancipation Nationale*, July 26, 1938.

"Vingt-deux ans en 1789." *Je Suis Partout*, June 9, 1939, p. 8. [On Saint-Just]

"Le Visiteur." *Drieu La Rochelle, Cahiers de l'Herne,* edited by Marc Hanrez. Paris: Editions de l'Herne, 1982, pp. 110–11.

"Le Vrai dix-neuvième siècle." *Je Suis Partout,* November 25, 1938, p. 8.

"Vrai socialisme français." *Le Fait,* December 7, 1940.

"La Violencia en Europa." *La Nación* (Buenos Aires), September 21, 1936, p. 8.

"Vocabulaire politique." *Littérature,* III (March, 1921), 17–18.

"Voyages." *Je Suis Partout,* November 26, 1937, p. 8.

"Les Voyages." *Petit Dauphinois,* April 18, 1940.

"Y a-t-il des siècles littéraires?" *Nouvelles Littéraires,* February 17, 1940, p. 1.

SECONDARY SOURCES

Books and Articles

For full publication data on exhibition catalogues and pamphlets listed below, see Exhibition Catalogues, the final category in this Bibliography.

Abetz, Otto. *Histoire d'une politique franco-allemande (1930–1950): Mémoires d'un ambassadeur.* Paris: Stock, 1953.

Adler, Renata. "The Perils of Pauline." *New York Review of Books,* August 14, 1980, pp. 26–36.

Agulhon, Maurice. "Politics, Images, and Symbols in Post-Revolutionary France." In *Rites of Power: Symbolism, Ritual, and Politics Since the Middle Ages,* edited by Sean Wilentz. Philadelphia, 1985, pp. 177–205.

Albérès, R.-M. *Histoire du roman moderne.* Paris: Albin Michel, 1962.

———. *Portrait de notre héros.* Paris: Le Portulan, 1945.

Alexandrian, Sariane. *Surrealist Art.* New York, 1985.

Altick, Richard. *The Shows of London.* Cambridge, Mass., 1978.

Andreu, Pierre. *Drieu, témoin et visionnaire.* Paris: Grasset, 1952.

———. "*Gilles,* une somme romanesque." *Magazine Littéraire,* No. 143 (December, 1978), 32–34.

Andreu, Pierre, and Frédéric Grover. *Drieu La Rochelle.* Paris: Hachette, 1979.

Aragon, Louis. *Aurélien.* Paris: Gallimard, 1944.

———. "L'Essai Max Ernst." In *Ecrits sur l'art moderne.* Paris: Flammarion, 1981, pp. 312–21.

———. *La Peinture au défi.* 1930; rpr. in *Les Collages.* Paris: Hermann, 1965.

Arland, Marcel. "*Etat civil,* par Pierre Drieu La Rochelle." *Nouvelle Revue Française,* XVIII (April, 1922), 491–95.

———. "*Drôle de voyage,* par Drieu La Rochelle." *Nouvelle Revue Française,* XL (June, 1933), 980–83.

————. "*Gilles*, par Drieu La Rochelle." *Nouvelle Revue Française*, LIV (March, 1940), 403–406.

————. "Sur un nouveau mal du siècle." *Nouvelle Revue Française*, XXII (February, 1924), 156.

Arnheim, Rudolph. *The Genesis of a Painting: Picasso's "Guernica."* Berkeley, 1962.

Balvet, Marie. *Itinéraire d'un intellectuel vers le fascisme: Drieu La Rochelle*. Paris: Presses Universitaires de France, 1984.

Baron, Jacques. "Mesure de la poésie." In *Pierre Drieu La Rochelle, Cahiers de l'Herne*, edited by Marc Hanrez. Paris: Editions de l'Herne, 1982, pp. 301–12.

Barr, Alfred H., Jr. *Picasso: Fifty Years of His Art*. New York, 1946.

————. *Picasso: Forty Years of His Art*. New York, 1939.

Barthes, Roland. *Essais critiques*. Paris: Editions du Seuil, 1964.

————. *Mythologies*. Paris: Editions du Seuil, 1957.

Bastier, Jean. *Pierre Drieu La Rochelle, soldat de la grande guerre 1914–1918*. Paris: Editions Albatros, 1989.

Benda, Julien. "Socialisme fasciste, par Drieu La Rochelle." *Nouvelle Revue Française*, XLVI (January, 1936), 295.

Berl, Emmanuel. *Mort de la pensée bourgeoise*. Paris: Grasset, 1929.

Beucler, André. "De Maupassant à Drieu La Rochelle." *Revue des Deux Mondes*, October, 1964, pp. 351–59.

Boisdeffre, Pierre de. *Les Ecrivains de la nuit, ou la littérature change de signe*. Paris: Plon, 1973.

————. "Faut-il réhabiliter Drieu?" *Figaro Littéraire*, November 25, 1978, pp. 88–89.

————. *Une Histoire vivante de la littérature d'aujourd'hui*. Paris: Le Livre Contemporain, 1958.

Bondy, François. "The Comeback of Drieu La Rochelle." *Encounter*, LIV (July, 1980), 44–46.

Bradby, David, Louis James, and Bernard Sharratt, eds. *Performance and Politics in Popular Drama*. Cambridge, Eng., 1980.

Brasillach, Robert. "Drieu La Rochelle, toujours amer." In *Les Quatre jeudis, images d'avant-guerre*. Paris: Les Sept Couleurs, 1951; rpr. in Brasillach, *Oeuvres complètes*. 10 vols. Paris: Au Club de l'Honnête Homme, 1964, vol. 8, pp. 309–14.

————. *Portraits*. Paris: Plon, 1935.

Brosman, Catharine Savage. "Les Nourritures Sartriennes." In *Littérature et gastronomie: Huit études réunies et préfacées par Ronald W. Tobin*, edited by Ronald W. Tobin. Tübingen, 1985, pp. 229–63.

Cabanne, Pierre. "La Leçon de Van Gogh." In Camille Bourniquel *et al.*, *Van Gogh*. Paris: Flammarion, 1968, pp. 259–73.

Cadwallader, Barrie. *Crisis of the European Mind: A Study of André Malraux and Drieu La Rochelle*. Cardiff, 1981.

Caws, May Ann. *The Eye in the Text: Essays on Perception, Mannerist to Modern*. Princeton, 1981.

———. *Reading Frames in Modern Fiction*. Princeton, 1985.

Clark, Kenneth. *Landscape into Art*. Boston, 1961.

———. *The Nude: A Study in Ideal Form*. Princeton, 1956.

Clark, T. J. *The Painting of Modern Life: Paris in the Art of Manet and His Followers*. New York, 1985.

Cobb, Richard. *French and Germans, Germans and French*. Hanover, N.H., 1983.

Colette. *Le Journal*, November 25, 1934. Quoted in Frédéric Grover, *Drieu La Rochelle*. Rev. Paris: Gallimard, 1979, pp. 219–20.

"Conversation [de Frédéric Grover] avec Aragon." In *Drieu La Rochelle, Cahiers de l'Herne*, edited by Marc Hanrez. Paris: Editions de l'Herne, 1982, pp. 395–400.

Crémieux, Benjamin. *"Fond de cantine."* *Nouvelle Revue Française*, XV (December, 1920), 948–51.

———. *"La Suite dans les idées; Le Jeune Européen; Les Derniers Jours*, par P. Drieu La Rochelle." *Nouvelle Revue Française*, XXIX (November, 1927), 671–76.

Crow, Thomas E. *Painters and Public Life in Eighteenth-Century Paris*. New Haven, 1985.

Cryle, P. M. *The Thematics of Commitment: The Tower and the Plain*. Princeton, 1985.

Cruickshank, John. *Variations on Catastrophe: Some French Responses to the Great War*. Oxford, 1982.

Daix, Pierre. *Aragon, une vie à changer*. Paris: Editions du Seuil, 1975.

Dale, Jonathan. "Drieu La Rochelle: The War as 'Comedy.'" In *The First World War in Fiction*, edited by Holger Klein. London, 1976, pp. 63–72.

De La Faille, J. B. "Les Faux de Van Gogh." *Formes*, December, 1929.

———. "Réponse à l'article de M. Elie Faure." *L'Art Vivant*, June 15, 1930.

Défense de l'Occident, special issue on Drieu La Rochelle, L (February, 1958).

Delagrange, Gérard. *Le Cas Pierre Drieu La Rochelle*. Paris: Imprimerie du Palais, 1969.

Demarcy, Richard. *Eléments d'une sociologie du spectacle*. Paris: Union Générale d'Editions, 1973.

Desanti, Dominique. *Drieu La Rochelle ou le séducteur mystifié*. Paris: Flammarion, 1978.

Descotes, Maurice. *Le Public du théâtre et son histoire*. Paris: Presses Universitaires de France, 1964.

Desnoyers, Jean. *Etude médico-psychologique sur Pierre Drieu La Rochelle.* Paris: Foulon et Cie, 1965.

Dijkstra, Bram. *Cubism, Steiglitz, and the Early Poetry of William Carlos Williams.* Princeton, 1969.

Dominique, Pierre. *Quatre hommes entre vingt: Montherlant, Morand, Cocteau, Drieu.* Paris: Le Divan, 1924.

Dorgelès, Roland. *Images.* Paris: Albin Michel, 1975.

————. "Utrillo, Drieu La Rochelle." *Revue des Deux Mondes,* November, 1975, pp. 282–89.

Dumur, Guy, ed. *Histoire des spectacles.* Encyclopédie de la Pléiade. Paris: Gallimard, 1965.

Duportail, Guy-Félix. "La Femme au perroquet." In *Pierre Drieu La Rochelle, Cahiers de l'Herne,* edited by Marc Hanrez. Paris: Editions de l'Herne, 1982, pp. 199–215.

Duret-Robert, François. "Destin de ses tableaux." In Camille Bourniquel *et al., Van Gogh.* Paris: Hachette, 1968, pp. 217–43.

"Entretien entre André Malraux et Frédéric Grover sur Drieu La Rochelle." (Paris, October, 1959.) In *André Malraux, I, du "farfelu" aux 'Antimémoires',* edited by Walter G. Langlois. Paris: Revue des Lettres Modernes, 1972, pp. 149–73.

Faure, Elie. "A propos des faux Van Gogh." *L'Art Vivant,* April 1, 1930.

Fell, John L. *Film and the Narrative Tradition.* Norman, Okla., 1974.

Fernandez, Ramon. "*Blèche,* par Drieu La Rochelle." *Nouvelle Revue Française,* XXXI (December, 1928), 867–69.

————. "*Une Femme à sa fenêtre,* par Drieu La Rochelle." *Nouvelle Revue Française,* XXXIV (May, 1930), 767–69.

————. "*L'Homme couvert de femmes,* par Drieu La Rochelle." *Nouvelle Revue Française,* XXVI (March, 1926), 356–57.

————. "*Plainte contre inconnu,* par Drieu La Rochelle." *Nouvelle Revue Française,* XXIV (January, 1925), 104–106.

Field, Frank. *Three French Writers and the Great War: Studies in the Rise of Communism and Fascism.* Cambridge, Eng., 1975.

Fitch, Noel Riley. *Sylvia Beach and the Lost Generation: A History of Literary Paris in the Twenties and Thirties.* New York, 1983.

Flagothier, François. "Le Point de vue dans l'oeuvre romanesque de Drieu La Rochelle." *Revue des Langues Vivantes,* XXXIV (1968), 170.

Flower, John E. *Writers and Politics in Modern France, 1909–1961.* London, 1977.

Frank, Bernard. *La Panoplie littéraire.* Paris: Julliard, 1958.

Fry, Edward. *Cubism.* New York, n.d.

Fry, Roger. *Vision and Design.* London, 1923.

Fussell, Paul. *The Great War and Modern Memory.* New York, 1975.

Gache-Potin, Sylvie, and Scott Schaefer. "Impressionism and the Sea." In *A Day in the Country: Impressionism and the French Landscape*, 273–98. Exhibition catalogue.

Gallagher, M. D. "Drieu et Constant: Une parenté." *Revue d'Histoire Littéraire de la France*, LXXIII (July–August, 1973), 666–75.

———. "Influences anglaises." In *Drieu La Rochelle, Cahiers de l'Herne*, edited by Marc Hanrez. Paris: Editions de l'Herne, 1982, pp. 337–54.

Gauthier, Xavière. *Surréalisme et sexualité*. Paris: Gallimard, 1971.

Gershman, Herbert S. *The Surrealist Revolution in France*. Ann Arbor, 1969.

Gillet, Louis. "A l'Exposition: Chefs-d'oeuvre de l'art français." *Revue des Deux Mondes*, September 15, 1937, pp. 274–303.

Girardet, Raoul. "Notes sur l'esprit d'un fascisme français, 1934–1939." *Revue Française de Science Politique*, V (June–September, 1955), 529–46.

Green, Mary Jean. *Fiction in the Historical Present: French Writers and the Thirties*. Hanover, N.H., 1986.

———. "Toward an Analysis of Fascist Fiction: The Contemptuous Narrator in the Works of Brasillach, Céline, and Drieu La Rochelle." *Studies in Twentieth Century Literature*, X (Fall, 1985), 81–97.

Grenier, Jean. "Une Conversation avec Drieu La Rochelle." *Nouvelle Nouvelle Revue Française*, I (December, 1953), 387–90.

Grover, Frédéric. "Céline et Drieu La Rochelle." In *Louis-Ferdinand Céline, Cahiers de l'Herne*. Paris: L'Herne, 1963, pp. 302–305.

———. *Drieu La Rochelle*. Paris: Gallimard, 1962; rev., Collection "Idées." Paris, 1979.

———. *Drieu La Rochelle and the Fiction of Testimony*. Berkeley, 1958.

———. "*Le Feu follet:* Un roman qui fait encore peur." *Magazine Littéraire*, No. 143 (December, 1978), 28–31.

———. "Malraux et Drieu La Rochelle." *André Malraux, I, du "farfelu" aux 'Antimémoires'*, edited by Walter G. Langlois. Paris: Revue des Lettres Modernes, 1972, pp. 61–93.

Hagstrum, Jean H. *The Sister Arts: The Tradition of Literary Pictorialism and English Poetry from Dryden to Gray*. Chicago, 1958.

Hammacher, A. M., and Renilde Hammacher. *Van Gogh, A Documentary Biography*. London, 1982.

Hanrez, Marc. "Le Dernier Drieu." *French Review*, XLIII, Special number (Winter, 1970), 144–57.

———, ed. *Drieu La Rochelle, Cahiers de l'Herne*. Paris: Editions de l'Herne, 1982.

Hanson, Anne Coffin. "Manet's Pictorial Language." In *Manet*, 20–28. Exhibition catalogue.

Haskell, Francis. *Rediscoveries in Art: Some Aspects of Taste, Fashion and Collecting in England and France.* Ithaca, N.Y., 1976.

Hecksher, William. *Art and Literature: Studies in Relationship.* Durham, 1985.

Heller, Gerhard. "La *NRF* de Drieu." In *Un Allemand à Paris, 1940–1944.* With the collaboration of Jean Grand. Paris: Editions du Seuil, 1981, pp. 40–58.

Herbert, Robert L. "Method and Meaning in Monet." *Art in America,* LXVII (September, 1979), 90–108.

Hervier, Julien. *Deux individus contre l'histoire: Drieu La Rochelle, Ernst Jünger.* Paris: Klincksieck, 1978.

———. "Drieu, l'Espagne, la guerre et la mort." *Revue de Littérature Comparée,* No. 236 (October–December, 1985), 397–407.

———. "Drieu La Rochelle ou le roman inachevé." *Magazine Littéraire,* No. 143 (December, 1978), 25–27.

———. "Le Romancier et ses doubles." In *Drieu La Rochelle, Cahiers de l'Herne,* edited by Marc Hanrez. Paris: Editions de l'Herne, 1982, pp. 127–46.

Hines, Thomas M. "Myth, Misogyny, and Fascism in the Works of Drieu La Rochelle." *Modern Fiction Studies,* XXIV (Summer, 1978), 197–207.

———. *Le Rêve et l'action: Une Etude de 'L'Homme à cheval' de Drieu La Rochelle.* Columbia, S.C., 1978.

Hughes, Robert. *The Shock of the New.* New York, 1980.

Huyghe, René. "Querelles muséographiques—pour ou contre l'exposition Van Gogh." *Micromégas,* October 10, 1937.

———. "Le Rôle des musées dans la vie moderne." *Revue des Deux Mondes,* October 14, 1937.

———. *Watteau.* Translated by Barbara Bray. New York, 1970.

Isaak, Jo Anna. *The Ruin of Representation in Modernist Art and Texts.* Ann Arbor, 1986.

Jaloux, Edmond. "'La Valise vide,' par Drieu La Rochelle." *Nouvelles Littéraires,* December 5, 1924.

Johnson, Lee. *The Paintings of Eugène Delacroix, A Critical Catalogue, 1816–1836.* Vol. I of 2 vols. Oxford, 1981.

Jouret, Jacques. "Quand Van Gogh inspirait Drieu La Rochelle." *Revue des Langues Vivantes,* XXIX (1973), 100–111.

Judkins, Winthrup. "Toward a Reinterpretation of Cubism." *Art Bulletin,* XXX (December, 1948), 270–78.

Kaplan, Alice Yaeger. *Reproductions of Banality: Fascism, Literature, and French Intellectual Life.* Minneapolis, 1986.

Kenny, Neil. "Changing the Language of the Theater: A Comparison of Brecht and Artaud." *Journal of European Studies,* XIII, Part 3, No. 82 (1983), 169–86.

King, Jonathan H. "Philosophy and Experience: French Intellectuals and the Second World War." *Journal of European Studies*, I (1971), 198–212.

Kunnas, Tarmo. *Drieu La Rochelle, Céline, Brasillach et la tentation fasciste*. Paris: Les Sept Couleurs, 1972.

Lansard, Jean. *Drieu La Rochelle ou la passion tragique de l'unité: Essai sur son théâtre joué et inédit*. 2 vols. Paris: Aux Amateurs de Livres, 1985–87.

————. "L'Homme de théâtre." In *Drieu La Rochelle, Cahiers de l'Herne*, edited by Marc Hanrez. Paris: Editions de l'Herne, 1982, pp. 164–80.

Leal, Robert Barry. "Aspects du moi dans la fiction de Drieu La Rochelle." *Revue d'Histoire Littéraire de la France*, LXXXV (March–April, 1985), 248–65.

————. *Drieu La Rochelle*. Boston, 1982.

————. "Drieu La Rochelle and Huxley: Cross Channel Perspectives on Decadence." *Journal of European Studies*, XV, Part 4, No. 60 (October, 1985), 247–59.

————. "Drieu La Rochelle and Malraux." *Australian Journal of French Studies*, X (May–August, 1973), 175–90.

————. *Drieu La Rochelle: Decadence in Love*. St. Lucia, Australia, 1973.

————. "Huxley and Drieu La Rochelle: Studies in Commitment and Mysticism." *Revue de Littérature Comparée*, No. 236 (October–December, 1985), 397–407.

————. "Le Thème du sacrifice chez Drieu La Rochelle." *Studi Francesi*, XXIX, fasc. III (September–December, 1985), 483–99.

Leprohon, Pierre. *Vincent Van Gogh*. Paris: Chiron-Diffusion, 1986.

Levey, Michael. "The Real Theme of Watteau's *Embarkation for Cythera*." *Burlington Magazine*, CVI (1961), 180–85.

Loss, Archie K. *Joyce's Visible Art: The Work of Joyce and the Visual Arts*. Ann Arbor, 1984.

Lucie-Smith, Edward. *A Concise History of French Painting*. New York, 1978.

Mabire, Jean. *Drieu parmi nous*. Paris: La Table Ronde, 1963.

Macleod, Alexander. *La Pensée politique de Pierre Drieu La Rochelle*. Paris: Editions Cujas, 1966.

Magazine Littéraire, special issue on Drieu La Rochelle, No. 143 (December, 1978).

Martin du Gard, Maurice. "Drieu et ses suicides." *Ecrits de Paris*, December, 1951.

————. *Les Mémorables*. 3 vols. Paris: Flammarion, 1957–60, Grasset, 1978.

Mauriac, François. "Drieu." *La Table Ronde*, June, 1949, pp. 912–17.

Mauriac, François, and Jacques-Emile Blanche. *Correspondance 1916–1942*. Paris: Grasset, 1976.

May, Gita. *Diderot et Baudelaire, critiques d'art*. Geneva: Droz, 1957.

McCorquodale, Charles. *Bronzino*. New York, 1981.

Meier-Graefe, Julius. *Vincent Van Gogh, A Biography.* Translated by J. Holroyd-Reece. 1922, 1933, 1936. rpr. New York, 1987.

Meyers, Jeffrey. *Painting and the Novel.* Manchester, 1975.

Mondor, Henri. *Mallarmé.* 2 vols. Paris: Gallimard, 1941.

M[ounier], E[mmanuel]. "Drieu La Rochelle: *Gilles.*" *Esprit,* VIII (April, 1940), 87–90.

Moureau, François. "Theater Costumes in the Work of Watteau." In *Watteau, 1684–1721.* Exhibition catalogue.

———. "Watteau in His Time." In *Watteau, 1684–1721.* Exhibition catalogue.

Nochlin, Linda. "Watteau: Some Questions of Interpretation." *Art in America,* LXXIII (March, 1986), 68–97.

Nourissier, François. "Maintenant il va falloir expliquer Drieu." *Gazette de Lausanne,* October, 1960, p. 17.

Ocampo, Victoria. "El Caso de Drieu La Rochelle." *Sur* (Buenos Aires), No. 180 (October, 1949), 7–27.

———. *Lawrence de Arabia y otros ensayos.* Madrid: Aguilar, 1951.

La Parisienne, special issue on Drieu La Rochelle, October, 1955.

Paulhan, Jean. *De la paille et du grain.* Paris: Gallimard, 1948.

Perloff, Marjorie. *The Futurist Moment: Avant-Garde, Avant Guerre, and the Language of Rupture.* Chicago, 1986.

Pérusat, Jean-Marie. *Drieu La Rochelle ou le goût du malentendu.* Frankfurt am Main, 1977.

Peyre, Henri. *French Novelists of Today.* New York, 1967.

Picon, Gaëtan. *Panorama de la nouvelle littérature française.* Paris: Gallimard, 1949.

Pompili, Bruno. "Pierre Drieu La Rochelle e i surrealisti." *Studi Urbinati,* I (1968), 164–90.

Pope-Hennessy, John. *The Portrait in the Renaissance.* Princeton, 1966.

Posner, Donald. *Antoine Watteau.* Ithaca, 1984.

———. *A Lady at Her Toilet.* London, 1973.

Poulet, Robert. "Deux portraits d'écrivains." *Ecrits de Paris,* No. 376 (January, 1978), 85–91.

Praz, Mario. *Mnemosyne.* Princeton, 1970.

Prideaux, Tom. *The World of Delacroix, 1798–1863.* Amsterdam, 1984.

Read, Herbert. *Picasso's Guernica.* Exhibition pamphlet. London, 1938.

Reboussin, Marcel. *Drieu La Rochelle et le mirage de la politique.* Paris: Nizet, 1980.

Reck, Rima Drell. "Drieu La Rochelle's *Etat civil* and the French Lost Generation." *French Review,* LVIII (February, 1985), 368–76.

———. "Drieu La Rochelle's *La Comédie de Charleroi:* A Long View on the Great War." *Romance Quarterly,* XXXIV (August, 1987), 285–96.

————. "Drieu's Theater Criticism of the Twenties: Rituals, Spectators, and Subtext." *French Review*, LXI (October, 1987), 50–59.

————. "Louis Aragon." *Dictionary of Literary Biography*, LXXII (1988), 3–25.

————. "Pierre Drieu La Rochelle." *Dictionary of Literary Biography*, LXXII (1988), 148–69.

————. Review of *Paris 1937, L'Art indépendant.* Exhibition catalogue. *French Review*, LXI (May, 1988), 998–99.

Reff, Theodore. "Manet's Portrait of Zola." *Burlington Magazine*, CXVII (July, 1975), 34–44.

Rewald, John. *Cézanne: A Biography.* New York, 1986.

————. "The Posthumous Fate of Vincent Van Gogh, 1890–1970." In *Studies in Post-Impressionism.* New York, 1986.

Richard, Lionel. "Drieu La Rochelle et la *Nouvelle Revue Française* des années noires." *Revue d'Histoire de la Deuxième Guerre Mondiale*, XXV (January, 1975), 67–84.

Rieuneau, Maurice. *Guerre et révolution dans le roman français, 1919–1939.* Paris: Klincksieck, 1974.

Robert, Marthe. "Le Génie et son double." In Camille Bourniquel *et al.*, *Van Gogh.* Paris: Hachette, 1968, pp. 171–97.

Roeder, George H., Jr. "What Have Modernists Looked At? Experiential Roots of Twentieth-Century American Painting." *American Quarterly*, XXXIX (Spring, 1987), 56–83.

Rosen, Charles, and Henri Zerner. *Romanticism and Realism: The Mythology of Nineteenth-Century Art.* New York, 1984.

Rosenblum, Robert. *Ingres.* New York, 1967.

Rouart, Jean-Marie. "Une Fraternité de la nuit." *Magazine Littéraire*, No. 143 (December, 1978), 44–45.

Roueché, Berton. "Cinnabar." *New Yorker*, December 8, 1986, pp. 94–102.

Rubin, William. *Picasso in the Collection of the Museum of Modern Art.* New York, 1972.

Russell, John. *Seurat.* London, 1965.

Saint-Ygnan, Jean-Louis. *Drieu La Rochelle ou l'obsession de la décadence.* Paris: Nouvelles Editions Latines, 1984.

Saisselin, Rémy. Introductory essay and commentaries to *Style, Truth, and the Portrait.* Exhibition catalogue.

[Sartre, Jean-Paul.] "Drieu La Rochelle ou la haine de soi." *Les Lettres Françaises*, No. 6 (April, 1943), 3–4.

Sartre, Jean-Paul. Preface to *Portrait de l'aventurier*, by Roger Stéphane. Paris: Editions du Saggitaire, 1950.

————. "Qu'est-ce que la littérature?" In *Situations, II.* Paris: Gallimard, 1948.

Schapiro, Meyer. *Van Gogh.* New York, n.d.

Schechner, Richard. *Between Theater and Anthropology*. Philadelphia, 1985.

Sebastien Lopez, Santiago. *El Guernica y otras obras de Picasso: Contextos Iconográficos*. Murcia, 1984.

Sérant, Paul. *Le Romantisme fasciste*. Paris: Fasquelle, 1959.

————. *Les Vaincus de la Libération*. Paris: Laffont, 1964.

Shattuck, Roger. *The Banquet Years*. New York, 1968.

Sheon, Aaron. Essays and plate commentaries to *Monticelli, His Contemporaries, His Influence*. Exhibition catalogue.

Simon, Pierre-Henri. *Histoire de la littérature française du XXe siècle*. Paris: A. Colin, 1956.

————. *Procès du héros: Montherlant, Drieu La Rochelle, Jean Prévost*. Paris: Editions du Seuil, 1950.

Singer, Barnett. "The Prison of a Fascist Personality." *Stanford French Review*, I (Winter, 1977), 403–14.

Sontag, Susan. "Writing Itself: On Roland Barthes." In *A Roland Barthes Reader*, edited by Susan Sontag. New York, 1980.

Soucy, Robert. "Drieu La Rochelle and Modernist Anti-modernism in French Fascism." *Modern Language Notes*, CX (May, 1980), 922–37.

————. *Fascist Intellectual: Drieu La Rochelle*. Berkeley, 1979.

Steinberg, Leo. "Picasso's Philosophical Brothel," Part 1. *Art News*, CXXI (September, 1972), 20–29.

————. "Picasso's Philosophical Brothel," Part 2. *Art News*, CXXI (October, 1972), 38–47.

Steiner, Wendy. *The Colors of Rhetoric*. Chicago, 1982.

————. *Exact Resemblance to Exact Resemblance: The Literary Portraiture of Gertrude Stein*. New Haven, 1978.

Suleiman, Susan Rubin. *Authoritarian Fictions: The Ideological Novel as a Literary Genre*. New York, 1983.

————. "Ideological Dissent from Works of Fiction: Towards a Rhetoric of the *roman à thèse*." *Neophilologus*, LX (April, 1976), 162–77.

Sypher, Wylie. *Rococo to Cubism in Art and Literature*. New York, 1960.

Thiher, Allen. "*Le Feu follet*: The Drug Addict as Tragic Hero." *PMLA*, LXXXVIII (January, 1973), 34–40.

Thomson, Richard. *Seurat*. Oxford, 1985.

Tintner, Adeline R. *The Museum World of Henry James*. Ann Arbor, 1986.

Tomkins, Calvin. "Colored Muds in a Sticky Substance." *New Yorker*, March 16, 1987, pp. 44–70.

Toussaint, Hélène. *Les Portraits d'Ingres*. Paris: Editions de la Réunion des Musées Nationaux, 1985.

Tucker, William R. "Fascism and Individualism: The Political Thought of Pierre Drieu La Rochelle." *Journal of Politics*, XXVII (1965), 153–77.

Turner, Victor. *From Ritual to Theater.* New York, 1982.

Uhde, Wilhelm. "La Vie et l'oeuvre de Vincent Van Gogh." Preface to *Van Gogh.* Selection of paintings, drawings and letters by Ludwig Goldscheider. London, 1936.

Updike, John. "Death's Heads." In *Picked-Up Pieces.* New York, 1975, pp. 260–69.

Van Gogh, Vincent. *The Complete Letters of Vincent Van Gogh.* 3 vols. London, 1958.

Vandromme, Pol. *Drieu La Rochelle.* Paris: Editions Universitaires, 1958.

Vlaminck, Maurice. *Le Ventre ouvert.* Paris: Corrêa, [1937].

Vollard, Ambroise. *Souvenirs d'un marchand de tableaux.* Paris: Albin Michel, 1937.

Waldberg, Patrick. *René Magritte.* Translated by Austyn Wainhouse. Brussels: André de Rache, 1965.

———. *Surrealism.* New York, n.d.

Wechsler, Judith. *A Human Comedy: Physiognomy and Caricature in 19th Century Paris.* Chicago, 1982.

Winner, Viola Hopkins. *Henry James and the Visual Arts.* Charlottesville, 1970.

Winock, Michel. "Une Parabole fasciste." *Mouvement Social,* LXXX (September, 1972), 29–47.

Wohl, Robert. *The Generation of 1914.* Cambridge, Mass., 1979.

Exhibition Catalogues

A Day in the Country: Impressionism and the French Landscape. Los Angeles: Los Angeles County Museum of Art, 1984.

Les Demoiselles d'Avignon. 2 vols. Paris: Musée Picasso, 1988.

Guernica. London: New Burlington Galleries, 1938.

Guernica—Legado Picasso. Madrid: Museo del Prado, 1981.

Manet. New York: Metropolitan Museum of Art, 1983.

Monticelli, His Contemporaries, His Influence. Pittsburgh: Museum of Art, Carnegie Institute, 1978.

Paris 1937, L'Art indépendant. Paris: Musée d'Art Moderne de la Ville de Paris, 1987.

Style, Truth, and the Portrait. Cleveland: Cleveland Museum of Art, 1963.

Van Gogh à Paris. Paris: Musée d'Orsay, 1988. [Published by the Réunion des Musées Nationaux.]

Vincent Van Gogh. New York: Museum of Modern Art, 1935; rpr. with the addition of *A Bibliography.* New York: Museum of Modern Art, 1966.

Watteau, 1684–1721. Washington, D.C.: National Gallery of Art, 1984.

Index

DATE DUE

DATE DUE	
SEP 2 1 1993	
UPI 261-2505	PRINTED IN U.S.A.